The Brightest Mirror of God's Works

Princeton Theological Monograph Series

K. C. Hanson, Charles M. Collier, D. Christopher Spinks,
and Robin A. Parry, Series Editors

Recent volumes in the series:

Riyako Cecilia Hikota
*And Still We Wait:
Hans Urs von Balthasar's Theology of Holy Saturday
and Christian Discipleship*

Guillaume Bignon
*Excusing Sinners and Blaming God:
A Calvinist Assessment of Determinism, Moral Responsibility,
and Divine Involvement in Evil*

Jeff McDonald
*John Gerstner and the Renewal of Presbyterian and
Reformed Evangelicalism in Modern America*

James P. Haley
*The Humanity of Christ:
The Significance of the Anhypostasis and Enhypostasis in
Karl Barth's Christology*

Karlo V. Bordjadze
Darkness Visible: A Study of Isaiah 14:3–23 as Christian Scripture

Graham H. Twelftree
The Nature Miracles of Jesus: Problems, Perspectives, and Prospects

William M. Marsh
*Martin Luther on Reading the Bible as Christian Scripture:
The Messiah in Luther's Biblical Hermeneutic and Theology*

Benjamin J. Burkholder
*Bloodless Atonement?
A Theological and Exegetical Study of the Last Supper Sayings*

The Brightest Mirror of God's Works
John Calvin's Theological Anthropology

Nico Vorster

☙PICKWICK *Publications* • Eugene, Oregon

THE BRIGHTEST MIRROR OF GOD'S WORKS
John Calvin's Theological Anthropology

Princeton Theological Monograph Series 236

Copyright © 2019 Nico Vorster. All rights reserved. Except for brief quotations in critical publications or reviews, no part of this book may be reproduced in any manner without prior written permission from the publisher. Write: Permissions, Wipf and Stock Publishers, 199 W. 8th Ave., Suite 3, Eugene, OR 97401.

Pickwick Publications
An Imprint of Wipf and Stock Publishers
199 W. 8th Ave., Suite 3
Eugene, OR 97401

www.wipfandstock.com

PAPERBACK ISBN: 978-1-5326-6024-5
HARDCOVER ISBN: 978-1-5326-6025-2
EBOOK ISBN: 978-1-5326-6026-9

Cataloguing-in-Publication data:

Names: Vorster, Nico, 1973–, author.

Title: The brightest mirror of God's works : John Calvin's theological anthropology / Nico Vorster.

Description: Eugene, OR : Pickwick Publications, 2019 | Princeton Theological Monograph Series 236 | Includes bibliographical references.

Identifiers: ISBN 978-1-5326-6024-5 (paperback) | ISBN 978-1-5326-6025-2 (hardcover) | ISBN 978-1-5326-6026-9 (ebook)

Subjects: LCSH: Calvin, Jean,—1509–1564. | Calvin, Jean,—1509–1564—Anthropology. | Theological Anthropology.

Classification: BX9418 .V665 2019 (print) | BX9418 .V665 (ebook)

Manufactured in the U.S.A.   MARCH 5, 2019

Contents

Acknowledgments | vii
Abbreviations | viii

　Introduction | 1
1　The Created Structure of the Human Being | 13
2　Sin and the Bondage of the Human Will | 33
3　Union with Christ | 59
4　The Boundaries of Human Knowledge | 100
5　The Anthropological Roots of Society | 121
6　Women in Church and Society | 147
7　Summary | 172

Bibliography | 181

Acknowledgments

This book is the culmination of a long journey involving extensive reading, writing, re-writing and incorporating comments of reviewers. Various persons and institutions played an important role in bringing this endeavour to fruition. Let me express my gratitude to Rudi de Lange for editing the Latin quotations in the book, Christien Terblanche for the language editing of the main text, and Celia Kruger for assisting in technical editing. Also a word of appreciation to my mother, Hannetjie Vorster, for double checking the footnotes, citations and bibliography; and my father, Koos Vorster, for encouraging me to persist. I value their guidance deeply. Lastly, a special word of thanks to my wife Christelle, son Thinus and daughter Lehani who supported me all the way. Pickwick Publications deserves mentioning for a highly efficient and professional management of the publication process. I hereby acknowledge the South African National Research Foundation (NRF) who provided funding for the project. The views expressed in this book do not necessarily represent the opinions of the NRF.

Abbreviations

CO *Ioannis Calvini Operae quae supersunt omnia: Ad fidem editionum principium et authenticarum ex parte*, edited by Gulielmus Baum; Eduartus Cunitz, Eduardus Reuss. Brunsvigae: Scwetschke, 1864–1900.

SC *Supplementia Calvinia: Sermons Inédit*. Moderated by James I. McCord. Neukirchen-Vluyn: Neukirchner Verlag, 1961.

LW *D. Martin Luther's Werke: Kritische Gesamtausgabe. Tischreden*. H. Böhlau, 1921.

WA *D. Martin Luthers Werke: Kritische Gesamtausgabe*. Weimar. 1883–.

MW *Melanchton's Werke in Auswahl: Bd. Humanistische Schriften*, edited by Robert Stupperich. C Bertelsmann, 1969.

ZSW *Zwingli Sämtliche Werke: Corpus Reformatorum*, Volume 88–101. Zwingli Verein: Zurich, 1927.

Introduction

THEOLOGY AND ANTHROPOLOGY ARE intimately interwoven. Whenever we ask questions about God, anthropological issues seem to arise: Are we divinely created beings? How does God relate to us? What is the role and place of the human person within a divinely created order? Do we have a divinely determined destiny? Calvin recognized this in the famous opening sentences of his 1559 *Institutes* when he closely linked knowledge of God and knowledge of ourselves:

> Our wisdom, insofar as it ought to be deemed true and solid wisdom, consists almost entirely of two parts: the knowledge of God and ourselves. But as these are connected together by many ties, it is not easy to determine which of the two precedes and gives birth to the other. For in the first place, no man can survey himself without forewith turning his thought towards the God in whom he lives and moves.[1]

The anthropological import of Calvin's remark is that human identity is intricately connected to our understanding of God. In fact, our knowledge of God is "foundational" to personal identity and self-understanding.[2] In a previous publication, I have stated that Calvin's anthropology pervades other doctrines of his theology.[3] The body and soul, for instance, serves as a microcosmic example of the ontological relation between the natural and supernatural; Calvin understood sin as having a strong noetic character because reason acts as the ruler of the soul; and he held that complete sanctification is not fully possible in the penultimate realm because the body is a

---

1. The *Calvin Opera* volumes are referenced in this book as *CO* with notice of the relevant volume and page, while the *Supplementa Calviniana* are referenced as *SC*, also with notice of page and volume. English quotations from John Calvin's 1559 *Institutes* are taken from Calvin, *Institutes of the Christian Religion* (2008). All the Latin translations and references come from the *Ioannis Calvini Operae*. "Tota fere sapientiae nostrae summa, quae vera demum ac solidata sapientia censeri debeat, duabus partibus constat, Dei cognition et nostril. Caeterum, quum multis inter se vinculis connexae sint, utra tamen alteram praecedat, et ex se pariat, non facile est discenere. Nam primo se nemo aspicere potest quin ad Dei, in quo vivit est movetur" (Calvin, *Institutes*, 1.1.1; *CO* 2.32).

2. Vorster, "Theocentric Premises," 104.

3. Vorster, "Theocentric Premises," 104.

"prison." When it comes to his doctrine of creation, Calvin understood the human being as the brightest mirror of God's glory in creation.[4]

The obvious question is whether a study of Calvin's theological anthropology is indeed a worthwhile enterprise. Some theologians regard Calvin's anthropology as outdated because it was informed by a "premodern setting and premodern concepts such as matter, form, substance and essence, which are no longer intelligible to modern people."[5] What can modern theologians learn from the anthropology of a premodern theologian who was unaware of modern paleontological discoveries, human evolution, neuroscientific data, ethnographical information or contemporary cultural-anthropological insights? Calvin, indeed, was a child of his time who was profoundly influenced by the premodern worldviews of the time and often uncritically appropriated the philosophical, conceptual and exegetical apparatus available to address the anthropological questions of his era. Some of these tools are methodologically outdated and no longer able to address modern questions.[6]

Despite these shortcomings, this book argues that Calvin's anthropology exhibits strengths that provide contemporary Christians with resources and impulses to address the systemic problems that modern societies face: human alienation, individualism, collective power abuse, systemic corruption, ecocide, and the fracturing of communities. Modern theologians ought to be cautious not to abandon all classical philosophical and anthropological concepts from the start.[7] Modern theological anthropology did not develop in a vacuum, but has its roots in the thoughts, reflections, and concepts of earlier theological epochs. As theologians, we need to be aware of our inevitable indebtedness to the historical chain of theological thought. If we discard theological traditions and simply attempt to practice theology *de novo*, we will not only repeat historical mistakes, but also impoverish ourselves by not engaging with a rich intellectual history. Theologians, of course, have to avoid the pitfalls in which previous theological generations fell, but we also must ask how earlier traditions can enrich us today and empower us to address new challenges.

A second concern often raised with regard to the relevance of Calvin's anthropology is the belief that Calvin's theocentrism subsumes the anthropological reflections his theological corpus.[8] According to this view,

---

4. Vorster, "Theocentric Premises," 104.

5. Vorster, "Theocentric Premises," 105–6; Kelsey, *Eccentric Existence*, 32.

6. Vorster, "Theocentric Premises," 106.

7. Vorster, "Theocentric Premises," 106.

8. Engel, *John Calvin's Perspectival Anthropology*, ix, 189; Vorster, "Theocentric Premises," 104.

Calvin emphasized God's sovereignty to such a degree that he risked obliterating creaturely integrity. It is therefore not possible to speak of "Calvin's anthropology" in the modern sense of the word. However, this argument rests on a highly simplistic reading of Calvin's doctrine on the relation between divine sovereignty and human agency. As will be shown later on, Calvin utilized the notions of relative necessity and the Aristotelian two-causes doctrine to safeguard divine sovereignty, whilst preserving human freedom and accountability. Calvin, moreover, employed the logic of *united but not mingled* as an ontological premise to relate the divine and human realms to each other, yet also to distinguish between them. Far from denying creaturely integrity, Calvin was adamant that the peculiar properties of both the divine and human natures ought to be respected. This is most evident in Calvin's doctrine on the two natures of Christ that allowed for no mingling between the divine and human natures of Christ; Calvin's refutation of the doctrines of the Manichees and Osiander, who held that God infuses his essence into the human being; Calvin's rejection of Luther's ubiquity doctrine; and Calvin's rebuff of the realism of Scholastic thought. The human person is, in Calvin's thought, a distinct other that can relate to God, respond to God, disobey God, and praise God. The Holy Spirit dwells in the believer, but his regenerating work in the believer does not entail becoming part of the essence of the believer. The Holy Spirit transforms the believer, but does not become the believer, nor does he coerce the human being by replacing her faculties.[9] Mary Potter Engel[10] rightly notes that theologians who tend to typify Calvin's theocentrism as subsuming his anthropology does not take into account the significance of Calvin's "pairing of God-knowledge and self-knowledge." She posits that self-knowledge is at the center of Calvin's theology and that his anthropology therefore pervades his theology. Calvin never "intended theology and anthropology to be mutually exclusive."

Thirdly, some theologians perceive Calvin's anthropology to display a Platonic type of dualism that does not take the bodily aspect of human existence sufficiently into account. This purportedly devalues the significance that can be attached to Calvin's anthropology, especially when compared to the rest of his theology.[11] Without denying the influence of Aristotle and Plato on Calvin, it ought to be noted that Calvin was first and foremost a biblical theologian. Dennis Tamburello[12] rightly notes that there are simi-

---

9. See *CO* 2.215.

10. Engel, *John Calvin's Perspectival Anthropology*, ix, 189.

11. See van Wyk, *Homo Dei*; Sewell, *Calvin, the Body and Sexuality*; Vorster, "Theocentric Premises," 105.

12. Tamburello, *Union with Christ*, 15.

larities between Calvin and Plato, but also vast differences. Calvin regarded Plato as the only philosopher who gave proper attention to the immortality of the soul. He also shared Plato's view on the body as a prison. Yet Calvin did not share Plato's notion that the body should be despised; he affirmed contra Plato that the body will be resurrected; and he rejected Plato's doctrine on the afterlife as consisting in phases of the purification of the soul. Calvin's use of the Aristotelian distinction between a human body and soul that consists of intellect and will is obviously no longer applicable within a modern setting, but we should not underestimate the holistic features and reach of his anthropology. Calvin, for instance, utilized the formula of *united but not mingled* (*unitis non confusis*) to describe the relation between body and soul. As will be argued later on, Calvin used this formula not only to differentiate between the body and soul, but also to relate them to each other. His doctrine on the Holy Communion also contains perspectives on the body that are far from denigrating.

Survey of Literature

Since anthropology is a primary concern in Calvin's theology and pervades all aspects of his theology, the consistency and intelligibility of his understanding of the human being is pertinent to the integrity of his theology as a whole. Calvin scholars disagree on the coherence of Calvin's anthropology. Some historians and theologians are of the opinion that Calvin's anthropology contains contradictions and inconsistencies that are not reconcilable. Paul Pruyser, for instance, posits that Calvin is an anthropological realist who "accepts some basic functional polarities in man and conceptualizes them as a network of lines in conflict."[13] Quistorp conjectures that Calvin's anthropology contain irreconcilable contradictions that can be attributed to Calvin's attempt to reconcile Platonic insights on the soul with Hebraic notions of the body,[14] while Bouwsma distinguishes between two Calvins who coexist "uncomfortably within the same historical personage."[15] According to Bouwsma, the "philosophical Calvin craved desperately for intelligibility, order and certainty," while the "rhetoric and humanist Calvin" was a "sceptical fideist" and a "revolutionary" who celebrated "the paradoxes and mystery at the heart of existence.[16]

---

13. Pruyser, "Calvin's View of Man," 57.
14. See Quistorp, *Calvin's Doctrine of the Last Things*, 101.
15. Bouwsma, *John Calvin*, 230.
16. Bouwsma, *John Calvin*, 230–31.

Some theologians have attempted to clarify the supposed inconsistencies and contradictions in Calvin's anthropology by analysing the structure of Calvin's anthropological thought. In his classical work, *Calvin's Doctrine of Man*, Thomas Torrance[17] argues that Calvin's anthropology must be understood from the perspective that God created the human being in order to behold his own glory in the human being as in a mirror. God is continually calling the human being from "non-being into being and life by the Word and will of the Creator." Calvin thus emphasized God's radical grace and the obligation on the human being to a thankful response to it.[18] Torrance furthermore distinguishes between Calvin's understanding of creation as exhibiting the wider image of God and the human being as displaying the narrower image of God by standing in a special relationship to the Word of God. He argues that Calvin grounded the wider image of creation in the narrower image, since the narrower image gives creation a voice in proclaiming the glory of God. Secondly, Torrance interprets Calvin as differentiating between the human's objective image as opposed to his subjective image. The objective image consists of the supernatural gifts God bestows on human beings, while the subjective image comprises the human beings' response to God's grace.[19]

In her 1988 book, Mary Potter Engel characterizes John Calvin's anthropology as perspectival in nature. According to Engel, Calvin's many contradictory, but also complementary assertions and judgements are "held together by a determinable set of distinct theological perspectives" to which she refers as the "dynamic perspectival structure" of Calvin's anthropology."[20] This structure is "determined by a distinction between the perspective of God and the perspective of humankind as it operates in both the doctrines of creation and redemption."[21] Engel typifies the perspective of God as "absolute" and of humankind as "relative."[22] Despite recognizing that this structure is not found explicitly in Calvin's works,[23] she proceeds in each of her chapters to illustrate how the bifocal distinction between God's absolute perspective and humankind's relative perspective permeates the various aspects of Calvin's anthropology. When Calvin approached a topic from the divine perspective, he came to different judgements than when he

---

17. Torrance, *Calvin's Doctrine of Man*.
18. Torrance, *Calvin's Doctrine of Man*, 41–42, 62–63.
19. Torrance, *Calvin's Doctrine of Man*, 69–70.
20. Engel, *John Calvin's Perspectival Anthropology*, xi.
21. Engel, *John Calvin's Perspectival Anthropology*, 1.
22. Engel, *John Calvin's Perspectival Anthropology*, 2.
23. Engel, *John Calvin's Perspectival Anthropology*, 9.

approached a topic from the human side of things. Yet, all these diverse perspectives culminate in a "rich portrait of humankind."[24] Engel[25] summarizes her argument as follows:

> The unity of Calvin's portrait of the self is no easy arrangement of balanced, symmetrical parts, no easily discernible ordering of consistent truths. Rather, it is "a unity with inner conflict," a unity incorporating inconsistent and contradictory truths about the self into a larger, ordered whole.

Van Eck's 1992 publication in Dutch titled *God, mens en medemens. Humanitas in de Theologie van Calvijn* also attempted to analyze the structure of Calvin's anthropology.[26] Van Eck argues that Calvin's anthropology was from the start profoundly influenced by his early humanist background—so much so that we can distinguish between a humanist and reformed line of thought in Calvin's theology. These two lines of thought co-existed in Calvin's theology, though the reformed line dominated his later works. According to Van Eck, Calvin's view of *humanitas* already crystalized in his commentary on Seneca and the first edition of his *Institutes*. After discussing the influences of classical authors on Calvin, Van Eck examines the development of Calvin's anthropology in the various editions of the *Institutes*. He finds that Calvin's notion of *humanitas* is profoundly influenced by his Christology. Humanity finds its destiny in the reconciliatory work of Christ, while Christ's human nature is the manifestation of true humanity.

Dennis Tamburello's 1994 book entitled *Union with Christ* investigates the similarities and differences between the mysticism of St Bernard and Calvin's understanding of the believer's union with Christ. Chapter 2 contains a comparison between St Bernard and Calvin's anthropology. Tamburello argues that Calvin's view on the intellect and will, as the two most important properties of the soul, are crucial to Calvin's anthropology.[27] Calvin regarded the will has having primacy over the intellect because the will can accept or reject the commands of reason. Yet, Calvin did not allow for any notion of a free will, because he considered humanity as wholly depraved and bondage to sin. The only natural endowments remaining after the fall is the *sensus divinitatis* that makes us aware of God, and the conscience that creates in as an intuitive understanding of good and evil. The *sensus divinitatis* and the conscience are "inerasable" even by sin and

---

24. Engel, *John Calvin's Perspectival Anthropology*, 194.
25. Engel, *John Calvin's Perspectival Anthropology*, 23.
26. Van Eck, *God, Mens en Medemens*.
27. Tamburello, *Union with Christ*, 29.

serves as a "point of contact" between the fallen human person and God's redeeming grace. As a result of sin, they are nevertheless, powerless to lead us to redemption.[28]

In 2004 Shu-Ying Shih published a dissertation entitled *The Development of Calvin's Understanding of the Imago Dei in the Institutes of the Christian Religion from 1536–1559*.[29] In this book, Shih argues that Calvin's understanding of the *imago Dei* consisted in a dialectical tension between temporal and eschatological motives. These motives eventually emanated in the 1559 *Institutes* in a doctrine of reciprocal participation.[30] According to Shih, Calvin distinguished between the sovereign autonomy of God and the limited autonomy of human beings. Human beings exercise their autonomy by partaking in God's life and reflecting his characteristics, while God's sovereign autonomy over human autonomy are reflected in the "created essence" of the *imago Dei* and the providence of God that governs the human will and uses evil as an instrument in his hands.[31]

Jason van Vliet attempts in his 2009 book *Children of God* to explain the supposed inconsistencies in Calvin's anthropological thought by paying attention to the "timeline of Calvin's theological development."[32] After a thorough chronological examination of all the relevant texts in the *Calvini Opera*, specifically with regard to the *imago Dei*, Van Vliet concludes that Calvin's anthropology was "always subject to correction and amelioration."[33] According to Van Vliet, Calvin's description of the *imago Dei* matures over time, but the core of his definition remains fairly consistent.[34] Calvin "changed his mind about certain aspects of the *imago Dei*, clarified other matters, and added things which were previously lacking."[35] Most notably, Calvin changed his position on the human's dominion over creation as a characteristic of the *imago Dei*.[36]

In her influential work, *Calvin's Ladder*,[37] Julie Canlis posits that Calvin understood the relationship between God and humanity from the perspective of *koinonia*, that is, a relationship "forged" in the person of Christ.

28. Tamburello, *Union with Christ*, 35, 37.
29. Shih, *Calvin's Understanding of the Imago Dei*.
30. Shih, *Calvin's Understanding of the Imago Dei*, 10, 279–80.
31. Shih, *Calvin's Understanding of the Imago Dei*, 11.
32. Van Vliet, *Children of God*, 23.
33. Van Vliet, *Children of God*, 127.
34. Van Vliet, *Children of God*, 253.
35. Van Vliet, *Children of God*, 256.
36. Van Vliet, *Children of God*, 256.
37. Canlis, *Calvin's Ladder*, 42.

She holds that Calvin's theology follows a synthetic structure of descent and ascent:

> Calvin brilliantly synthesized the two movements of ascent and descent into one primary activity: the ongoing story of God himself with us. God has come as man to stand in for us (descent), and yet as man he also leads us back to the Father (ascent). The entire Christian life is an outworking of this ascent – the appropriate response to God's descent to us – that has already taken place in Christ.[38]

Canlis holds that many of the misunderstandings of Calvin's view on creaturely reality are due to a failure to "see how communion governs all of Calvin's theology of mediation" through the twofold movement of descent and ascent that are essentially "the movements of God."[39] According to Canlis, Calvin framed his anthropology in such a way that anthropology becomes an "occasion for constant communion" with God.[40] If we do not realize that participation in God is for Calvin the end goal of humanity, Calvin's anthropology can be easily obscured.[41]

The most recent book publication on Calvin's anthropology is entitled *Calvin, the Body, and Sexuality: An Inquiry into His Anthropology*.[42] In this book, Alida Leni Sewell investigates Calvin's notion of the body, specifically Calvin's Platonist references to the soul as a prison of the body. Sewell discusses the role that this metaphor fulfils in Calvin's eschatology and compares his use if this metaphor to that of Augustine and Plato. After a thorough investigation that takes into account Calvin's late Renaissance context, his educational upbringing, personal physical tribulations and his doctrine of the *imago Dei*, she concludes that Calvin mainly regarded the body as an auxiliary to the faculties of the soul, which consist of reason, will and conscience. This, however, does not mean that Calvin was a Platonist in a pure and unadulterated sense.

Besides the abovementioned book publications on the structure and main trajectories of Calvin's anthropology, there also have been intense debates in scholarly essays on specific aspects of Calvin's anthropology. Examples are the discussions on the exact nature of Calvin's relational understanding of the *imago Dei*; his conception of the various human faculties and their interrelationship; his notion of the body-soul relation; his

---

38. Canlis, *Calvin's Ladder*, 3.
39. Canlis, *Calvin's Ladder*, 62, 92.
40. Canlis, *Calvin's Ladder*, 63.
41. Canlis, *Calvin's Ladder*, 64.
42. Sewell, *Calvin, the Body, and Sexuality*.

construction of the effects of sin on the human being's image; his view on the relationship between divine sovereignty and human agency; the possible presence of *theosis* in his doctrine on the believer's union with Christ; the logical sequence of justification and sanctification in human salvation; the connection between Calvin's anthropology and his social philosophy; his view of gender; and his understanding of the Christian's social calling. Obviously, these debates are too wide-ranging and the literature too comprehensive to explicate in an introductory chapter, but they will receive attention throughout the course of the book.

Specific Contribution of this Book

This book does not attempt to provide an exhaustive account of every aspect of Calvin's anthropology, but rather addresses the interchange between the main motifs of Calvin's theology and his anthropology. The key questions are: How did Calvin's anthropology influence his theological outlook and how did his theological agenda determine his understanding of the human being? Two examples illustrate the relevance of this question: Calvin's doctrine on sin and grace profoundly influenced Calvin's formulation of the relationship between the human intellect and will. By affirming the bondage of the human will to sin, and the primacy of the human will to human reason, Calvin closed the door to Pelagian doctrines of salvation. In this case, Calvin formulated his anthropology in a manner that serves his theology of sin and grace. Conversely, Calvin also used his anthropology to clarify theological positions. He, for instance, modeled the relationship between the two natures of Christ and the two kingdoms of God on the relation between the two substances of the human being.[43]

Secondly, this book aims to engage with the most recent and important scholarly debates on Calvin's anthropology; specifically with regard to Calvin's view of divine sovereignty and human accountability, the possible presence of *theosis* in Calvin's soteriology, the relation between human justification and sanctification; Calvin's two kingdoms doctrine; and his scepticism of reason. Though these debates were always contentious in Calvin scholarship, recent times have seen scholars putting forward new arguments and interpretations.

Thirdly, this contribution intends to identify those features of Calvin's anthropology that exhibit constructive potential and provide us with possibilities to address some burning modern issues. Again the aim is not to provide an exhaustive account of Calvin's relevance for today, but simply

---

43. See chapters 3 and 6.

to single out impulses in Calvin's anthropology that may stimulate scholarly debate. Weaknesses in Calvin's anthropology are identified, but due consideration are also given to themes in Calvin's anthropology that could invigorate modern Reformed reflections on the human being and her destiny. Many of the challenges that modern theological anthropology face are in fact old questions in new disguises. The debate on the relation between God and human evolution, for instance, pertains in essence to our understanding of the relation between God's sovereignty and creaturely freedom. Though pre-modern theologians did not have to contend with the modern ethical issues emanating from an evolutionary perspective on reality, they did develop theories to explain and relate divine sovereignty and creaturely freedom to each other. These theories can be utilized or reformulated to address modern theological problems emanating from the phenomenon of evolution. Premodern understandings of creation as gift of God; the intimate relation between the transcendent and immanent realities; the nature of sin; Christian vocation; marriage as a covenantal institution; the spiritual significance of the family; the boundaries of reason and the importance of virtues are other examples of premodern theological-anthropological insights that might be helpful in the endeavour to develop intelligible modern Christian anthropologies.

Method

Richard Muller's thesis that Calvin's *Institutes* must be read in an organic and "developmental" relationship with his exegetical work is widely accepted in modern Calvin scholarship.[44] According to Muller, Calvin moved from biblical topics to "doctrinal discourse in the form of loci, communes or disputations."[45] He, for instance, significantly revised his 1539 *Institutes* whilst working on his Commentary on Romans.[46] The historical development of Calvin's exegetical work also needs to be kept in mind. Calvin's Commentary on Genesis 2 and 3 seems to be influenced by his earlier Commentary on 1 Corinthians, as well as, his debate with Pighius on the bondage of the Will. Calvin's early work on the soul, *Psychopannychia*, which was drafted in 1534 and finally published in 1542, shows traces of scholasticism and exhibits less maturity on the topic than his commentary on Genesis 1 and 2, as well as chapter 15 of his 1559 *Institutes*.[47] The 1536 and 1539 edi-

---

44. Muller, *Unaccommodated Calvin*, 116.
45. Muller, *Calvin and the Reformed Tradition*.
46. Muller, *Calvin and the Reformed Tradition*, 205.
47. See Gamble, "Calvin's Bibliography," 427.

tions of Calvin's *Institutes* referred to the image of God in human beings as destroyed by the fall, but Calvin restated his position in the 1554 Genesis Commentary and the 1559 *Institutes* by describing the image as corrupted.[48] These examples indicate that Calvin's *Institutes* ought to be interpreted in light of the historical development of his exegetical work, whilst keeping in mind the chronological order of the works and the various debates to which Calvin was exposed.

A second important methodological consideration relates to the social context of sixteenth-century Europe and specifically the effects of the Renaissance and Christian humanism on Calvin's thought. Sixteenth-century Europe experienced an intellectual revolution caused by the natural scientific discoveries of Galileo, Kepler and Copernicus that led to the downfall of the Ptolemaic worldview. The resulting paradigm shift challenged Aristotelian physics profoundly, specifically the notion that reality is undergirded by stable patterns that reside in the essence of things. The Renaissance questioned the sterility of the contemplative rationality of medieval thinkers and sought after an instrumental rationality that would inspire the reconstruction of societies. Calvin rejected late-medieval realist ontology, the Scholastic dependence on the organization of truths in rational intelligible systems; and philosophical speculations on God's divine nature. He shared the Renaissance quest to return to the classical sources; his writings sought practical rather than speculative knowledge; he prioritized the education of the young; and followed the humanists in attempting to reshape society. Nonetheless, the influence of social context on Calvin's thinking must not be overestimated. The key characteristic of Calvin's theological method was to return to "the pre-eminent source of theology" which he regarded as Scripture.[49] Calvin attempted to produce a biblical theology that stays true to the main tenets of Scripture and he therefore showed little interest in intellectual debates or philosophical discourses governed by non-theological interests. This caveat does not mean that Calvin was untouched by the discourses of his day. In fact, he used the philosophical tools available in his day when it suited his argument. Yet, Calvin made deliberate attempts to present his arguments in a way that is grounded in Scripture or that at least display the logic of Scripture.

A last methodological concern relates to the axioms and theological premises that Calvin utilized in his theology without attempting to proof their truth. Calvin, for example, asserted that Scripture is the Word of God and that it does not contradict itself; that God is good and just and not the

---

48. See Van Vliet, *Children of God*, 253.
49. Billings, "Calvin's Theology of Grace," 94.

Author of sin; that all events in history and human life are part of God's greater, sometimes, incomprehensible plan; and that creation contains a natural order that governs human relationships.[50] Calvin simply accepted these axioms as true and made little effort to substantiate them rationally. It is important to take these basic assumptions in Calvin's theology into account, because they determine to a large extent the patterns of his theological thought and his approach to moral questions.

---

50. See Gamble, "Calvin's Bibliography," 427.

The Created Structure of the Human Being[1]

Introduction

CALVIN CLAIMED THAT THE human being can only truly be understood in relation to God. The result was an anthropology that decenters the human being. The basic premise of Calvin's anthropology is that we are not our own, but centered outside ourselves to live in communion with God and our neighbours. We exist in God through the grace of God to heighten the glory of God. This does not mean that Calvin's anthropology was immune to the popular philosophical notions of the time on the nature of the human being. In fact, he drew strongly on the Aristotelian understanding of the makeup of the human being's psychological faculties by holding that the human soul consists of an intellect and a will. Calvin made no attempt to devise a unique anthropology in psychological terms; neither did he spend much time on deconstructing the popular notions of the time, except when it compromised his theological agenda. Calvin's anthropology was driven by theological intentions, and he utilized the psychological terminology of his day to serve his theological argument.

Calvin repeatedly insisted that philosophers and theologians err by not making a distinction between the created structure of the human being, and her condition after the fall.[2] The aim of this chapter is to provide a broad overview of Calvin's understanding of the created structure of the human being in its original state. Subsequent chapters will provide a deeper reflection on specific issues such as his scepticism of the powers of reason, his understanding of the depravity of the human will and gender. This chapter explicates Calvin's understanding of the human's place in creation, the human's original state, her created relation to Christ, the relation between

---

1. This chapter is a modified and extended version of a published article by Nico Vorster entitled "Calvin on the Created Structure of Human Nature" in the *Journal of Theology for Southern Africa* 151 (2015) 162–82. Used by permission.
2. Lane, "Did Calvin Believe in Free-Will," 73.

body and soul, the relationship between the various human faculties, as well as the meaning of the *imago Dei*. The chapter concludes with a critical evaluation of Calvin's understanding of the created structure of the human being, while also identifying those insights considered as promising for modern theological-anthropological reflections.

The Created Attributes of the Human Being

Calvin consistently described creation as a "theatre" of God's glory and the human being as created in order to adore God's glory in this theatre by living in communion with God.[3] Some passages depict creation as a "mirror" that reflects God's works and power and compels us to contemplate God, who is in essence invisible.[4] These depictions of creation are in accordance with the central motive of Calvin's theology: to demonstrate and heighten God's glory.[5] By contemplating God's works the human develops a sense of God's infinite grace that is displayed by the glorious God condescending to us and adorning a creature "so miserable as man."[6] Creation also teaches us "reverence" and "fear" for God and induces us to "ask every good thing from God," since humanity is the "workmanship" of God, while God is the "origin and fountain of all goodness."[7] In fact, creation displays God's works so gloriously that "none, however dull and illiterate, can plead ignorance as their excuse."[8]

In Calvin's thought, both creation and humanity are "mirrors" of God. Whereas creation as a whole shines forth the macrocosmic image of God; the human being, as a created part of nature, constitutes a microcosmic image of God. Yet, within the hierarchy of created "mirrors" in God's creation, the mirror of the human being reflects God's glory the "brightest,"[9] because, contrary to all other creatures, the human is inhabited by an immortal

---

3. See Calvin, *Sermons on Genesis 1–11*, 6; SC 11.15; Calvin, *Institutes*, 1.14.18; CO 2.123.

4. Cf. CO 23.23; CO 5.325; CO 31.92. Calvin characterized God's works in creation as manifestations of God's wisdom, power, justice, and goodness. See in this regard CO 2.132.

5. See Miles, "Theology, Anthropology," 303–23.

6. Calvin, *Book of Psalms*, 100; CO 31.91: "miseros homines."

7. Calvin, *Institutes of the Christian Religion 1536*, 1.2.2; CO 2.35: "bonorum omnium fontem esse et originem."

8. Calvin, *Institutes*, 1.5.1, 2.6.2; CO 2.41, 2.249: "verum singulis operibus suis certas gloriae suae notas insculpsit, et quidem adeo claras et insignes ut sublata sit quamlibet rudibus et stupidis ignorantiae excusatio."

9. CO 21.88; CO 2.43; SC 11.476.

spirit.[10] Calvin maintained this view consistently from his earliest works, such as *Psychopannychia*, through to his later works.

According to Calvin, the human person must be considered, first of all, from the "condition of innocence in which he was created."[11] In doing so, we acquire an awareness of God's goodness, while also realizing that we depend fully on God since nothing exists apart from God.[12] Knowledge of the primeval dignity of human beings is theologically important, because it stimulates us to pursue the original end for which we were created.[13] As pinnacle of God's creation the human being was created good; sin was in no sense part of the "substance" of the human being.[14] Calvin emphasized the accidental nature of sin, because any notion to the contrary would not only diminish God's glory, but would also locate the origin of sin in the Creator.

The original goodness of humans consisted, first of all, in their ability to live in full communion with God; but it also involved them being able to display supernatural virtues such as the ability to discriminate between good and evil and to exercise purity, prudence, integrity, uprightness, righteousness, holiness, wisdom, perseverance and truth; as well as to apply natural virtues, such as the ability to reason, understand and to act.[15] Calvin regarded these virtues and abilities not as inalienable innate properties, but as gifts (*dona*). He thereby highlighted, in the words of Denlinger, the "gratuitous and adventitious character of these faculties."[16] In fact, after the fall the human lost most of these virtues and abilities, not because of some natural disintegration, but because God decided, as a form of punishment, to denude human beings from the gifts they possessed.[17]

Related to Christ from the Beginning

For Calvin, the entire structure of the world finds its grounding in Christ as the Origin of all things:

---

10. *CO* 2.134.
11. Calvin, *Bondage and Liberation*, 46; *CO* 6.263: "in ea integritate, in qua conditus fuit." Calvin made the same assertion at the start of his discussion in the *Institutes* on created human nature. See *CO* 2.134.
12. See his sermon on Gen 1:1–2; *SC* 11/1.1–12.
13. *CO* 47.70. See Torrance, *Calvin's Doctrine of Man*, 16.
14. *SC* 11/1.8; *CO* 6.284.
15. *SC* 11/1.8; *SC* 11/1.55, 57, 59; *SC* 11/1.325; *CO* 23.25–26; *CO* 6.263, 402.
16. *CO* 2.181. See Denlinger, "Adam's Relationship to His Posterity," 239.
17. Cf. Calvin, *Bondage and Liberation*, 46–47; *CO* 6.263.

> Inasmuch as he is the Eternal Word of God, he is the first born of every creature, not because he is created, or is to be reckoned among the creatures, but because the entire structure of the world, such as it was from the beginning, when adorned with exquisite beauty, had no other beginning, then inasmuch as he was made man.[18]

Even before the world existed, all things were connected to God.[19] This is also true of the human who is related to Christ from the beginning of Creation.[20] Calvin regarded life not as an intrinsic good of the human being, but as proceeding from God in who we exist, live and move. Literally everything that the human possesses is gift. Calvin specifically related the gift of life to Christ, who is the "Fountain and Origin of life" that "breathes life and energy into all creatures," but especially "human beings who are conjoined with reason and intelligence."[21]

Christ is an eternal Mediator who from the start preserves and directs the *telos* of Creation and unites humanity with God. God loves no human being outside of Christ, since the love of the Father dwells in Christ, and from Christ is extended to us.[22] For Calvin, true being is life in relation to Christ; there is no such thing as autonomous humanity who can determine their own destiny or have communion with God outside the Mediator. Canlis[23] rightly notes that Calvin's theocentrism is "relentless at work" here, because even a perfect being constantly has to be united to the Mediator. Without the Mediator, human existence is frail. The "perfectness" of the primeval being is, in fact, bound up with his relationship to the Mediator.

By relating the human being to Christ from the start, Calvin linked knowledge of ourselves to knowledge of God. Humans cannot truly know themselves if they do not know the foundation of their being and the origin of their existence. Upending the essential relationship with the Eternal Mediator would not only lead to alienation from the Fountain of life, nor simply risk obstructing the continuous flow of gifts from the Giver, but it

---

18. Calvin, *Institutes*, 2.12.7; *CO* 2.346: "quatenus aeternus est Dei sermo, primogenitum esse omnis creaturae, non quod creatus sit, vel numerari inter creaturas debeat; sed quia integer mundi status, qualis ab initio fuit summa pulchritudine insignis, non alium principium habuit; deinde quatenus homo factus est."

19. *CO* 47.1.

20. Calvin expounded this view consistently from the 1536 *Institutes* onwards.

21. Calvin, *Institutes*, 4.17.8; *CO* 2.1007–8: "vitae fontem et originem, unde omnia ut viverent semper acceperunt . . . illum etiam tum creaturas omnes influentem, vim spirandi et vivendi eis instilasse." Also see *CO* 47.1.

22. Cf. *CO* 2.387.

23. Canlis, *Calvin's Ladder*, 56, 64.

would also lead to a distorted kind of self-knowledge that results in sinful pride.

The Soul and Body

Calvin consistently upheld the soul as the primary seat of the *imago Dei*, since it is "a spirit with a permanent structure."[24] As seat of the image, the soul is superior to the body.[25] Yet, Calvin's definitions of the soul vary. Sometimes he identified the soul with spirit, while distinguishing between soul and spirit on other occasions.[26] At times he described the soul as the seat of affections,[27] on other occasions he identified it with reason and intelligence.[28]

His most consistent stance was that the soul consists of intellect and will.[29] In maintaining this view, Calvin dispensed with Augustine's notion of the memory as a third faculty of the soul.[30] The intellect makes moral judgements, while the will makes choices in accordance with the judgments of the intellect.[31] The soul thus regulates human conduct.[32] In its original state the soul was sound of mind, capable of choosing the good and able to ascend to God and experience God's eternal happiness.[33] Since the soul is spiritual in nature, it is capable of resembling God, who himself is Spirit. Yet, this does not mean that human and divine nature can be identified with each other. Against Osiander and the Manichees, Calvin maintained that the soul consists of a created essence, not a transfused essence emanating from God, since it is created by God out of nothing and does not share in any sense the substance of God.[34] The soul is thus "as much a creature as the body."[35] For Calvin, the most outstanding characteristic of the soul is

24. Calvin, *Sermons on Genesis 1–11*, 145; SC 11/1.97; Calvin, *Commentary on Philippians, Colossians and Thessalonians*, 211; CO 52.121.

25. Engel, *John Calvin's Perspectival Anthropology*, 42.

26. See CO 55.50: "ad divisionem usque animae et spiritus." CO 2.135; CO 52.178–79.

27. CO 31.53: "Ergo anima sedem affectuum mihi significat."

28. SC 11/1.56.

29. Calvin, *Institutes*, 1.15.7; CO 2.142: "Sic ergo habeamus: subesse duas humanae animae partes, quae quidem praesenti institute conveniant, intellectum et voluntatem."

30. See Tamburello, *Union with Christ*, 29.

31. CO 2.142; CO 2.148; SC 11/1.56.

32. CO 2.140–41.

33. CO 2.148.

34. CO 2.139–40.

35. Torrance, *Calvin's Doctrine of Man*, 26.

that it is immortal, not liable to death, and therefore capable of an existence apart from the body.[36] This feature of the human being separates him from animals and makes her unique. Immortality, however, does not mean that the soul is able to exist without God's agency. The immortality of the soul is a gift; the soul is not by nature immortal, but immortality is infused by God, who is the Source of life to the soul.[37]

Calvin's understanding of the relationship between the body and soul tends to be ambiguous. At times he described the body as a mere extension of the soul, an accessory.[38] Yet, in the 1559 *Institutes* he compared the relation between the body and soul to the relation between the two natures of Christ. As the human and divine natures in Christ were not confounded in substance, but retained their own properties while being united in the person of Christ, the soul and body are separate substances that retain their own properties, yet are united in one person. Calvin stated it as follows:

> We maintain that the divinity was so conjoined and united with the humanity, that the entire properties of each nature remain entire, and yet the two natures constitute only one Christ. If in human affairs, anything analogous to this great mystery can be found, the most apposite similitude seems to be that of man, who obviously consists of two substances, neither of which, however, is so intermingled [permixta est] with the other as that both do not retain their properties. For neither is soul body, nor body soul.[39]

Calvin consistently regarded the soul as the life-giving principle in the human being that "imparts breath to the body, and gives it vigour and motion," while the body provides habitation to the soul.[40] In fact, God gives life to the soul, whereupon the soul invigorates life in the body.[41] The metaphor that Calvin employed most to describe the function of the body is that of a "tabernacle" that houses the soul, until the human finds his destination in God's tabernacle.[42] When describing the human in his fallen state he depicted the

36. *SC* 11/1.479; *CO* 2.135; *CO* 5.184.
37. *CO* 5.221; *CO* 2.140.
38. *SC* 11/1.54–67.
39. Calvin, *Institutes*, 2.14.1; *CO* 2.353: "Si quid in rebus humanis tanto mysterio simile potest reperiri, hominis similitudo appositissima videtur, quem ex duabus substantiis conspicimus constare; quarum neutra tamen sic alteri permixta est, ut non retineat naturae suae proprietatem. Neque enim aut anima corpus aut corpus anima est."
40. Calvin, *Commentaries on Genesis*, 1:112; *CO* 23.35: "quae corpus inspirat, et illi dat vigorem et motum." See *CO* 2.141; *CO* 5.178.
41. Calvin, "Psychopannychia," 441; *CO* 5.195.
42. Calvin, "Psychopannychia," 439; *CO* 5.193.

body as a "prison" of the soul that incapacitates the human being by "weighing" down and "confining" the soul.[43] Consequently, the human cannot enjoy full communion with God while living within the body.[44]

Whereas the soul consists of immortal essence, the body is "motion devoid of essence" because it has no spiritual properties.[45] In his earlier work, *Psychopannychia*, Calvin postulated that the body does not exhibit the image of God in any manner since God "cannot be represented by any bodily shape." However, in his later works beginning with his Commentaries on Genesis, he revised this position by describing the body as radiating God's glory in a secondary sense.[46] In the 1559 *Institutes* he states that though God's glory is manifested in the human's outward appearance, "the proper seat of the image is in the soul."[47] Miles rightly notes that the real significance of the body lies for Calvin in its ability "to reflect the dynamics of the soul."[48]

There can be no doubt that the body occupies an inferior position to the soul in Calvin's anthropology. It is, in the words of Miles,[49] "that part of a human being that is without affectivity, without psychological predicates, without animation." Yet, Calvin's notion of the body is not consistently negative, since he also refers to the beauty of God's workmanship in the body, the body as a temple of God and the body as participating in the resurrection.[50]

Calvin's view on the relationship between body and soul exhibited dualistic elements. He did not want to confuse body and soul and also regarded the soul as of "immeasureably higher value than the body in the sight of God."[51] Why Calvin entertained dualistic anthropological notions is difficult to assess. It is possible that he read the anthropology of Paul through the spectacles of Greek philosophy. Calvin referred quite extensively to Plato in his *Institutes*. Not only did he borrow his understanding

---

43. Cf. Calvin, "Psychopannychia," 443; *CO* 5.196; *CO* 5.336; *CO* 2.450.

44. *CO* 2.526: "Si corpus animae est carcer, si terrena habitatio, compodes sunt: quid anima soluta hoc carcere, exuta his vinculis? Nonne sibi redditur, et quasi se colligit? Ut dicere liceat, tantum illi accrescere, quantum decrescit corporis."

45. Calvin, *Institutes*, 1.15.2; *CO* 2.135: "Motus sine essential."

46. *CO* 5.180–81; *SC* 11/1.54–67.

47. Calvin, *Institutes*, 1.15.3; *CO* 2.137: "Quamvis enim in homine externo refulgeat Dei gloria, propriam tamen imaginis sedem in anima esse dubium non est."

48. Miles, "Theology, Anthropology," 318.

49. Miles, "Theology, Anthropology," 311.

50. *CO* 2.135; *CO* 3.737.

51. Calvin, *Institutes*, 2.8.40; *CO* 2.295: "animae . . . quae in immensum coram Domino praecellit."

of the soul as consisting of intellect and will from Plato's *Phaedrus*,[52] but the notion of the body as a "prison" is also quintessential Plato. As noted in the introduction, Calvin's use of Platonist categories and language does not mean that he was a Platonist; in fact his first inclination was to disassociate himself as far as possible from Greek philosophers in order to do justice to Scripture. Yet, his use of Platonic anthropological distinctions indicates that he did not escape the sixteenth century's cosmological and philosophical understandings of human nature.

A clear theological and cosmological motif can also be detected behind Calvin insistence that the body and soul ought not to be confused. This motif appears in his polemic against Osiander, who stated that the human being's essence emanates from the essence of God. Consequently, both the body and soul possess the image of God. In response, Calvin accused Osiander of "mingling heaven and earth."[53] According to Calvin, the soul and body do not exhibit the image of God in an equal sense, since the image pertains to spiritual things. Osiander blurred the distinction between heavenly and earthly things, by depicting body and soul as imaging God in the same degree. Calvin insisted that the heavenly and earthly realms should be *kept* apart. Once the heavenly and earthly is fused, the much needed distance between God and creation is breached and the spiritual is subsumed by the temporal.[54] Calvin opposed any kind of monism that fuse divine and human essence, join the spiritual and material realms, or compromise the much needed divide between God and creation. He thus took refuge in dualistic categories that safeguard the distinction between the divine and creaturely realms and prevent nature from being deified. Calvin's dualism, though, is moderate in nature. He did not dissolve soul and body, but differentiated in order to relate.

The Faculties of the Soul

Late medieval theology was characterized by debates on the existence or non-existence of a human free will. In essence, the issue related to the relationship between God's sovereign grace and the integrity of human nature. How does God's omnipotence and sovereignty relate to creaturely freedom? Is it possible to sustain both concepts at the same time? The various polemical dispositions on these issues affected the ways in which theologians

---

52. Cf. *CO* 2.142.

53. Osiander, *Gesamtausgabe*, 176–79. Calvin, *Institutes*, 1.15.3; *CO* 2.137: "coelom terrae miscet."

54. See Miles, "Theology, Anthropology," 310.

constructed their anthropological positions, specifically with regard to the interrelationship between the various faculties of the soul. Two main approaches crystallised. The intellectual approach posited the primacy of reason over the will, while the voluntarist tradition maintained the priority of the will.[55]

The Scholastic tradition held that the human intellect rules the human will and that humans are therefore able to attain their divinely appointed destiny if they follow the prescripts of reason under the guidance of God's Spirit. On the other hand, the magisterial Reformers followed a voluntarist route by highlighting the will's primacy over reason. Though human reason might instruct the human will to execute certain actions, it does not follow that the human will always comply. The human ability to distinguish between good and evil does not necessarily result in a choice not to do evil. In fact, the will tends to follow its own desires and passions after the fall. The theological motives behind the various faculty psychologies are quite evident. The concern of the Scholastic tradition was to maintain a realist ontology. Voluntarism would seriously jeopardize the realist notion that the human soul participates in divine life through the intellect, which is capable of discerning God's will. The Reformers, conversely, attempted to avoid all avenues that could result in either Pelagianism or Semi-Pelagianism.

Muller rightly notes that Calvin did not single out the relation between the various faculties as a "distinct topos," yet the frequency with which he raised the issue indicates that he regarded it as an important issue.[56] As noted earlier, Calvin followed the tradition of the day in identifying reason and will as the two faculties of the soul:

> The office of the intellect [is to] distinguish between objects, according as they seem deserving of being approved or disapproved; and the office of the will, to choose and follow what the intellect declares to be good, to reject and shun what it declares to be bad.[57]

As the abovementioned passage suggests, Calvin regarded reason as the faculty of understanding whereby God enables human beings to discern God's moral order and to make judgements that guide their behaviour. In

---

55. Muller, *Unaccommodated Calvin*, 162.

56. Muller, *Unaccommodated Calvin*, 161–62.

57. Calvin, *Institutes*, 1.15.7; *CO* 2.142: "Sic ergo habeamus subesse duas humanae animae partes, quae quidem praesenti instituto convenient, intellectum et voluntatem. Sit antem officium intellectus, inter obiecta discernere, prour unum quodque probandum aut improbandum visum fuerit; voluntatis autem, eligere et sequi quod bonum intellectus dictaverit; aspernari ac fugere quod ille improbarit."

its original state, reason was sound of mind and able to distinguish between good and evil. By endowing the human being with reason, God enabled the human being to "discern good from evil," justice from injustice and most importantly, to restrain his sensual passions.[58] Reason is therefore "one of the essential properties of our nature" that distinguishes us from "lower animals" and "inanimate objects."[59] In a sermon on Genesis 5:1-25 Calvin exclaimed: "Is there anything more excellent and noble than the reason and understanding which are in us?"

Though unique, reason is not an end in itself, but its purpose is to direct us to God. The defining feature of reason before the fall was that it allowed the human person not only to govern earthly life, but also "to rise up to God and eternal happiness."[60] The human was in fact capable of "comprehending his eternal destiny," which signifies an ability to stand in an immediate relation to God, who is the source of life.[61] This capacity of reason to "ascend" to God was for Calvin the most important feature of reason in its original state.

Reason contains, according to Calvin, the *conscientia* which is an innate ability to distinguish between right and wrong. *Conscientia* is closely related to the *sensus divinitatis*, that is, an innate sense of the divine that all human beings possess. Though affected by sin, the *conscientia* and *sensus divinitatus* cannot be erased by sin. At the same time, they do not provide us with salvational knowledge, nor a point of contact with God or a means to ascend to God outside of Christ.[62] Instead, they render us inexcusable before God. Thus while the *conscientia* serves a positive function because it provides us with a sense of justice and order, it has a negative accusatory function with regard to our relationship with God.

Calvin followed the voluntarist tradition of locating choice in the will, not in the intellect. The will signifies the human ability to choose and execute the judgements of reason.[63] Calvin's position should not be misconstrued

58. Calvin, *Institutes*, 1.15.8; *CO* 2.142; Calvin, *Bondage and Liberation*, 76; *CO* 6.285: "Ergo animam hominis Deus mente instruxit, qua bonum a malo, iustum ab iniusto discerneret."

59. Calvin, *Institutes*, 2.2.17; *CO* 2.199: "Haec summa sit, in universo genere humano perspici, naturae nostrae propriam esse rationem, quae nos a brutis animalibus discernat, sicut ipsa sensu differunt a rebus inanimatis."

60. Calvin, *Institutes*, 1.15.8; *CO* 2.143: "His praeclaris dotibus excelluit prima hominis conditio, ut ratio, intelligentia, prudentia, iudicium, non modo ad terrenae vitae gubernationem suppeterent, sed quibus transscenderent usque ad Deum et aeternam felicitatem."

61. Calvin, *Institutes*, 2.1.1; *CO* 2.175: "Aeterna vitae meditationem."

62. See *CO* 2.36; *CO* 2.39; *CO* 2.40.

63. *CO* 2.187.

as guided by a dichotomist distinction between reason and the will, as if reason is driven by cognition and the will by affections. Muller rightly points out that Calvin regarded both reason and will as involved in all cognitive and affectionate decisions and actions:

> Calvin does not oblige any neat "head/heart," intellective/affective, rational/experiential dichotomy; what is "sealed upon our hearts" is the "firm and certain understanding" or "cognition." Nor can there be genuine "persuasion," "sincere feeling" or "effectual confidence" unless heart as well as mind is involved in the cognitive act. We are here directed toward the assumption of traditional faculty psychology that the will is itself rational."[64]

Muller furthermore remarks that Calvin gave temporal priority to reason in the sense that the will only can execute after reason has made a judgement; but he did not follow the intellectualist tradition's causal understanding of the reason-will relationship.[65] The will is free to accept or reject the judgements of reason, and in fact, often does so. In Calvin's thought, reason and will stand in a judgement/choice relationship to each other, not a cause/effect or cognitive/affective association.

The Human Being as Image of God

Calvin's understanding of the original created structure of the human being was strongly informed by his concept of the nature of the *imago Dei*; a theological theme that constituted one of the major areas of his dispute with the Scholastic tradition. Following Irenaeus, the schoolmen distinguished between the image of God in a natural sense (imago) and a supernatural sense (similitudo). They based this distinction on the two words, "image" and "likeness," used in Genesis 1:26 to describe the *imago Dei*. According to them, the image as *similitudo* refers to the original righteousness of the human being, lost during the fall, whereas *imago* denotes the various qualities of the human being retained after the fall such as the ability to know God and to lead a virtuous life.[66] By speaking of natural "habits" infused by God's grace that enable human beings to understand the human *telos*, the schoolmen located grace partly in the innate capacities of the human being. Calvin, however, understood the two words as synonyms used together for

---

64. Muller, *Unaccommodated Calvin*, 164.
65. Muller, *Unaccommodated Calvin*, 170.
66. Van Vliet, *Children of God*, 125.

the sake of explanation and accentuation.[67] By doing so he attempted to stay clear of any understanding of the *imago Dei* as a natural endowment; instead, he regarded the *imago Dei* as "spiritual" and therefore as relational and dynamic in nature.[68] Though Calvin modified his position on the precise location of the *imago Dei* over time, he consistently maintained that the *imago Dei* does not connote any natural property in the human being. This was probably due to his twofold concern that an understanding of the *imago Dei* as "being" could lead to a fusion of human and divine natures,[69] as well as provide an avenue for a Pelagian soteriology.

Central to his relational understanding of the *imago Dei* is the notion that the *imago Dei* exalts the human above the animal realm, the difference being that the human is created to have spiritual communion with God, while animals have no such relationship with God.[70] Yet for Calvin, the human's ability to have communion with God is not located in human nature being ontologically continuous with divine nature, but in the status that God bestows on human beings by entering through the Eternal Son into a relationship with humanity. Canlis[71] states Calvin's position well:

> Anthropology is bound up with participation in the Eternal Son, not because of an innate Godward movement or point of contact, but because of God's own self-gift.

The question could rightly be asked whether it is possible for a relation to be forged on the basis of gift alone without the existence of natural properties in human nature that help to actualize such a relationship? Too be fair, Calvin did not deny that natural faculties such as reason can reflect God's glory, nor that they are essential to live in communion with God; but these properties do not image God in a functional sense; instead, they resemble God's works when they, moved by God's grace, make conspicuous God's works.[72] Reflecting God's glory is dependent upon God's gift; it is not something innately present in the properties themselves. For Calvin, the image of God appears in conduct, not in capacities. Calvin's relational approach to the *imago Dei* is reflected in him referring to the *imago Dei* both as a "mirror" and as an expression of the filial relationship between God and the human being.

67. *CO* 23.25–26.
68. Cf. *CO* 2.137.
69. Cf. Van Vliet, *Children of God*, 104, 226.
70. *CO* 2.138; *CO* 23.35.
71. Canlis, *Calvin's Ladder*, 71.
72. *CO* 2.138.

Calvin used the "mirror" image to convey two features of the *imago Dei*, namely that the image resembles God and that the human is a living object in who the glory of God can be contemplated and observed.[73] He differentiated between a "picture image" and a "mirror image." The human being is not a static lifeless "picture" image of God, but a living "mirror" image, since the human represents God's majesty in possessing reason and understanding and being able to distinguish between good and evil.[74] In contrast to the creation that is mute, the human being is able to respond in gratitude to God.[75] Congruent with the image of the "mirror," true obedience to God consists in the "imitation" of God.[76] However, since the human's original image was utterly defaced after the fall, we can only understand how to imitate God by focusing on Christ, the second Adam, through whom God manifests himself and draws the faithful close to him.[77] Based on his exegesis of Colossians 3:10 and Ephesians 4:24, Calvin identified knowledge (wisdom), righteousness and goodness (holiness) as the core virtues of God that the *imago Dei* ought to reflect, yet he did not limit human reflections of God to these virtues.[78] The end goal of the human's imaging is not only that humankind may rejoice in the glory of God they see in each other, but that God himself can behold his own glory in the human being as in a mirror.[79]

Calvin's filial definition of the *imago Dei* as an expression of the Father-child relationship between God and the human being is an important and integral part of the anthropology that he introduced as early as 1536.[80] Calvin used this metaphor within three fields of meaning. First of all he regarded humankind as "God's lineage."[81] Being in the lineage of God entails that the human is a child of God who, in distinction from animals, possesses noble features that allows him to live in a Father-child relationship with God. These noble attributes are reason and understanding, wisdom, the power to discriminate between good and evil, possessing the seed of religion, and above all, immortality.[82] Though Calvin utilized the filial metaphor, he emphasized that the God-human relationship was a resemblance

73. Cf. Calvin, *Sermons on Genesis 1–11*, 93; SC 11/1.57.
74. Cf. SC 11/1.744; SC 11/1.495.
75. Gerrish, "Mirror of God's Goodness," 211–22.
76. Cf. *Commentary on the Fist Book of Genesis*, 106; CO 23.32–33.
77. Cf. Torrance, *Calvin's Doctrine of Man*, 37.
78. CO 52.121; CO 50.208–209.
79. CO 2.558.
80. See Van Vliet, *Children of God*, 32, 36.
81. Calvin, *Sermon on Gen 1:26–28*, 98; SC 11/1.55.
82. SC 11/1.347; SC 11/1.481.

of attributes, not a resemblance of essence. Only the relationship between the Father and Son can be a resemblance of essence.[83] The difference is, thus, not only a distinction in "degree", but in "category."[84] Secondly, the filial metaphor expresses the human being's utter dependence on God, the realization of which draws the human to live a life of gratitude towards God, who is pleased to look upon the human as his child.[85] God the Father in his goodness bestows gifts on his children and the children continuously respond to the gifts through a life of gratitude. Lastly, the filial relationship entails that the human being, as child of God, is heir of God. The faithful are after all elected in Christ before the foundation of the world in order to inherit the eternal kingdom of God.[86] It is precisely this eschatological orientation of human life that distinguishes the human from animals and that establishes the human as the noblest of creatures.[87]

With regard to the human being's relationship with animals and creation, Calvin held that the human being as God's representative, exercises dominion over the world.[88] In his early work, *Psychopannychia*, Calvin described human dominionship as not part of the image. Later on he modified his position to include dominion as a "very small" part of the image.[89] Calvin grounded human dominionship both in divine calling and God's endowment of the human being with reason. Reason distinguishes the human from "lower animals" and enables her to rule.[90] Human dominion, however, has limits and must always be exercised in obedience to God. Creation is the theatre of God's works and the beautiful order of things must be preserved, respected and adored.[91] This naturally entails that the human has no right to exploit God's creation.

As far as gender relations were concerned, Calvin, rather inconsistently, depicted dominion as an important part of the image.[92] Calvin

---

83. *CO* 55.35. See Van Vliet, *Children of God*, 89.

84. Van Vliet, *Children of God*, 89.

85. Torrance, *Calvin's Doctrine of Man*, 31, 35.

86. *CO* 51.147.

87. *SC* 11/1.99.

88. *CO* 31.92.

89. Calvin, *Commentaries on Genesis*, 1:94; *CO* 23.25–26: "Est quidem haec imaginis Dei aliqua portio, sed perquam exigua."

90. Calvin, *Institutes*, 2.2.17; *CO* 2.199: "Haec summa sit, in universo genere humano perspici, naturae nostrae propriam esse rationem, quae nos a brutis animalibus discernat."

91. *CO* 31.92.

92. See chapter 6.

maintained that both male and female are created in the image of God,[93] but he struggled to reconcile Gen 1:26-28 that refers to both sexes as image of God with 1 Corinthians 11:7 that only refers to the male as image of God.[94] In order to harmonize the biblical data at his disposal, he distinguished between the heavenly and earthly facets of the male-female relationship. With respect to heavenly matters such as God's grace, male and female are equal sharers, but in earthly matters, the male is created as head of the female and has superiority over the woman.[95]

Though Calvin regarded both male and female as created in the image of God, he referred in his comments on Gen 2:18 to the woman as image of God "in the second degree."[96] When one reads this comment together with his expositions on Eph 5 and 1 Cor 11:7, it becomes clear that Calvin believed that the woman as "ornament" of her husband reflected God's image to a lesser degree than the husband, especially with regard to the exercise of authority in earthly matters. In such matters the male reflects the Son's headship in a way that the female does not. This requires that the woman subordinate herself to the man, not only in marriage, but in all social relationships.[97]

Calvin's understanding of the female role in earthly matters was partly due to Calvin's comprehension of Genesis 2. He deduced from the account of creation in Genesis 2 that the female was created from the substance of the male. This not only suggests a "holy union among the human race" and a "mutual bond of love,"[98] but it also implies that the "order of nature"[99] designates women as "helpers" of their husbands, since God did not create women for themselves, but to help their husbands.[100]

---

93. Calvin considered cases where Paul only refers to the male as created in the image of God as pertaining to political matters. He believes that the creation narratives clearly designate both male and female as image of God. See CO 2.138-39; CO 23.46.

94. SC 11/1.62; CO 23.46.

95. Cf. Van Vliet, *Children of God*, 85, 120.

96. Calvin, *Commentaries on Genesis*, 1:129; CO 23.46: "Negari certe non potest quin mulier quoque, licet secundo gradu, ad imaginem Dei creata sit."

97. Calvin, *Commentaries on Genesis*, 1:100; SC 11/1.62. See Calvin, *Commentary on the Epistles of Paul*, 357; CO 49.476.

98. Calvin, *Commentaries on Genesis*, 1:180-81; SC 11/1.125-26.

99. Calvin, *Commentaries on Genesis*, 1:129; CO 23.46.

100. Calvin, *Sermons on Genesis 1-11*, 183; SC 11/1.127. Chapter 6 discusses Calvin's doctrine on gender in more detail.

Evaluation and Reflection

Calvin's view of the created structure of the human being exhibits various difficulties but also contains promising avenues for contemporary Reformed theologians. The most pertinent question is whether Calvin's understanding of the human/body relationship and his notion of the interrelationship between the human faculties agreed with the language of Scripture. As Muller rightly notes, Calvin simply presumed that his Aristotelian-derived faculty psychology corresponded with the language of Scripture:

> Calvin assumes that the language of the New Testament corresponds with the terms given to him by classic and scholastic faculty psychology and that the Old Testament, despite the differences between its language and that of the New Testament, offers the same perspective.[101]

Calvin's notion of personhood was governed to some degree by the Christian-Aristotelian philosophical tradition. This is clearly illustrated when Calvin quotes both Aristotle and Plato in distinguishing between the functions of the intellect and will.[102] The biblical traditions, in contrast, are largely informed by holistic Hebraic notions of human existence. The Hebrew word for "soul" denotes a living being as opposed to an inanimate being or corpse. In Pauline thought the term "flesh" signifies the whole human being as living in isolation from God, while "spirit" describes the human being who is invigorated by God's Spirit.[103] The biblical traditions do not make dichotomistic distinctions between the soul and body or intellect and will. Calvin, however, tended to "cluster" all the energies and faculties of the human being in the soul, while the body serves as a habitation for the soul, and provides a secondary reflection of the dynamics of the soul.[104] Admittedly, Calvin's doctrine on the Supper does allow for the Spirit's quickening of the body and Calvin also proclaimed the resurrection of the body. In general, though, Calvin exhibited little concern for the body, and tended to regard the spiritual aspect of reality as more important than the physical realm.

Calvin's typical pre-modern notion of a soul that animates the body and the body that provides habitation to the soul stands in stark contrast to discoveries within the modern neurosciences. Neuroscience indicates that the human body contains intricate neural and endocrine communicative systems that carry messages to and from the brain to various parts of the

---

101. Muller, *Unaccommodated Calvin*, 169.
102. *CO* 2.142.
103. See Nürnberger, *Informed by Science*, 148.
104. Miles, "Theology, Anthropology," 311.

body. Clearly, the human body is not animated by a non-biological entity such as the soul, but human consciousness, emotions and intellect all subsist within the "biological infrastructure of the brain."[105] Hence, spirituality cannot be isolated from our biological existence.[106] Though Calvin acknowledged that the soul consists of created essence, he followed most of his contemporaries in arguing that the soul contains an immortal quality that can escape the body after death. In fact, Calvin did not allow for a fusion between the properties of the soul and body, because such a fusion would hinder the ability of the soul to endure after death.[107] Such a stance, though, is theologically problematic because it uses anthropological categories to create an avenue for a doctrine on immortality. Stated differently, the possibility of an eternal life is grounded in some indestructible characteristic of the human composition. Van den Brink and Van der Kooi rightly indicates that medieval and late-medieval notions of an immortal soul were inspired by Greek-Philosophical concepts rather than the more holistic perspectives of Scripture.[108] A better theological approach, in my view, would be to ground the doctrine of an eternal life and bodily resurrection wholly in the doctrine of God, that is, in the power and work of God who alone is able to create *ex nihilo* and to re-create despite death. Theologians ought to stay clear from attempts to explain the doctrine of resurrection from a biological or anthropological vantage point. Such an approach can only engender undue speculation and emanate in highly problematic anthropological concepts. Instead we need to accept the resurrection as a promise of a faithful God who will bring his promise to fruition in ways that extend beyond our comprehension.

A second problematic issue relates to Calvin's hierarchical view of both the natural and social environments that govern human existence. As noted earlier, Calvin posited that creation consist of brighter and dimmer mirrors of God's glory; that the image of God denotes those features that distinguish human beings from animals; that the female reflects God's image only to a secondary degree; and that authoritative relations in society are determined by fixed creational orders.[109] While both social and biotic egalitarianism are highly problematic for reasons we cannot discuss at present, human history is testimony to the dangers inherent to hierarchical forms of thought. Environmental degradation; state authoritarianism; and racial, social and

---

105. Nürnberger, *Informed by Science*, 146.
106. Nürnberger, *Informed by Science*, 143.
107. *CO* 2.135–36.
108. van den Brink and van der Kooi, *Christelijke Dogmatiek*, 248.
109. See *CO* 23.46; *CO* 51.222; *CO* 31.88; *CO* 2.134.

gender inequalities have been justified and perpetuated by hierarchical notions of reality that locate certain forms of power in "the way things are" and were "intended" by God. Though Calvin's theology contributed a great deal to the affirmation of human freedom in the political, social and moral realm, his theology does contain vestiges of the hierarchical lines of thought so typical of late medieval theology.

What do we gain from Calvin's reflections on the created structure of the human being? The most promising feature of Calvin's theological anthropology, in my view, is the theocentric premise of his anthropology. Calvin subordinated claims about human beings to claims about God.[110] Our dignity and self-worth as human beings are not anchored in our innate capabilities or human consciousness; but we live, breath and move due to God's Spirit that invigorates us and communes with us. The result of Calvin's theocentric approach was a dynamic anthropology that understands the human as a creature constantly renewed and re-invigorated in his relation to God by the Spirit of God. The human is not a static being, but a responsive counterpart to God that stands in a direct living relationship with God.

The inherent danger to theocentric anthropological approaches is that they often conflate divine and human nature leading to the divine being subsumed in human nature or human nature being taken up in divine existence. Panentheistic and pantheistic anthropologies tend to fall in this trap. Calvin's theocentrism did not go that far. While he grounded human existence in God's creative and consummative work, he consistently maintained that God and creature are ontologically different and distinct from each other.[111] This caveat in Calvin's anthropology is important. Conflating God's being with creaturely reality could compromise God's sovereignty, holiness and goodness and, conversely, may endanger creaturely integrity and freedom.[112] Calvin avoided both a cosmological dualism and monism by grounding the divine-human encounter in a reciprocal relationship of divine grace and human response. This construction allowed Calvin to differentiate between Creator and creature, while also relating them to each other, thus preserving both human creaturehood and divine otherness

Calvin's theocentric yet ontological differentiating approach to anthropology is important because it safeguards theology from reductionist anthropologies. Reductionisms such as individualism, subjectivism, anthropocentrism, collectivism and naturalism emerge when proximate

---

110. See Vorster, "Theocentric Premises," 107.
111. Vorster, "Theocentric Anthropology," 107.
112. Vorster, "Theocentric Anthropology," 107.

physical and social contexts are treated as if they are ultimate contexts.[113] Theological anthropology, in contrast, holds that human beings cannot be understood apart from their relationship to God, because this relationship orients all other human relationships. Schwöbel[114] rightly cautions us against making inherent human characteristics the exclusive determinant factor of human existence or to embed personhood in inter-human relations characterized by the "dislocation" that sin brings. Such anthropologies are prone to descent into extremes, because the multi-dimensional features of reality are not adequately taken into account. What we need are non-reductionist anthropologies that relate the individual, communities and natural environments to each other, while preserving individual autonomy, social interests and the integrity of nature at the same time. This balance, I argue, can only be maintained if we follow Calvin's example and relate the I, We and It to a loving God who through his grace orients and directs all creaturely life. Without a faithfull response to God's love, inter-human and creaturely relations are destined to become disjointed.

The question of course is, how can we relate our penultimate contexts to the ultimate reality of God? Calvin's simple but profound approach is to refer to Christ as the "paradigmatic example," the second Adam, who shows us "what imaging God is all about."[115] For Calvin authentic personhoods and identities are grounded Christ's identity. This, in my view, is what Christian theological anthropology is all about. Kelsey rightly describes theological anthropology as a discipline that attempts to comprehend God "in ways that are decisively normed by descriptions in canonical Christian Scripture of what and who Jesus of Nazareth is."[116] Calvin understood that Christology provides access to God; that it safeguards theological anthropology against ontological speculation and abstraction, and that following Christ's loving mode of existence liberate us from sectarianism and inhumanity. We can only stand in an appropriate relationship to ourselves, fellow human beings and other creatures if we realize that I, We, They and It are God's handicraft, his gifts to reality and mirrors of God's glory. Such knowledge should encourage self-respect, because I am a mirror of God's glory. It should also engender in me a sense of calling and responsibility because I am God's gift to the other. At the same time it kindles in me respect for otherness, because the other is God's gift to reality precisely in his/her or its' otherness.

113. The distinction between proximate and ultimate contexts is borrowed from Kelsey, *Eccentric Existence*, 4. See Vorster, "Theocentric Premises," 110.
114. Schwöbel, "Human Being as Relational Being," 154.
115. Vorster, "Theocentric Premises," 111.
116. Kelsey, *Eccentric Existence*, 1008.

Esteeming otherness means respecting the autonomy and freedom of the other, allowing him/her, they or it to be the gift God intended. When I disrespect otherness it often amounts to me expecting the other to image me rather than Christ. Conversely, tolerance has limits and should always be principled because—for the believer—Christ's image remains the directive principle for our actions and attitudes. When the other engages in harmful acts that blemishes God's glory, the believer needs to take a moral stance.

A last, perhaps unintended, impulse of Calvin's theocentric anthropology is its potential for developing ecosensitive perspectives. Though Calvin leant towards emphazising the importance of spiritual reality at the expense of corpearility, he also related natural reality directly to mirroring God's glory. For Calvin creation is not only a "theatre of God's glory" but all natural things have inherent qualities that point to God.[117] Moreover, as Kelsey rightly notes, Calvin did not regard humans as mere spectators in God's theatre but as themselves part and parcel of God's theatre.[118] This unexpected ecosensitive consequence of Calvin's approach should not come as a surprise because theocentric anthropological discourses opens up avenues that personalist or anthropocentric approaches do not explore. Calvin's anthropology may yet prove to be useful for developing ecosensitive values.

Conclusion

Calvin's understanding of the created structure of the human being is by no means problem-free. The most troubling feature of his anthropology is the manner in which he read Scripture's understanding of the human's created structure through the glasses of Greek philosophy. His anthropology also contains vestiges of hierarchicalism that are not helpful for modern debates on equality. Notwithstanding, Calvin's anthropology contains promising features. His theocentric approach infuses his anthropology with a dynamic relational quality and enables us to avoid anthropocentrism; his relational understanding of the *imago Dei* counters reductionist anthropological propositions; his Christocentric intuitions encourages us to develop a practical and pastoral perspective on human existence; and his notion of creation as God's theatre fosters ecosensitive perspectives. Though all of these themes are not fully developed in Calvin's theology, they do provide promising impulses that can be fruitfully explored.

---

117. Vorster, "Theocentric Premises," 113. *CO* 2.41.
118. See Kelsey, *Eccentric Existence*, 316; Vorster, "Theocentric Premises," 113.

2

Sin and the Bondage of the Human Will[1]

Introduction

CALVIN IS WELL-KNOWN FOR his rather negative and pessimistic, if not denigrating, depictions of human nature. We need only mention a few passages to prove the point: in his sermon on Genesis 1:26–28, Calvin called the human being a "rubbish bin" and a "slave of Satan;"[2] in article 4 of his 1538 Catechism, he depicted the human as inherently "impure, profane and abominable to God;"[3] while he referred in his commentary on Psalm 8 to human persons as "poor worms."[4] In other passages he ranked human beings lower than vermin and insects.[5]

However, before we characterize Calvin's theological anthropology as profoundly pessimistic, even downright antagonistic, we need to note the numerous passages in his works where he celebrated human nature in lofty language. He referred to the human being as the "brightest mirror" of God's works,[6] a "noble" creature "above all others"[7] and the "most excellent" of all God's works.[8]

---

1. This chapter is a modified and extended version of a published article by Vorster entitled "Assessing the Consistency of John Calvin's Doctrine on Human Sinfulness" in *HTS Teologiese Studies* 71.33 (2015) 1–8. AOSIS Publishers allows for the reuse of journal material published by them under a CC-BY license. See https://creativecommons.org/licenses/by/4.0/.

2. Calvin, *Sermons on Genesis 1–11*, 96; SC 11/1.59.

3. Calvin, *Catechism or Institution of the Christian Religion*, art. 4; CO 5.325: "nihil nisi impurum, profanum, ac Deo abominabile spectare liceat."

4. Calvin, *Book of Psalms*, 101; CO 31.80.

5. See Calvin, *Sermons on Job*, 33; CO 33.104; Calvin, *Sermons on Genesis 1–11*, 490; SC 11/1.327.

6. CO 31.88: "humanum genus . . . est maxime illustre speculum in quo perspicere licet eius gloriam."

7. Calvin, *Sermons on Genesis 1–11*, 90; SC 11/1.55.

8. CO 23.25–26: "opus omnium praestantissimum."

These examples of contradictory statements on human nature can probably be explained by attributing it to Calvin's rhetorical intent, as well as his understanding of human nature before and after the fall.[9] Yet, there seem to be other systemic inconsistencies in his doctrine on human sinfulness that are more difficult to harmonize. A few examples will suffice: in certain passages, it seems as if he regarded the *imago Dei* as totally annihilated by sin, while in others he referred to remnants of the image that survived after the fall.[10] At times he depicted human reason as totally blind and perverted, yet in other passages he extolled the praiseworthy attributes of natural philosophers and scientists.[11] Calvin also grounded the event of the fall in the will and ordainment of God, yet he maintained that God is not the Author of sin.

These seeming contradictions and inconsistencies have led some scholars to depict Calvin's doctrine on sin as deterministic, inconsistent, contradictory, and culpable of making God the Author of sin.[12]

The aim of this chapter is to assess the logical consistency of Calvin's doctrine on human sinfulness. The first section discusses the theological-rhetorical intent of Calvin's doctrine on sin, the second his understanding of human bondage and accountability, and the third his view on the relation between sin and the *imago Dei*. After making a finding on the logical consistency of Calvin's understanding of human sinfulness, the chapter concludes by reflecting on the constructive potential of Calvin's doctrine on sin.

Calvin's Rhetorical and Theological Intent

Calvin deliberately developed his theological anthropology, both rhetorically and theologically, to emphasize the sovereignty and glory of God. In order to extol God's glory and goodness, he used sin and grace as corollaries—the radical, all-encompassing nature of sin requires radical divine grace. By relentlessly stripping humans from all desert, he endeavoured to display the purity of God's goodness and grace.[13] Calvin considered any

---

9. Compare *CO* 6.264 with *CO* 2.138–39.

10. Cf. Calvin, *Bondage and Liberation*, 47; *CO* 6.264 with Calvin, *Institutes*, 1.15.4; *CO* 2.138.139. In his reply to Pighius, Calvin consistently depicted human nature as "evil."

11. Compare *CO* 2.38 with *CO* 23.22.

12. For examples of these criticisms see König, *God waarom lyk die Wêreld so?* [God why does the World look like this?], 127; Taylor, *Secular Age*, 78, 624; Gregory, *Unintended Reformation*, 207–8; Cf. Berkhof, *Christian Faith*, 203.

13. Cf. Calvin, *Institutes*, 2.2.1: "man cannot arrogate anything, however minute, to himself, without robbing God of his honor." *CO* 2.185: "Rursum vel minutulum illi quidpiam arrogari non potest, quin et Deo praeripiatur suus honor." Also see *CO* 6.372.

SIN AND THE BONDAGE OF THE HUMAN WILL

notion of human merit in the God-human relationship as compromising the profundity of God's grace.[14] This is well illustrated by the following passage in article 6 of his 1538 Catechism.

> This knowledge (of sin), though it strikes man with terror and overwhelms him with despair, is nevertheless necessary for us in order that stripped of our own righteousness, cast down from confidence in our own power, deprived of all expectation of life, we may learn through the knowledge of our own poverty, misery and disgrace to prostrate ourselves before the Lord, and by the awareness of our own wickedness, powerlessness, and ruin may give all credit for holiness, power and salvation to Him.[15]

Calvin's affirmation of the deep-rooted sinfulness of the human race not only served as a tool to underscore the overwhelming nature of God's glory, sovereignty, omnipotence, and goodness, but it also "compels us to turn our eyes upward" by creating in us a sense of humility and vulnerability.[16] For Calvin, awareness of sin was of utmost importance for salvation, because—without a sense of our predicament—there will be no desire in us to seek God's mercy and grace.[17] Only through self-denial can our relationship with God be reoriented. We cannot aspire to God until we have begun to be displeased with ourselves.[18]

The downside of Calvin's didactical method is that it is easy to be misled by his debasing and denigrating depictions of human nature after the fall into thinking that he totally devalued the human; that is, if such passages are not understood within the context of his rhetorical and theological intent to accentuate God's glory. The reality is that grace enjoyed precedence in Calvin's thought over sin. Gerrish[19] states it well:

---

14. *CO* 2.566.

15. Calvin, *Catechism*, art. 6. (*De Peccato et Morte*), *CO* 5.326: "Haec cogitatio quanquam hominem terrore consternat, ac desperatione obruit, nobis tamen necessaria est: quo propria iustitia exuti, propriae virtutis fiducia deiecti, omni vitae exspectatione depulsi, discamus paupertatis, miseriae, ignominiae nostrae conscientia coram Domino consternari, iniquitatis, impotentiae, ruinae nostrae agnitione, omnem illi sanctitatis, virtutis, salutis gloriam deferre."

16. Calvin, *Institutes*, 1.1.1; *CO* 2.31: "Praesertim miserabilis haec ruina, in quam nos deiecit primi hominis defectio, sursum oculos cogit attollere, non modo ut inde ieiuni et famelici petamus quod nobis deest, sed metu experge facti humilitatem discamus."

17. Cf. *CO* 2.185.

18. *CO* 2.33.

19. See Gerrish, "Mirror of God's Goodness," 211.

The restoration of man in Christ has dogmatic precedence even over the doctrine of the original estate, since, so he argues, we know of Adam's blessedness only by viewing it in Christ, the Second Adam.

Sin, Bondage, and Accountability

When speaking about sin, Calvin often used the term "flesh" as a synecdoche. In Calvin's thinking, "flesh" denotes the human being in "the fallen condition of sinfulness" before regeneration.[20] It is the principle of bondage that governs the whole of human nature and subjects the human to his fallen state through the tyrannical superiority of carnal lusts and desires.[21] Despite being vitiated by sin, the body as motion devoid of essence plays no role "in the corruption of the soul, or its own corruption", but is the "helpless victim" of the "destructive hegemony of flesh."[22] Sometimes Calvin used the term "body" synonymously with "flesh" as an indication of the human being's sinful existence. For instance, when he spoke of the body as a prison he essentially referred to the fallen condition of temporal life, not the human being's corporeal existence.[23]

Calvin regarded the human soul as one of a kind, because it possesses a "unique potential for relationship with God."[24] It is therefore not surprising that Calvin also located the corruption of sin in the soul.[25] This does not mean that other parts of the human being are not vitiated by sin, but the soul as the seat of the *imago Dei* and the source of human action is the principle location of sin.[26] By locating sin in the soul's faculties of reason and will, Calvin underscored both the noetic and volitional aspects of sin.[27] He consistently used the metaphor of "blindness" to explain sin's hegemony over human reason. Sin "darkens our understanding" and "blinds our hearts."[28]

---

20. Calvin, *Romans*, 230; *CO* 49.111. See Miles, "Theology, Anthropology," 311.
21. *CO* 2.413. See Calvin, "Psychopannychia," 443; *CO* 5.196.
22. Miles, "Theology, Anthropology," 314.
23. *CO* 49.111.
24. Pitkin, "Protestant Zeno," 353.
25. *CO* 2.193.
26. Cf. *CO* 2.182; 2.184.
27. See Pitkin, "Protestant Zeno," 355–56.
28. Calvin, *Institutes*, 2.3.1, *CO* 2.210: "Nam quod gentes omnes scribit (Eph. 4, 17. 18) ambulare in vanitate mentis suae, obtenebratas esse intelligentia, alienatas a vita Dei, propter ignorantiam quae in ipsis est, et caecitatem cordis sui, minime est dubium quin competat in eos omnes quos Dominus ad rectitudinem suae tum sapientiae, tum iustitiae nondum reformavit."

Human reason is cut off from its source of knowledge and deprived of the light of God and therefore becomes "carnally" minded.[29] The "blindness" that sin brings forth not only corrupts the human mind, but it also leads to idols being created and venerated in the place of God.[30] The human being is inclined to "fashion for himself an idol or spectre in place of God."[31] Actually, reason itself becomes an idol. No longer are human beings content to consult God's will and to confine reason to the boundaries of God's will, but reason itself is elevated above God.[32] The result is a loss of communion with God. For Calvin, the human's pride and self-adoration is the exact opposite of the image of God that is directed towards reflecting God's virtues and heightening God's glory.

According to Calvin, the sin-infected mind is not able to direct the will towards rejecting sin. The will as the volitional principle in the human being is also totally prone to sin.[33] Yet, Calvin insisted that the will is not coerced by sin in the sense that it is dragged unwillingly into corruption. As a matter of fact, it is bound by sin, which means that because of its corruptness it willingly and of its own accord chooses nothing but evil. The will's corruption is self-determined because it sins voluntarily.[34]

Since sin is self-inflicted it can in no sense be imputed to God, neither by attributing it to created human nature,[35] nor to the order of nature. Such an inconceivable notion would be an affront to God's goodness.[36] The human is evil because of his own wrongdoing by which he "brought wretchedness upon himself."[37] According to Calvin, sin makes the human liable to condemnation and this leads to a loss of communion with and participation in God.[38] Our alienation from God is demonstrated by death, which is God's curse on sin. Death denotes that the human being is cut off from its "Fountain of life" and thus lives in a state of demise.[39]

29. Cf. Calvin, *Institutes*, 2.3.1; CO 2.209: "Affectus enim carnis . . . mors est."

30. Calvin, *Institutes*, 1.15.12; CO 2.49: "humanae mentis caecitas."

31. Calvin, *Institutes*, 1.15.12; CO 2.49: "vix unus unquam repertus est qui non sibi idolum vel spectrum Dei loco fabricaret."

32. CO 2.51-52.

33. CO 31.206.

34. CO 6.280.

35. Calvin vehemently opposed the idea of the Manicheans that evil is part of the substance of the human. Instead, he regarded evil as accidental to human nature, a corruption that occurred through the human's own fault. See CO 6.263.

36. SC 11/1.55; CO 2.32.

37. Calvin, *Bondage and Liberation*, 47; CO 6.263: "qua miseriam hanc sibi accersavit."

38. CO 23.32.

39. Calvin, *Commentaries on Genesis*, 1:127; CO 23.454: "a Deo vitae fonte."

The question is: How can this curse be imposed on all of humankind because of the sin of their primeval parents? Calvin explained that Adam was not merely a "progenitor" but "a root" who, through his corruption, vitiated the whole human race.[40] Sin is, therefore, systemic in nature; when Adam sinned, he "transmitted the contagion to all his posterity."[41] Adam's posterity is liable to God's punishment; not because Adam's sin pertains to them, but because they are infected by the same corruption.[42] The question Calvin faced was: How can human beings be held liable by God if their actions are necessitated by their corrupted nature?

In his commentary on Genesis, Calvin suggested that God created the human with an ability to choose between good and evil. Tragically, the human chose to be independent from God and to depart from God's perfect wisdom resulting in bondage to sin.[43] In creating the human being with the ability to choose, God not only allowed for the possibility that humans could revolt against him,[44] but in fact, God ordained that they be tempted:

> Adam did not fall without the ordination and will of God, I do not take it as if sin had been ever pleasing to Him, or as if He simply wished that the precept which he had given should be violated. So far as the fall of Adam was the subversion of equity, and of well constituted order, so far as it was contumacy against the Divine Law Giver, and the transgression of righteousness, certainly it was against the will of God; yet none of these things

---

40. Calvin, *Institutes*, 2.1.6; *CO* 2.180: "Ita certe habendum est: fuisse Adamum humanae naturae non progenitorem modo, sed quasi radicem." See Denlinger, "Calvin's Understanding," 242. Calvin shifted the debate on the transmission of sin from Augustine's biological categories to noetic categories. For Calvin, sin is first of all moral and religious blindness, not something transmitted through sexual concupiscence as posited by Augustine. According to Calvin, we share a corporate solidarity in sin and death because our being is corrupt. The mere fact that we are born corrupted makes us guilty before God. It is thus important to note that Calvin does not distinguish, as some federalists do, between the human's original guilt in Adam and the actual perversion of sin that gradually follows through time. Perversion and guilt are closely interconnected. The perversion of sin brings guilt, while guilt brings perversion. In any case, Calvin did not regard the debate on the nature of the transmission of sins as of theological import. In his commentary on Psalm 51:7 (*CO* 31.54), Calvin states that the question on the transmission of sins is not important and that it is not sensible to enter into such mysterious discussions.

41. Calvin, *Institutes*, 2.1.6; *CO* 2.181: "Sic ergo se corrupit Adam, ut ab eo transierit in totam sobolem contagio."

42. Calvin, *Institutes*, 2.1.6; *CO* 2.180.

43. Calvin, *Commentaries on Genesis*, 1:118; *CO* 23.38. According to Calvin, the root of humanity's defection from God was infidelity and a desire to exalt themselves against God by acquiring illicit knowledge. See *CO* 23.60–61; *CO* 2.188.

44. *CO* 23.59–60.

render it impossible that, for a certain cause, although to us unknown, he might will the fall of man.⁴⁵

In his *Institutes*, Calvin used stronger terms. God not only "foresaw the Fall" but actually "arranged" it.⁴⁶

This position of Calvin was due to his unrelenting belief in God's omnipotent providence; nothing can occur outside of God's will. Though God created human beings with the ability to choose, they are not able to act outside God's eternal decree.⁴⁷ While Calvin consistently maintained the position that God is not the Author of sin, he struggled to reconcile this with his belief in God's omnipotence that entails that everything happens according to God's will and eternal counsel. The following quotation reveals the inner tension that Calvin experienced on the matter:

> It offends the ears of some, when it is said that God willed this Fall; but what else I pray is the permission of Him, who has the power of preventing, and in whose hand the whole matter is placed, but his Will?⁴⁸

Calvin held that, even though God willed the temptation, he cannot be regarded as the Author of sin, since the human sinned voluntarily.⁴⁹ Two questions naturally arise: firstly, how can God ordain something, but not be regarded as complicit in the outcome of the action? Secondly, how can human nature sin voluntarily if their actions are necessitated by an ordination of God?

Calvin addressed this conundrum by employing the Scholastic distinction between absolute and relative necessity. In contrast to Luther's view of necessity as compulsion, Calvin explicitly supported in the 1559 *Institutes* the notion of relative necessity.⁵⁰

---

45. Calvin, *Commentaries on Genesis*, 1:144; *CO* 23.55: "Sed quum dico non sine Dei ordinatione et nutu lapsum fuisse Adam, non ita accipio quasi peccatum illi unquam placuerit, aut simpliciter voluerit praeceptum quod dederat violari. Quatenus recti et bene compositi ordinis eversio fuit Adae lapsus, quatenus in Deum legislatorem contumacia, et iustitiae transgressio: Dei voluntati fuisse adversum certum est. Horum tamen nihil obstat quominus certa de causa, licet nobis incognita, hominem labi voluerit."

46. Calvin, *Institutes*, 3.23.7; *CO* 2.704: "Nec absurdum videri debet quod dico, Deum non modo primi hominis casum, et in eo posterorum ruinam praevidisse, sed arbitrio quoque suo dispensasse."

47. Lane, "Did Calvin Believe in Free-Will," 75.

48. Calvin, *Commentaries on Genesis*, 1:144; *CO* 23.55: "Offendit quorundam aures, quum dicitur, Deum voluisse: sed quid, obsecro, aliud est eius permissio qui prohibendi ius habet, imo cuius in manu res est posita, quam voluntas?"

49. *CO* 23.64.

50. Calvin, *Institutes*, 1.16.8–9; *CO* 2.152–53: "ubi Dei voluntatem summam esse

> God is the supreme and primary cause of all things ... at the same time that which God has determined, though it must come to pass, is not, however, precisely, or in its own nature, necessary ... there was good ground for the distinction which the Schoolmen made between necessity, secundum quid, and necessity absolute, also between the necessity of consequent and of consequence.

Relative necessity entails that, though God controls all things, it is fortuitous to us. From a divine perspective all things are determined, but from a human perspective the future is contingent. Marko[51] elucidates well what the Reformers understood under contingency:

> An absence of necessity, not to be equated with chance, but rather to be understood as the free operation of secondary causes. In a contingent circumstance, an effect results from clearly definable causes, though the effect could be different, given an entirely possible and different interrelation of causes. In short, a contingent event or thing is a non-necessary event or thing that either might not exist or could be other than it is.

That which God has determined is thus, from a human point of view, not absolutely necessary.[52] Even though humans sin "necessarily," they do not sin by absolute necessity, because they are not coerced by external compulsion. Necessity does not mean that sin is committed without "willful and evil intent."[53] Calvin stated it as follows:

> Man, since he was corrupted by the Fall, sins not forced or unwilling, but voluntarily, by a most forward bias of the mind; not by violent compulsion, or external force, but by the movement of his own passion; and yet such is the depravity of his nature, that he cannot move and act except in the direction of evil. If

---

probat et primam omnium causam ... Interea quod statuit Deus, sic necesse est evenire ut tamen neque praecis, nequesuapte natura neccesarium sit. Unde iterum videmus, non temere in scholisinventas fuisse distinctions de necessitate secundum quid, et absoluta; item consequentis et consequential."

51. Marko, "Free Choice," 41.

52. See CO 2.152. Also see Lane, "Did Calvin Believe in Free-Will," 72–90. Lane notes that, in Calvin's thought, the fallen will is not free in the sense that it can choose between good and evil, but it is also not "coerced" by external impulses. Instead it is "self-determined" in that we choose of our "own accord." See Pitkin, "Protestant Zeno," 365.

53. Calvin, *Institutes*, 2.4.1; CO 2.224: "dum necessario peccat, nihilo tamen minus voluntarie peccare." See Pitkin, "Protestant Zeno," 365.

this is true, the thing not obscurely expressed is, that he is under a necessity of sinning.[54]

Closely related to the argument on necessity, was the two-causes argument that Calvin borrowed from the broader Christian-Aristotelian tradition to explain why God cannot be regarded as the Author of evil. In order to avoid dualism, classical theology distinguished between the *causa prima*, the *causa secundae* and the *causa finalis*. The *causa prima* refers to God as the first cause of all things who, through his eternal decree, takes the initiative in the creation of all things. There can be no other *causa prima* than God. All other causes that emanate from the first cause are relative to the first cause and are themselves always taken up in a wider network of other causes.[55] Though second causes are contingent, God still is actively involved in his creation. Muller states it aptly:

> Calvin indicates that it would be quite "absurd" to claim that there is no contingency in the world: on the one hand what God ordains necessarily occurs – but the things God has ordained are not necessary in their own nature. Although "the order of nature" is "ordained" by God, this ordination does not exclude contingency so that his "certain providence" is conjoined with contingencies: providence does not bind the hands of human beings.[56]

Applied to the relation between God and sin, the two-causes argument entails that, though God is the principal cause, he is not the immediate author of all actions, since secondary causes that flow from the primary cause have their own integrity and can be regarded as contingent.[57] In his *Letter Concerning the Eternal Predestination of God*, Calvin made it clear that the hardening of the human will should not be ascribed to God:

> We do not make the minds of men to be impelled by force external to them so that they rage furiously; nor do we transfer to God as the cause of hardening, in such a way that they did

---

54. Calvin, *Institutes*, 2.3.5; CO 2.214: "Haec igitur distinctionis summa observetur, hominem, ut vitiatus est ex lapsu, volentem quidem peccare, non invitum nec coactum; affectione animi propensissima, non violenta coactione; propriae libidinis motu, non extraria coactione; qua tamen est naturae pravitate, non posse nisi ad malum moveri et agi. Quod si verum est, peccandi certe necessitati subiacere non obscure exprimitur."

55. See Beek, *Een Lichtkring om het Kruis*, 359.

56. Muller, *Divine Will and Human Choice*, 190–91. See van de Beek, *Een Lichtkring om het Kruis*, 359, 369.

57. See Engel, *John Calvin's Perspectival Anthropology*, 135–36 for various examples in Calvin's works where he uses this argument.

> not voluntarily and by their own wickedness and hardness of heart spur themselves on to obstinacy. What we say is that men act perversely not without God's ordination that it be done, as Scripture teaches.[58]

In his commentary on Isaiah, Calvin further elucidated his view:

> If God controls the purposes of men, and turns their thoughts and exertions to whatever purpose he pleases, men do not therefore cease to form plans and to engage this or the other undertaking. We must not suppose that there is a violent compulsion, as if God dragged them against their will, but in a wonderful and conceivable manner he regulates all the movements of men, so that they still have the exercise of their Will.[59]

The question is: How should we regard evil? Is it a cause of its own? Thomas Aquinas held that evil is *privatio boni*, because it has no *causa finalis* of its own. Evil is accidental in nature, it derives from the chain of secondary causes, and it affects the chain of events, but it has no meaning of its own nor can it change the *causa finalis* determined by God.[60]

Calvin, similarly, employed the two-causes argument to state that, since God is not the "Author of evil but the first cause, human beings remain free from compulsion."[61] Relying on these philosophical premises, Calvin posited that the human "held captive under bondage of sin" possesses no free choice, while also maintaining that even though we are powerless to avoid sin, it is nonetheless voluntary.[62]

---

58. Calvin, *Concerning the Eternal Predestination*; CO 8.357–58: "quando neque extrinseco motu impelli fingimus hominum animos, ut violenter ferantur, neque in Deum transferimus indurationis causam, ac si non sponte propriaque militia duri et immites, se ipsos ad pervicaciam acuerent: sed quod perverse homines faciunt, non nisi Deo ordinante fieri, scriptura docet."

59. Calvin, *Isaiah*, 352; CO 36.222: "Nec enim si Deus hominum consilia sibi subiicit, et studia conatusque vertit. In quemqunque visum est finem ideo consilia agitur et hoc vel illud moliri desinunt homines, quando hic violenta coaction fingendo non est, ac si Deus traheret nolentes: sed mira et incomprehensibili ratione omnes hominum temperat, ut tamen illis maneat sua voluntas."

60. See Beek, *Een Lichtkring om het Kruis*, 369–70.

61. Engel, *Calvin's Perspectival Anthropology*, 135.

62. Calvin, *Bondage and Liberation*, 37; CO 6.263: "Nunc quidem captivum teneri sub peccati servitude arbitrium nostrum asserimus." In his reply to Pighius, Calvin uses the example of a sick person. A person might be sick of his own accord. Hence it was possible for him not to become ill, but when he became ill it is no longer possible for him to undo his sickness caused by an unrestrained life. In the same manner humankind sinned voluntarily, but through the voluntary sin, became entangled in the bondage of the sin. Humankind's bondage in sin is not attributable to God, but to human

Calvin was adamant that nothing can happen or exist outside of God's will. God does not merely allow sin, because he is not a passive God, but he actively willed the fall because he always acts as the *causa prima*. All events are thus causally related to each other and therefore always have meaning.[63] Yet, Calvin also maintained that we need to make a distinction between what God wills and what he commands. God willed that Adam sinned, but he did not command Adam to sin. Adam thus is guilty of his own voluntary actions.[64]

The objection might be leveled against Calvin's theory that God still acts immorally if he sets in motion a primary cause that might result in a distorted secondary event. The argument is that an individual or person that is a principal author of an action by instigating, arranging, ordaining or permitting an action cannot be absolved from being culpable of the consequences that might ensue. However, Calvin held that God acts in this way in order to preserve the own integrity of creation and human beings. God willed the fall in a way that included Adam's free will. Calvin, hence, affirmed secondary causes and their contingency, whilst recognizing human responsibility and agency.[65] God does not use humans as if they are inanimate creatures that can neither act nor choose, nor are they externally coerced to sin. Their inclination to sin necessarily arises from their own nature and choice.[66] Secondly, God's decrees as first causes are good because the *causa finalis* of his decree is good and to the benefit of the whole creation. If God did not will a fall, there would be no opportunity for God to show his love towards humankind through Jesus Christ and for human beings to know God through Christ. The secondary actions of Adam thus ought to be seen in relation to God's *causa finalis* in Christ.[67] Thirdly, Calvin did not regard God and human beings as operating on the same ontological level.[68] The logic that applies to human conduct thus cannot necessarily be applied to God. Since God and human beings operate in different ontological levels, the primary/secondary causation distinction is for Calvin a necessary construction and allowed him to state that God is absolutely sovereign, while humans are at the same time totally responsible for their actions. God's

---

nature because the origin of the bondage is due to an initial voluntary act. See Calvin, *Bondage and Liberation*, 144–45; CO 6.335.

63. See Beek, *Een Lichtkring om het Kruis*, 361.
64. CO 2.172. Beek, *Een Lichtkring om het Kruis*, 363.
65. See Muller, *Divine Will and Human Choice*, 187.
66. See Lane, "Did Calvin Believe in Free-will," 78.
67. CO 2.170–71.
68. See CO 2.157.

omnipotence entails that he has the power to establish the contingency of second causes, and since second causes are contingent in nature, humans are culpable of their sins. Even if God is the origin of evil, in a human sense, that evil is good because it serves our best interests.[69]

The Westminster Confession of Faith followed Calvin in relying heavily on the two-causes distinction to affirm both God's absolute sovereignty and the responsibility of humanity for its sin. Article 3.1 states:

> God from all eternity, did by the most wise and holy counsel of His own will, freely and unchangeably ordain whosoever comes to pass: yet so, as thereby neither is God the author of sin, nor is violence offered to the will of the creatures, nor is the liberty or contingency of second causes taken away, but rather established.

In article 5.2 the Westminster Confession comments as follows on the providence of God:

> Although in relation to the foreknowledge and decree of God, the first cause, all things come to pass immutably and infallibly; yet by the same providence, He ordereth them to fall out, according to the nature of second causes, either necessarily, freely, or contingently.

In article 5.4 the Confession proceeds to use the same distinction to state that, though the fall is part of the "ordering and governing" of God, its sinfulness proceeds only from the creature.

Though Calvin was cautious not to speculate, he also used the two-causes argument to explain how sin fits within God's purpose. Calvin's proposition was that the sins of wicked people are like saws in God's hand that moves, turns and directs them where he will; yet their doing of evil originates from them and is to be imputed only to them.[70] God is not the Author of evil when he uses the ungodly to "accomplish and execute his works through them, but rather a wonderfully expert craftsman who can use bad tools as well."[71]

Admittedly, the relation between God's goodness and omnipotence and human accountability for sin is a deep mystery that defies human explanation. We indeed risk overstepping the boundaries of human reason by

---

69. See Beek, *Een Lichtkring om het Kruis*, 390.

70. CO 6.264.

71. Calvin, *Bondage and Liberation*, CO 6.258: "Tum intelligemus, nec Deum fieri malorum autorem, quum dicitur impios agere quo vult, et per illos opus suum peragere et exsequi: sed potius confitebimur esse eximium et mirificum artificem, qui bene etiam malis intrumentis utatur."

trying to explain this mystery. Yet, the critique that Calvin's theology makes God the Author of sin, in my view, does not sufficiently take into account Calvin's two-causes argument and his view that God and human beings operate on different ontological levels. By using the two-causes argument, Calvin attempted to maintain the ontological distance between God and the world of the second causes. Calvin's contribution, and for that matter Thomas Aquinas, exists therein that they maintained the sovereignty of God by not recognizing evil as an independent power that exists alongside God. Evil is accidental in nature, it cannot function outside of God's will and it eventually serves God's destination with his creation.

Sin and the *Imago Dei*

According to Van Vliet, Calvin's description of the *imago Dei* matures over time, but the core of his definition remains fairly consistent.[72] Van Vliet states that Calvin "changed his mind about certain aspects of the *imago Dei*, clarified other matters, and added things which were previously lacking."[73] Calvin's initial position regarding the effect of sin on the *imago Dei*, was that sin totally destroys the image of God in the human.[74] In the 1536 edition of his *Institutes* he simply stated that the image of God was "effaced" by sin; in his 1538 Catechism he described the image as "wiped" out, while in the 1539 edition of the *Institutes* he made no effort to alter the position.[75] Pighius entered into debate with Calvin on this point, accusing Calvin of turning human beings into "brute beasts."[76] In his response, Calvin called attention to his rhetorical intent. He stated that his teaching on sin serves to remind human beings that they should not fix the blame elsewhere when finding the root of evil in themselves; secondly, they must give God credit when doing good; and third only God in his omnipotence is able to restrain and bridle sin. The believer thus should find comfort in God's omnipotence,

---

72. Van Vliet, *Children of God*, 253.

73. Van Vliet, *Children of God*, 256.

74. According to Engel, Calvin spoke from the perspective of God as judge when he pronounced the image as lost, while he used the softer language of "corrupted human nature" when approaching the topic from the relative perspective of humankind. I find this thesis somewhat unconvincing and superficial, since Calvin's references to human nature as "corrupted but not destroyed" enters his works relatively late in his career. See Engel, *John Calvin's Perspectival Anthropology*, 57–59.

75. Calvin, *Institutes of the Christian Religion 1536*, 16; CO 1.28: "haec imago et similitudo Dei inducta et obliterata est"; *Catechism*, art. 4 (*De Homine*); CO 5.325: "obliterata Dei similitudine."

76. Calvin, *Bondage and Liberation*, 38; CO 6.257: "homines vertuntur in pecudes."

not in his own capacity to fight evil.[77] By proclaiming the total annihilation of the *imago Dei*, Calvin's intention was clearly not to dehumanize the human being. Human dignity is not dependent upon the survival of the *imago Dei* in us, but of God upholding our status as human beings.

Possibly as a result of his debate with Pighius, Calvin restated his rhetoric on the total destruction of the *imago Dei*. The challenge he faced was to reconcile his doctrine on sin with his anthropology in a manner that did not diminish God's radical grace by ascribing too much to human capacity, but that, conversely, also avoided dehumanizing the human being to such a degree that virtuous behaviour and a shared social ethics becomes impossible.

Calvin's restated position was that the *imago Dei* is totally corrupted but not destroyed. Corruption entails that depravity is diffused after the fall through all parts of the human's soul and body.[78] It does not "reside in one part only, but pervades the whole soul, and each of its faculties."[79] The human is thus divested from all the distinguishing gifts he once possessed and is reduced to a condition of destitution.[80] What remains after the fall, according to Calvin, is only a miserable "ruin" that reminds us of our original excellence in the same manner that a ruin is reminiscent of the original beauty of a building.[81] In defining the extent of our corruption, Calvin is careful to allow no avenue for semi-Pelagianism. While the "ruins" of the *imago Dei* work in us a longing for restoration in Christ, it is in no sense a sufficient tool to attain salvation through our own efforts. In order to be restored, human nature needs to be renovated by God[82]:

> Although we grant that the image of God was not utterly effaced and destroyed in him, it was, however so corrupted that anything which remains is fearful deformity, and therefore our deliverance begins with that renovation which we obtain from Christ.[83]

---

77. *CO* 6.257.

78. *CO* 23.59.

79. Calvin, *Commentaries on Genesis*, 1:155; *CO* 23.62: "Corruptionem non subsidere una tantum in parte docet, sed totam animam et singulas eius partes occupare."

80. Calvin, *Psalms*, 1:104; *CO* 31.93: "Dei imago . . . ex summa excellentia ad tristem foedamque inopiam redacti."

81. Calvin, *Sermons on Genesis 1–11*, 489; *SC* 11/1.326.

82. Calvin, *Institutes*, 2.1.9; *CO* 2.183.

83. Calvin, *Institutes*, 1.15.4; *CO* 2.138: "Quare etsi demus, non prorsus exinanitam ac deletam in eo fuisse Dei imaginem, sit corrupta fuit, ut quidquid superest, horrenda sit deformitas. Ideoque recuperandae salutis nobis initium est in ea instauratione quam consequimur per Christum."

Though utterly depraved, the "ruin" of human nature still possesses some remnants of the *imago Dei*, which gives us a perception of the "liberality" that God displayed when creating the human.[84] These remnants remind us of God's great mercy, but also create in us an awareness of sin and the utter misery in which we find ourselves.[85] Torrance rightly observes that Calvin turned the original meaning of the *imago Dei* into its opposite; it now actually becomes a symbol of disgrace.[86] Yet, by recognizing the survival of remnants of the *imago Dei* in us, Calvin stressed that sin does not dehumanize the human being.[87] In his sermon on Genesis 9:3–7, Calvin stated that, despite the fall, the human—though depraved—still possesses the image of God. We must therefore "honor and revere" God's image in our fellow human beings and human life must be held sacred.[88] He then proceeds to state:

> Although that image is almost completely destroyed in us, we see clearly how God still shows it in our neighbors and distinguishes them from the brute beasts and demonstrates they possess a nobility and dignity above all creatures.[89]

It might be argued that Calvin does not go far enough to preserve the *humanitas* of the human being after the fall, since he ascribed a very limited role to the remnants of the image that survived. After all, what is noble and dignified about a "ruin"? To be fair, we need to realize that Calvin was primarily concerned with the issue of salvation, not human dignity. From a salvational point of view the "remnants" serve no purpose; the image is basically obliterated, but this should not be misunderstood as amounting to a low view of natural human ability. In fact, in some passages he used quite generous language to rejoice in the admirable skills and abilities of "ungodly" humans as displayed in the arts and sciences.[90] Gerrish states it well:

> What he (Calvin) was concerned to establish was, not that man is utterly bad, but that the taint of sin vitiates even his best and leaves no corner of his life unblemished. And Calvin tried to

---

84. Calvin, *Psalms*, 1:108; *CO* 31.95.
85. *SC* 11/1.55; *SC* 11/1.175.
86. Cf. Torrance, *Calvin's Doctrine on Man*, 101.
87. See Gerrish, "Mirror of God's Goodness," 219.
88. Calvin, *Sermons on Genesis 1–11*, 733; *SC* 11/1.476.
89. Calvin, *Sermons on Genesis 1–11*, 745; *SC* 11/1.485.
90. Cf., for instance, Calvin, *Institutes*, 2.2.25; 2.2.16; *CO* 2.206; 2.199.

demonstrate this thesis, in turn, with respect to both man's intellectual and his moral achievements.[91]

Secondly, Calvin defined good works in a very narrow sense. Only works aimed at glorifying God are regarded by him as virtuous.[92] Beneficial and humanitarian deeds for the sake of humanity or other interests do not qualify as good works, since they are driven by wrong inner intentions.[93]

Calvin carefully delineated his position on the nature of the "remnants" that survive after the fall by distinguishing between the natural and supernatural gifts of the *imago Dei*.[94] The supernatural gifts pertain to those heavenly gifts "above nature" that are "sufficient for the attainment of heavenly life" such as faith, pure knowledge of God, love to God, charity towards the neighbour, righteousness and holiness, while the natural gifts relate to matters of the earthly realm such as intelligence, art, the ability to discern between good and evil, the creation of social bonds, practicing politics and economics, and possessing a sense of becoming and of shame.[95] The effects of sin on the two categories of gifts are dissimilar; the natural gifts were corrupted by sin. Though not destroyed, they were severely weakened and impaired.[96] The supernatural gifts, in contrast, were totally "withdrawn" by God, which makes humans incapable of salvaging themselves.[97] Conse-

---

91. Gerrish, "Mirror of God's Goodness," 219.

92. *CO* 2.565.

93. *CO* 2.565.

94. Calvin took the distinction between supernatural and natural gifts over from scholasticism, but modified it to serve his theology. He, for instance, did not share the Schoolmen's optimism regarding the ability of natural reason to comprehend the human *telos*.

95. Cf. *CO* 2.196; *CO* 31.91.

96. *CO* 2.196.

97. Calvin, *Institutes*, 2.2.12-13; *CO* 2.196-97. The following quotation in *Institutes*, 2.2.13, provides a clear example of Calvin's understanding of the difference between natural and supernatural gifts: "We have one kind of intelligence of earthly things, and another of heavenly things. By earthly things, I mean those who do not relate to God and his kingdom, to true righteousness and future blessedness, but have some connection with the present life, and are in a manner confined within its boundaries. By heavenly things, I mean the pure knowledge of God, the method of true righteousness, and the mysteries of the heavenly kingdom. To the former belong matters of policy and economy, all mechanical arts and liberal studies. To the latter belong the knowledge of God and of his will, and the means of framing the life in accordance with them." See *CO* 2.197: "Sit ergo haec distinctio, esse aliam quidem rerum terrenarum intelligentiam, aliam vero coelestium. Res terrenas voco, quae ad Deum regnumque eius, ad veram iustitiam, ad futurae vitae beatitudinem non pertingunt, sed cum vita praesenti rationem relationemque habent, et quodammodo intra eius fines continentur. Res coelestes, puram Dei notitiam, verae iustitiae rationem, ac regni coelestis mysteria.

quently, the "remnants" only refer to the vestiges of the natural gifts that the human originally possessed, not to spiritual gifts. This distinction enabled Calvin to preserve the *humanitas* of all people, including unbelievers, and to sustain the possibility of a shared social ethics,[98] while affirming the doctrine of salvation through faith in Christ alone without any human merit.[99]

Calvin's attributed the loss of the supernatural gifts to God's punishment: alienated from his Creator God, the human being was "stripped" of the "excellent gifts" with which he had been previously "adorned."[100] He stated quite explicitly that the human's corruption was not due to some process of natural degeneration, but to God's will:

> For the human race has not naturally derived corruption through his descent from Adam; but that result is rather to be traced to the appointment of God, who, as he had adorned the whole nature of mankind with most excellent endowments in one man, so in the same man he again denuded it.[101]

Calvin's position can be ascribed to his firm belief that the human being lives, moves and exists in God and that nothing occurs outside God's will. This position of Calvin might be regarded by some as ambiguous. If the corrupted nature of *the imago Dei* is due to God denuding the human being from his excellent gifts, is God not made instrumental in the sinful effects of the fall? How can the human be held liable for sin if God denudes him of the very qualities he needs to know and serve God? Calvin's answer is that

---

In priore genere sunt politia, oeconomia, artes omnes mechanicae, disciplinaeque liberales. In secundo, Dei ac divinae voluntatis cognitio, et vitae secundum eam formandae regula."

98. Calvin's understanding of the possibility of a shared social ethics after the fall is illustrated by the following quotation from *Institutes*, 2.2.13: "Since man is by nature a social animal, he is disposed, from natural instinct, to cherish and preserve society; and accordingly we see that the minds of all men have impressions of civil order and honesty. Hence it is that every individual understands how human societies must be regulated by laws, and also is able to comprehend the principles of those laws." See *CO* 2.19: "quoniam homo animal est natura sociale, naturali quoque instinctu, ad fovendam conservandamque eam societatem propendet; ideoque civilis cuiusdam et honestatis et ordinis universalis impressionis inesse omnium hominum animis conspicimus. Hinc fit ut nemo reperiatur qui non intelligat, oportere quosvis hominum coetus legibus contineri, quique non earum legume principia mente complectatur."

99. See Gerrish, "Mirror of God's Goodness," 213.

100. Calvin, *Sermons on Genesis 1–11*, 95; *SC* 11/1.57; Calvin, *Commentaries on Genesis*, 1:155; *CO* 23.63.

101. Calvin, *Commentaries on Genesis*, 1:156; *CO* 23.62: "Neque enim naturaliter ex Adae progenie corruptionem traxerunt posteri: sed id potius ex Dei ordinatione pendet: qui sicuti totam humani generis naturam in uno homine ornaverat praestantissimus dotibus, ita in eodem ipsam nudavit."

our supernatural endowments are gifts and God has the right to take away gifts whenever he wants:

> Now if any should object that it is unjust for the innocent to bear the punishment of another's sin, I answer, whatever gifts God had conferred upon us in the person of Adam, he had the best right to take it away, when Adam wickedly fell.[102]

Calvin's argument was that if Adam truly had a choice and the full ability to obey God, God is just in holding Adam and those he represented liable for their inevitable disobedience, since it was their own guilt that prompted the punishment. Since God has the right to punish, he also has the right to choose the instrument of punishment.

Calvin ascribed the preservation of some remnants of the natural gifts in humankind to God's common grace;[103] in doing so, he attempted to avoid creating an opportunity for any teaching that denies the total and radical nature of sin. For Calvin, the survival of "remnants" of the image is not a result of some innate capability within the human that was capable of surviving the onslaught of sin, but it is wholly due to God who sustains the "remnants" and acts for the "common benefit of mankind."[104] Torrance's criticism that Calvin's doctrine on the total corruptness of the human being cannot be reconciled with his doctrine on remnants of the *imago Dei* surviving after the fall is not quite legitimate.[105] Berkouwer[106] rightly points out that Calvin

---

102. Calvin, *Commentaries on Genesis*, 1:156; CO 23.62: "Nunc si quis obiiciat, iniquum esse ut poenam alieni peccati luant insontes: respondeo, quidquid donorum nobis in Adae persona contulerat Deus, potuisse iure optimo auferre, quum ille impie descivit."

103. Calvin himself does not use the term common grace, but the idea is present in his works. The term "common grace" (*algemeene gratie*) was developed most extensively by the Dutch theologian Abraham Kuyper, who utilized Calvin's distinction between different forms of grace to develop a social doctrine that differentiates between various social spheres governed by different forms of grace. While both kinds of grace come from the one God, they differ both in reach and effect. Specific grace is a salvational kind of grace, whereas common grace has a universal scope and a preservative, providential, and non-salvational effect. God displays his special grace through the Holy Spirit that regenerates believers by working faith in them, while he uses his common grace to preserve the created order amidst the effects of sin. God's preservation of creation exist therein that he governs in his providence "the counsels and wills of men" as to "move exactly in the course which he has destined" (Calvin, *Institutes*, 1.16.8). CO 2.151: "eius providentia . . . hominum etiam consilia et voluntates gubernari sic asserimus, ut ad destinatum ab ea scopum recta ferantur."

104. Calvin, *Institutes*, 2.2.16; CO 2.199: "bona, quae in publicum generis humani bonum, quibus vult, dispensat."

105. See Torrance, *Calvin's Doctrine of Man*, 93.

106. See Berkouwer, *De Mens het Beelds God*, 160–62

was not working with substantive terms, but that he regarded the remnants as gifts of God. Actually, for Calvin, there is nothing praiseworthy that does not proceed from God.[107] Hence, though radical and comprehensive, sin does not involve an "ontological break" with God, because God keeps affirming his gracious intentions towards his creation.[108] Common grace is the result of God keeping his original purpose with creation in mind.[109] Calvin stated it as follows:

> Had God not spared us, our revolt would have carried along with it the entire destruction of human nature.[110]

The Spirit is the primary instrument in God's bestowal of common grace. While not working faith in all men, the Spirit "fills, moves and invigorates" all people and provides them with a sense of right and wrong in order to preserve order.[111] With regard to the earthly realm no "man is devoid of the light of reason."[112] In fact, the human mind "is still adorned and invested with admirable gifts from its Creator."[113] Calvin deduced from Romans 2 that the natural law is naturally "engraved" on the minds of all people, even Gentiles.[114] This is displayed in the ability of Gentiles to distinguish between right and wrong, have a "sense of judgment" and maintain "some integrity among themselves."[115] This natural knowledge of right and wrong, though, is not sufficient for salvation; it bears no relation to the renewal of the human being in Christ, but only serves the maintenance of the earthly realm.[116] As a

107. *CO* 2.197.

108. See Torrance, *Calvin's Doctrine on Man*, 83, 92.

109. *CO* 23.63.

110. Calvin, *Institutes*, 2.2.17; *CO* 2.199: "nisi nobis pepercisset, totius naturae interitum secum traxisset defectio."

111. Calvin, *Institutes*, 2.2.16; *CO* 2.199: "replet, movet, vegetat omnia eiusdem spiritus virtute."

112. Calvin, *Institutes*, 2.2.13; *CO* 2.197: "nullum destitui luce rationis hominem."

113. Calvin, *Institutes*, 2.2.15; *CO* 2.198: "eximiis tamen etiamnum Dei donis vestitam esse et exornatam."

114. Calvin, *Institutes*, 2.2.22; *CO* 2.203.

115. Calvin, *Sermons on Genesis 1–11*, 745; *SC* 11/1.485.

116. *CO* 2.203. Calvin states that human beings are "blinder than moles" when it comes to knowledge of God as he is in himself and in relation to us. See Calvin, *Institutes*, 2.2.18; *CO* 2.200. VanDrunen rightly notes that Calvin's use of the concept of natural law must be understood in relation to his two kingdoms doctrine. In the two kingdoms natural law serves both a negative and positive function. With regard to the earthly realm the function of natural law is essentially positive. It sets forth standards for "legal and political endeavors." In the heavenly realm its function is negative; it makes us aware of our sins and leaves as guilty before God. See VanDrunen, "Context of Natural Law," 505.

matter of fact, Calvin related the remnants of natural knowledge directly to his doctrine on double predestination. The remnants serve as a justification for God's punishment, since it renders all sins inexcusable.[117] Thus, because all people have enough natural knowledge to distinguish between right and wrong, the non-elect are liable for punishment.

Evaluation and Reflection

The doctrine of sin is probably the most difficult theological theme to deal with. Though we see the reality of evil and sin all around us, its origin and nature is, as Calvin himself contended, a mystery. Any reflection on sin is therefore bound to be plagued by impasses, ambiguities and inconsistencies. Yet, theology cannot escape reflecting on sin because it is so fundamentally part of human nature.

To give a fair assessment of Calvin's doctrine on sin, we need to take account of some mitigating factors. A defining feature of Calvin's doctrine on human sinfulness is the dialectical nature of its construction. Because Calvin used the sinfulness of human nature as a foil for the radical nature of God's grace, his theology is simultaneously profoundly pessimistic about humanity, but also pervasively optimistic. From one point of view "we are nothing, and from the other how magnified."[118] That is why Calvin was able to call human beings at once "vermin" but also God's most "noble" creatures.[119] Yet, it is important to note that in Calvin's theology, God's grace eventually overwhelms human sinfulness.[120] This fundamental position of Calvin can easily become obscured and his theological anthropology can undeservedly be made out as "pessimistic" if the dialectical construction of his theological anthropology is overlooked.

Secondly, it is important to note that Calvin's theology evolved through time. He consistently enhanced and amended his doctrines in response to the criticisms he received and the debates in which he was involved. Notably, in response to the criticisms of Pighius, Calvin restated his earlier position on the destruction of the image after the fall to one of a total corruption of the image. This turn provided Calvin's theology with greater coherence

---

117. *CO* 2.203, 565.

118. Calvin, *Institutes*, 3.2.25; *CO* 2.419: "iam si utraque consideration diligenter inspexerimus nos quid sumus, imo in una quam nihil, in altera quam magnificati."

119. Cf. Calvin, *Sermons on Job*, 33; *CO* 33.127–52 and Calvin, *Sermons on Genesis 1–11*, *SC* 11/1.54–67.

120. His placing of the doctrine of sin in the second book of the *Institutes*, which deals with soteriology, is evidence of this.

and helped him to integrate his doctrine on sin with his doctrines on the two kingdoms of God and God's special and general grace.

The device Calvin applied most often to explain the dialectic between human beings' total corruption and their ability to act morally despite sin, is the distinction between the natural and supernatural. With regard to the natural realm Calvin affirmed human freedom. He extolled the natural gifts of fallen man in various disciplines such as the sciences, arts, economics and politics. The corruption of the *imago Dei* does not entail that humans are dehumanized or capable of nothing but sin. The human's natural gifts endure because of God's common grace and universal providence that preserves creation and humanity despite sin. Humans still have the natural law encrypted in their minds to give them a sense of right and wrong and, notwithstanding sin, they still possess an earthly wisdom that allows them to seek the good. Yet, with regard to the supernatural realm, Calvin allowed little space for human freedom. Humans are unable to turn to God by themselves, to conquer sins through their own efforts, to attain salvation based on merit, or to attain heavenly wisdom by themselves. Calvin stressed the inability of human beings with regard to the supernatural to such a degree that he sometimes created the impression that human existence is fallen in all areas, and totally incapable of any good or virtue. As a matter of fact, overzealous rhetoric often led Calvin to make strong statements that are not reconcilable with his theology as a whole. This peculiar characteristic of Calvin's writings makes his works difficult to interpret and demands that interpreters pay special attention to the various contexts within which he uttered his words.

A fundamental question pertaining to Calvin's doctrine on sin is whether Calvin's relative necessity and two-causes doctrines recuse him from the charge of determinism? Albert Schweitzer, for instance, accused Calvin of emphasizing God's primary causation to such a degree that secondary causations are totally subsumed. God eventually becomes the sole Actor who determines all things.[121] Lane, however, rightly notes that we need to employ the term "determinism" carefully. Calvin's doctrine on providence implied that "man's choices are in some sense determined by God," but Lane argues that Calvin did not subject human beings to a "deterministic fate" as if their actions are simply the result of "a fixed process of cause and effect", nor did Calvin hold to a notion of absolute necessity, but allowed for the "real secondary causality of man."[122] Lane also remarks that "Calvin preserved the human will and made man the real agent in all

---

121. See Muller, *Divine Will and Human Choice*, 20.
122. Lane, "Did Calvin Believe in Free-Will," 72.

that he does."[123] Stated differently, Calvin argued that the bondage of the human will to sin does not mean that they are coerced to sin. Though humans sin inevitably, they sin voluntarily, of their own accord; not because of any external compulsion. Sin is wholly a self-determined choice of the human being and inevitably carries with it devastating consequences.

Admittedly, by relating the fall on some occasions too directly to God's will, Calvin came very close to compromising God's goodness. Calvin was a "determinist" thinker in that he did not allow for chance, nor was he willing to locate certain events outside of God's providence or control. Yet, Calvin was not a "determinist" in an absolute deistic fashion. Calvin resisted the "fatalist cosmology of the Stoics and the otiose deity of the Epicureans."[124] He claimed that God's eternal decrees do not coerce or destroy the human will; but create the necessary conditions for human choice, contingency and responsibility by allowing for secondary operations. Muller rightly notes that freedom and contingency is in Calvin's theology not only "compatible with an eternal decree that ordains all things, but also depends on it."[125] I would add that Calvin's idea of primary causation contains a positive dimension in that it allows him to deny the independent existence of evil, to emphasize the accidental nature of sin, to uphold the transcendence of God, and to preserve the unity of history that finds its consummation in Christ.

Despite some difficulties, Calvin's doctrine on sin contains important impulses that might profit modern theological anthropologies. The premise of Calvin's doctrine on sin was that sin stands under God's judgement; yet "Christ is more powerful in restoring than Adam in destroying."[126] This premise to the doctrine on sin is important for Reformed anthropological reflection, because God's power over sin is the key source for the Christian hope that humans are not condemned to fate, that human history has meaning and that all things will not end in despair but in eschatological consummation.

Three other aspects of Calvin's description of the effects of sin are, in my view, relevant for contemporary theological reflection on sin; namely, his understanding of sin as a systemic force that puts us in a state of personal, historical and collective guilt before God; his understanding of self-deception, self-idolatry and abuse of power as the ultimate effects of sin;

---

123. Lane, "Did Calvin Believe in Free-Will," 72.
124. Muller, *Divine Will and Human Choice*, 184.
125. Muller, "Grace, Election and Contingent Choice," 252–78 at 267.
126. Calvin, *Psychopannychia*, CO 5.205: "Christum fuisse potentiorem in restituendo, quam Adam in perdendo."

and his explanation of the relation between divine sovereignty and human accountability.

Calvin articulated the systemic and comprehensive nature of sin through concepts such as original sin and total depravity. These terms designate humans as beings born into sin, experiencing total bondage by sin, and therefore standing in a personal, historical and collective state of guilt before God. Modern secular culture increasingly tends to resist the notions of personal, historical and collective guilt. In fact, feelings of guilt are often seen as pathological in nature. This is not surprising because the notion of guilt becomes an empty concept if there is no God to hold us accountable. Instead, interior feelings of guilt are replaced by a superficial and exterior sense of shame when one is exposed. The absence of guilt naturally leads to a lack of accountability and an unwillingness to accept responsibility. This is especially true when it comes to collective and historical guilt. The aftereffects of colonialism, genocides, political oppression, economic exploitation and eco-devastation are often difficult to manage, because generations of people are not willing to take collective and historical responsibility for what went wrong. Obviously, people cannot be held accountable for wrongs they themselves did not commit. This would separate accountability from human agency. Yet, where people supported oppressive systems openly or tacitly (by voting for it), failed to oppose them or profited from them, they need to accept responsibility for what went wrong and make attempts to right the wrongs.

Besides the dominion that fleshly desires exercise over us, Calvin attributes the systemic nature of sin to our inability to understand transcendent reality and to penetrate the mystery and wisdom of God's kingdom. This inability has a "carnal" and "blinding" effect on us.[127] Since we no longer have the epistemological ability to "ascend" to God through our reason, our thinking becomes "carnally minded." Materialism naturally ensues when humans become carnally minded. No longer being able to relate to God, we are only able to relate to material reality fashioning all sorts of idols and spectres in the place of God.[128] This leads to an endless cycle of power abuse, because if there is no God or transcendent reality, we ourselves have to become god to safeguard our interests.[129] Zachmann[130] rightly states that Calvin regarded our blind self-love as "the driving engine behind our pride, arrogance and ambition, whereby we seek the meaning of our lives in power,

---

127. Calvin, *Institutes*, 2.3.1; CO 2.209.
128. CO 2.49.
129. Cf. CO 2.51.
130. Zachmann, "Deny Yourself," 467.

health and honour." A blind self-love and self-idolatry after all entails that there can be no space for others and that a power struggle naturally has to ensue. In order to entertain our selfish desires, we need to subject others to attain power and to erect our own kingdoms. Modern anthropologies need to take cognizance of the dangers of a purely immanent understanding of reality. Various contemporary problems of power are, amongst other things, closely tied to the materialism that emanates from the lack of a transcendental outlook on reality. The contemporary philosophies of Neo-Liberalism, Marxism, Fascism and Communism, as well as the modern trends of individualism and consumerism, are all characterized by a materialist-oriented mindset combined with a specific notion of power to attain material goals. At their core, all these philosophies are nihilist in nature. This is not to argue that obedience to God entails the abandonment of power. Kelsey rightly notes that such a notion would "amount to the denial of our creatureliness" since human creatures are "centres of finite power," participating in "exchanges of energy."[131]

The issue of evolution remains a major challenge to Reformed theological anthropology. Van den Brink and Van der Kooi[132] correctly state that theologians can't escape the theological implications of natural scientific theories on evolution. Issues at stake are evolution's implications for our understanding of God, the goodness of creation and the authority of Scripture. Though Calvin utilized a certain version of Aristotelian causation theory for theological purposes and certainly could not have foreseen the questions that natural science would bring to the fore, his notion of relative necessity as well as his two-causes argument might provide us with tools to comprehend something of the mysterious relation between God, evolution and creation. The contribution of early modern reformed theologians, and for that matter Thomas Aquinas, exists therein that they overcame ontological dualism and maintained the sovereignty of God by not recognizing evil as an independent power that exists alongside God. Evil is privation and emanates from the chain of secondary causes. Calvin maintained that evil is accidental in nature, it cannot function outside of God's will and it eventually serves God's destination with his creation.[133] By using causation theory Calvin and fellow reformed scholars such as Vermigli, Ursinus and Zanchi attempted to maintain a distance between God and the world of the second causes, whilst proclaiming God's sovereignty over all things. Van de

---

131. Kelsey, *Eccentric Existence*, 265.
132. van den Brink and van der Kooi, *Christelijke Dogmatiek*, 210–11.
133. *CO* 6.262.

Beek[134] rightly notes that modern theologians often err by locating God and his actions in the field of the second causes; God then becomes a player in history, a second cause himself.

A Christian theory on God and evolution might consider distinguishing between God's will as the *prima causa* and evolution as a *secunda causa* which emanates in God's *causa finalis* which is consummated reality. God's intent with evolution is good, but as a second cause evolutionary processes are contingent in nature. As *prima causa* God's creative acts put in place processes that bring forth living creatures. In doing so, he allows for the contingency and fortuitous nature of evolutionary processes in order to safeguard the integrity of creation and to give rise to "creaturely selves."[135] Evolution is therefore not driven by absolute necessity but a relative necessity. God's good intent with evolutionary processes has a shadow side in the suffering it causes. Such suffering, though foreseen by God and part of God's providence, is not coerced by God but emanates from the complex operations of second causes. Yet, the suffering and intrinsic competition that accompanies evolutionary processes serve a good outcome in that they make possible complex forms of life able to transcend themselves and capable of relating to God. Admittedly, such a theory will not fit easily within Calvin's creational theology, but it might provide a possible theological answer to a problem that a theologian from a pre-Darwinist era couldn't have foreseen.

Conclusion

Calvin's doctrine on sin is characterized by a fine balancing act that attempts to hold various theological tenets together. He emphasized the totality of human depravity in order to extol the glory and all-comprehensive nature of God's grace. At the same time, he claimed that sin does not destroy the human person's *humanitas* and maintained that the dignity of humans must be upheld despite their sinful nature. The endurance of *humanitas* after the fall is, according to Calvin, not due to humans possessing innate abilities or capacities that are untouched by sin, but to God's common grace that prevents humanity from descending into total chaos by graciously bestowing his gifts on them. Calvin unashamedly maintained the absolute sovereignty and omnipotence of God as the One who determines the origins and outcomes of all things; but he also attempted to preserve creaturely integrity and human choice by locating human actions in the contingent operations of secondary causes. Calvin, in my view, made a valiant and plausible attempt to provide

134. van de Beek, *Een Lichkring Rondom het Kruis*, 345.
135. Southgate, "Responses to Darwin," 381.

a coherent doctrine on sin and the relation between divine sovereignty and human responsibility. Though his understanding of sin might be challenged and criticized, his doctrine is fairly consistent and his arguments plausible enough to warrant serious consideration.

3

Union with Christ[1]

Introduction

CALVIN BELIEVED THAT TRUE humanity is only possible when the human being lives in union with God. Billings[2] describes Calvin's use of the phrase "union with Christ" as follows:

> The phrase "union with Christ" is best seen as a shorthand for a broad range of themes and images which occur repeatedly through a wide range of doctrinal *loci*. These images are often clustered together – like participation in Christ, ingrafting in Christ, union with Christ, adoption and participation in God. Yet, the images function differently in different doctrinal and at times, polemical contexts.

The believer's union with God denotes in Calvin's thinking a highly affective relationship with God. Calvin interpreted being engrafted in Christ as Christ dwelling in us through his Spirit so that we become "one" with him. Accordingly, he is called "our Head" and the "first born among the brethren."[3] Our union with Christ is at the same time union with the "fullness of the Godhead," because the Father and the Spirit are one with Christ.[4]

---

1. Some sections of this chapter has been published in an essay by Vorster entitled "'And Behold a Ladder': Descent and Ascent in Calvin's Soteriology" in *In Luce Verbi* 49.1 (2015) 1–8. AOSIS Publishers allows for the re-use of journal material published by them under a CC-BY license. See https://creativecommons.org/licenses/by/4.0/. Other parts have been published in the Journal *Dialog*, and permissions for re-use have been attained from Wiley Periodicals. The full reference is Nico Vorster, "John Calvin on the Christian's Social Responsibility: Cultural Activist or Modest Social Reformer?," *Dialog: A Journal of Theology* 56.4 (2018) 441–48.

2. Billings, "Multifaceted 'Sum' of the Gospel," 429.

3. Calvin, *Institutes*, 3.1.1; CO 2.393: "Ideo et caput nostrum vocatur, et primogenitus inter multos fratres (Eph. 4, 15; Rom. 8, 29)."

4. Calvin, *Institutes*, 3.11.5; CO 2.531: "pater et spiritus in Christo sunt; et sicut in ipso habitat plenitudo divinitatis, ita in ipso possidemus totum Deum."

The doctrine on our union with Christ is fundamental to Calvin's theology, and can even be described as the nerve center that brings together various facets and themes in his theology. To be sure, his anthropology cannot be understood apart from his Christology and soteriology. Right at the beginning of Book 3 of the 1559 *Institutes*, Calvin stated that we cannot become part of Christ as long as he remains outside of us; Christ has to become ours by dwelling in us through the Spirit. As long as we are not spiritually united with Christ, Christ's salvational work will be of no avail.[5]

This chapter analyzes Calvin's understanding of our union with Christ in light of his Christology and the descent-ascent motive in his soteriology. The first section of this chapter deals with Calvin's notion of the two natures of Christ. Issues addressed are Calvin's Chalcedonian approach to the two natures of Christ; his criticisms of Nestorianism, Eutychianism, Stancarism, and the Lutheran doctrine on ubiquity; and the Christological and ontological presuppositions that underlie his concept of the divine-human relationship. The next section examines Calvin's soteriology, specifically his understanding of Christ's descent to humanity through his incarnation and atoning work, and his exposition of the believer's ascent to God through the Spirit. Topics discussed are Calvin's view of atonement, the Spirit's role as the bond between Christ and believers, and the logical order of justification and sanctification. Then we turn to Calvin's understanding of the Christian life as a continuous cycle of self-mortification and vivification. The three main characteristics of the Christian life, namely self-denial, cross-bearing, and meditation on the future life is discussed, as is Calvin's views on prayer and the sacraments as instruments of God's grace, and the bodily resurrection as constituting our final ascent to God. The final part of the chapter reflects on the constructive potential of Calvin's doctrine on union with Christ for modern reformed anthropology.

The Two Natures of Christ

Calvin employed the formula *unitis non confusis* in the Christological sections of the various editions of the *Institutes*, as well as in his 1545 reply to Pierre Caroli to explain his understanding of the relationship between Christ's two natures. Pierre Caroli charged Calvin, Pierre Viret, and Guillaume Farel in 1537 with expounding an Arian doctrine of the Trinity in their Genevan Confession of Faith (1537). Calvin responded in the same year by demonstrating that his Trinitarian theology complied fully with

---

5. Calvin, *Institutes*, 3.1.1; CO 2.392.

creedal Christianity.⁶ After distinguishing between the three persons and one essence of God and affirming that the Son and Spirit are fully part of the one essence of God but distinguishable from each other in their persons, he refers to the two natures of Christ. Following Chalcedon, Calvin stated that the divinity of Christ, which has existed from eternity, was united with his humanity in such a way that each nature maintains its own integrity; yet from these two natures one Mediator is formed. Calvin emphasized that the union of the two natures is expressed in the Person of Christ, not, as the Euthychianists maintained, the mixture of the two natures. Christ's human and divine natures do not communicate their properties to each other. Instead, the distinctive properties of each nature are predicated to the person of the Mediator.

Caroli responded by expressing concern about Calvin's doctrine on the aseity of Christ; that is Christ's eternal existence before the incarnation.⁷ In his 1545 reply to Caroli on the topic of the Trinity, Calvin twice employed the *unitis non confusis* formula.⁸ On both occasions, Calvin referred to Christ as the Son of God who had existed from eternity and who was part of the one indivisible essence of God. The Person of the Son entered human nature through the incarnation in a way that unites, but does not mingle (*unitis non confusis naturis*) the two natures of Christ. Christ's divine nature extends beyond the finite realm so that his divinity, despite being clothed in the flesh, fills the heaven and earth as before the incarnation.⁹

In his debate with Caroli, Calvin utilized the *unitis non confusis* formula to defend what later became known as the *extra Calvinisticum*. Since the two natures of Christ are not mixed, the divine nature of Christ is not limited by his human nature, but extends beyond the physical realm. Christ exists eternally in the form of the Logos, despite having assumed human nature at the incarnation.¹⁰

More *unitis non confusis* formulae are found in the Christological sections of the various editions of the *Institutes*. In the 1536 edition, Calvin used the term *unitis non confusis naturis* to explain the relation between two natures of Christ, while the 1559 edition modified the particular passage to read:

---

6. See Calvin, "Confession on the Trinity," 4.
7. See Carmichael's introduction to "Confession on the Trinity," 1.
8. CO 7.310, 325.
9. CO 7.125. Also see Calvin, *Institutes*, 1.13.8; CO 2.96; Calvin, *Institutes*, 4.17.30; CO 2.1031.
10. See Helm, *John Calvin's Ideas*, 64.

> He who was the Son of God became the Son of man, not by confusion of substance, but by unity of person [*non confusione substantiae sed unitate personae*]. For we maintain, that the divinity was so conjoined and united with the humanity, that the entire properties of each nature remain entire, and yet the two natures constitute only one Christ.[11]

After describing Christ's hypostatic union as a *non confusione substantiae sed unitate personae*, Calvin proceeded to refute a literal understanding of the *communicatio idiomata*, which claimed that properties of Christ's divine nature can literally be communicated to his human nature and vice versa. Calvin's concern was that the integrity of Christ's human nature would be compromised if divine properties, such as omnipresence, were ascribed in a metaphysical and ontological sense to Christ's human nature, while his divine nature would be jeopardized if human qualities were assigned to that which properly belongs to the realm of the divine. Calvin identified four modes of speech in Scripture on the two natures of Christ. First, Scripture speaks of qualities that refer primarily to his humanity; second, there are qualities applied exclusively to Christ's divinity. On occasions, figures of speech are used that embrace both natures; while at times, a mode of speaking is employed that attributes both divine and human qualities to the office of the Mediator.[12]

Calvin emphasized that when Scripture ascribes qualities to Christ that embrace both natures, it is done improperly, in other words as a manner of speech and not fact:

> There is a communication of ἰδώματα or properties when Paul says, that God purchased the church "with his own blood" (Acts 20:28), and that the Jews crucified the Lord of glory (1 Cor 2:8) . . . God certainly has no blood, suffers not, cannot be touched by hands; but since that Christ who was true God and true man shed his blood on the cross for us, the acts which were performed in his human nature are transferred improperly but not ceaselessly, to his divinity.[13]

---

11. Calvin, *Institutes*, 2.14.1; CO 2.353: "et qui filius erat Dei, filius hominis factus est, non confusione substantiae, sed unitate personae. Siquidem ita coniunctam untamque humanitate divinitatem asserimus, ut sua utrique naturae solida proprietus maneat, et tamen ex duabus illis unus Christus constituatur."

12. CO 2.353-54.

13. Calvin, *Institutes*, 2.14.2; CO 2.354: "Communicatio autem idiomatum sive proprietatum est, quod dicit Paulus (Act. 20, 28), Deum suo sanguine acquivisse sibi ecclesiam, et, Dominum gloriae crucifixum (1 Cor. 2:8). Deus certe nec sanguinem habet, nec patitur, nec minibus tangi potest; sed quoniam is qui verus erat Deus et homo,

Calvin's point was that when Scripture ascribes human qualities to Jesus's divine nature and divine qualities to his human nature, it uses figurative forms of speech, not metaphysical statements of fact, to "keep in balance the varied Scriptural witness of the One Person of Christ."[14] In reality, there is no ontological interchange between the respective natures of Christ, only a predication of human and divine attributes to the concrete Person of Christ.[15] This insight is important, because the notion that properties of Christ's divine nature can be communicated ontologically to his human nature and vice versa, would revive the Eutychian heresy that the Council of Chalcedon intended to refute. Richard Muller rightly notes that Calvin's view on the *communicatio idiomata* should be seen as the expression of a "consistent ontology," namely that the integrity of the divine and human realms should be guarded.[16]

We encounter the *unitis non confusis* formula again in *Institutes*, 2.14.4, where Calvin presented it as a correction of the extremes of both Nestorianism and Eutychianism:

> Christ, therefore, as God and man, possessing natures which are united, but not confused (*unitis sed non confusis*), we conclude He is our Lord . . . . we must put far from us the heresy of Nestorius, who presuming to dissect rather than distinguish between the two natures devised a double Christ . . . We must beware also of the insane fantasy of Eutyches, lest, when we would demonstrate the unity of the person, we destroy the two natures.[17]

In his commentary on John 1:14, Calvin presented the same argument:

> The two natures of Christ were so united in one Person in Christ, that one and the same Christ is true God and true man. The second is that the unity of person does not hinder the two natures from remaining distinct, so that His divinity retains all

---

Christus sanguinem suum pro nobis crucifixus fudit, quae in humana eius natura peracta sunt, ad divinitatem improprie, licet non sine ratione, transferuntur."

14. Willis, *Calvin's Catholic Christology*, 67.
15. Edmondson, *Calvin's Christology*, 34.
16. Muller, "Christ in the Eschaton," 38.
17. Calvin, *Institutes*, 2.14.4; CO 2.356: "Christum ergo, ut Deus est et homo, unitis, licet non confusis, naturis constans, Dominum nostrum verumque Dei . . . Procul enim abigendus est a nobis Nestorii error, qui dum naturas distrahere potius quam distinguere volebat duplicem Christum ita comminiscebatur . . . Cavendum et ab eutychiana insania, ne dum volumus personae unitatem demonstrare, utramque naturam destrucamus."

that is peculiar to itself and his humanity holds separately whatever belongs to it.[18]

In an effort to understand Calvin's approach, it is pertinent to reflect on the late medieval distinction between nature and person. Classic late medieval theologians such as Thomas Aquinas (1225–1274), Duns Scotus (1266–1308) and William of Ockham (1287–1347) regarded natures as denoting the essential properties and characteristics of a species or type of being. Whereas persons are concrete acting agents, natures do not act. Instead, persons act in relation to the attributes and properties of their nature.[19] Stephen Edmondson notes that we find the same logic in Calvin's understanding of Christ's mediating work. Calvin holds that "mediation is an activity carried out by a person, not his natures, though his person is only able to carry out this activity on the basis of his natures."[20]

Calvin understood the two natures of Christ as predicating their properties without mingling to Christ's person, while Christ's person acts with respect to the properties of the two natures as Mediator. It is therefore permissible to ascribe both human and divine properties to Christ as Mediator. In the dedication to his Commentary on Jeremiah, Calvin makes a distinction between union (*unio*) and unity (*unitas*). *Unio* expresses a unity in distinction without blending, while *unitas* denotes a single agent. According to Calvin, *unio* applies to the two natures of Christ that are united but distinct, while *unitas* pertains to the Person of the Mediator, who possesses one identity as God-man and acts in a singular manner.[21] Helm notes that Calvin's understanding of the Mediator is characterized by "functional reduplication" in contrast to "ontological reduplication." For Calvin, Christ as Mediator is at once divine and human. The Mediator can forgive sins as God, while at the same time performing human actions. While the natures of Christ can be separately discussed, his actions as Mediator cannot be separately understood.[22]

Why did Calvin regard it as so important that Christ's two natures should not be mingled? The clearest answers are, perhaps, found in Book

---

18. Calvin, *Commentary on John*, 1:46; CO 47.14: "sic in unam personam coaluisse duas in Christo naturas, ut unus atque idem Christus verus sit Deus et homo."

19. See Aquinas, *Summa Theologiae*, III.16.1.3. See Oberman, *Dawn of the Reformation*, 253n78. Also see Fisk, "Calvin's Metaphysics," 309–13.

20. Edmondson, *Calvin's Christology*, 31.

21. Calvin, *Commentaries on Jeremiah and Lamentations*, 1:xx. Also see Edmondson, *Calvin's Christology*, 205.

22. Helm, *John Calvin's Ideas*, 69.

Four of the *Institutes*,²³ where Calvin rejected Luther's ubiquity doctrine, and in his 1561 reply to Francesco Stancaro (1501-1574). In response to the Lutheran doctrine of ubiquity, Calvin upheld the integrity of Christ's human nature, while he defended the divine nature of the Mediator in his reply to Stancaro.

During his exposition of the meaning of the Supper, Calvin argued that the doctrine of ubiquity introduces a new kind of Eutychianism that converts "God into man and man into God."²⁴ By assigning divine properties to Christ's human nature in an ontological sense, the doctrine of ubiquity compromises the integrity of Christ's human nature. Calvin stated that "no property [should] be assigned to his body inconsistent with human nature. This is done when he is said to be infinite, or made to occupy a variety of places at the same time."²⁵

Christ has to be a partaker of flesh and blood to be a Mediator, because a human has to atone for the sins of humanity. Calvin was adamant that human nature, and it alone, is liable for human sin and ought to pay for it. Christ's sacrifice means nothing to us if his two natures are so conflated that he is not like us in every respect, except for sin.²⁶ A human nature that possesses divine attributes, such as omnipresence, is not truly human. Hence, in the incarnation, Christ fully identifies himself with our human nature without diluting or compromising the integrity of our humanity.²⁷ Since the integrity of Christ's human nature should be preserved, Calvin held that Christ's glorified human body is not omnipresent, but is still limited to space.²⁸ Although the Eternal Son is everywhere according to his divine nature, including being united with human nature, he is not everywhere in terms of his human nature.²⁹

Calvin defended the integrity of Christ's divine nature in his comments on Stancarism. Stancaro held that Christ was not a Mediator between God and humanity with respect to his divinity, because this would subordinate the Son to the Father.³⁰ Since all three persons within the Trinity share the divine nature equally, it would be demeaning to Christ's divine nature to

---

23. Also see Calvin's response to Hesuchius in *CO* 9.463-23.

24. Calvin, *Institutes*, 4.17.30; *CO* 2.1031: "quod neque Deus esset, neque homo."

25. See Calvin, *Institutes*, 4.17.19; *CO* 2.1017: "Haec enim naturae humanae veritati non obscure repugnant. Istas, inquam, duas exceptions nunquam patiamur nobis eripi."

26. *CO* 2.342; *CO* 2.348-49; *CO* 2.352.

27. See Oberman, *Dawn of the Reformation*, 255.

28. *CO* 2.1031; *CO* 20.75.

29. *CO* 2.1032.

30. See Tylenda, "Christ the Mediator," 1.

"stand between" God and humanity in a mediating role.[31] His solution was to posit that Christ is Mediator only according to his human nature, while his divine nature shares in the Trinity's salvific work.[32] In his letter to the Polish Reformed ministers, Calvin responded to the revival of Stancarism in some regions by stating that Christ cannot be Mediator if he is not truly God and man. The Mediator has to be divine so that he can act as Judge. God's power of judgement cannot be transferred to human nature because that would bestow glory on the human being that only belongs to God.[33] Moreover, the human being does not have the capability to overcome death and overcome the devil. The same principle applies with respect to the Mediator's priesthood. Divinity is an essential precondition for the Mediator's office of priesthood, because only God can guide us to the Father.[34]

Calvin's refutations of the ubiquity doctrine and Stancarism indicate that he resisted a confusion of Christ's two natures because this would compromise Christ's work as Mediator. If Christ's human nature is not in every aspect truly human, his sacrifice would not be sufficient to appease God's anger. Conversely, if human properties are assigned to Christ's divine nature, we compromise his divine glory. Lastly, if the incarnation is understood as an event where Christ relinquished some of his divine attributes for the sake of his human nature, Christ would cease to be God in all respects.[35]

But if the two natures of Christ cannot be mingled or blended, how did Calvin avoid making Christ's human nature an autonomous reality independent from God? Here we should take note of Calvin's distinction between communicable and incommunicable divine attributes. In *Institutes*, 1.13.6, Calvin distinguished between God's essence (*essentia*) that consists of the three persons sharing the same divine nature; and the various subsistences (*subsistentiam in Dei essentia*) within the divine being that refer to the Father, Son and Spirit's distinctive properties that are incommunicable (*incommunicabiles*) to one another. Though Calvin did not use the exact same terms with regard to the relation between God and human beings, later Reformers did apply the terminology to the divine-human relationship. They held that divine attributes such as omnipotence and omnipresence cannot be communicated to human beings. However, attributes such

---

31. Edmondson, *Calvin's Christology*, 14.
32. Edmondson, *Calvin's Christology*, 27
33. *CO* 9.355–56.
34. *CO* 9.355.
35. See *CO* 47.290–92.

as holiness, love and mercy can be transferred to believers, who are indeed called to follow the example of Christ in this regard.[36]

There are hints of the same kind of distinction in both Calvin's anthropology and Christology. For Calvin there was no such thing as a human nature that could exist without the agency of God's Spirit. God's Spirit is diffused "over all space, sustaining, invigorating, and quickening all things, breathing into them being, life and motion."[37] Though God's Spirit does not regenerate all human beings, he literally breathes life and energy into all human beings and infuses their souls with an immortal spirit.[38] Calvin, though, quickly added that the Holy Spirit's operation does not entail a transfusion of God's essence to human nature, nor a "secret influx of God's divinity (*arcanum divinitatis influxum*)." Divine nature, after all, is not liable to "passion and change (*mutationi esse obnoxiam et passionibus*)."[39] The spiritual and immortal qualities of our souls are due to God adorning us with his endowments. Instead of confusing the divine and human nature through a transference of essence, the Spirit communicates a divine "quality" (*qualitatem*) to the human being that is something distinct from God himself.[40] Here we see that Calvin distinguished between qualities of God that could be communicated to human beings and essential attributes of God that are incommunicable: God's unchangeable and perfect nature cannot be communicated to human beings, yet God through his Spirit is able to endow human beings with the divine quality of immortality without fusing divine essence with human nature.

When it comes to the human nature of Christ, Calvin asserted that God's Spirit imparts certain *qualities* to Christ's human nature without fusing the two natures of Christ. In Book 2 of the *Institutes*, Calvin discussed the sinless quality of Christ's human nature. After affirming that Christ had a body and soul like all human beings,[41] Calvin ascribed Christ's sinless human nature[42] to the sanctifying work of the Spirit:

---

36. See Helm, *John Calvin's Ideas*, 89

37. Calvin, *Institutes*, 1.13.14; CO 2.102: "Ille enim est qui ubique diffuses omnia sustinet, vegetat et vivificat in coelo et in terra."

38. CO 5.221; CO 2.136–37; CO 2.395.

39. Calvin, *Institutes*, 1.15.5; CO 2.140.

40. CO 55.446.

41. Calvin, *Institutes*, 2.13.2; CO 2.348–49; Calvin, *Institutes*, 2.13.4; CO 2.352.

42. Calvin held that sin is accidental to human nature. Since Adam and Eve were initially created without sin, Christ's sinlessness does not detract from his true humanity. See CO 6.263.

> It is childish trifling to maintain that if Christ is free from all taint, and was begotten of the seed of Mary, by the secret operation of the Spirit, it is therefore not the seed of the women that is impure, but only that of the man. We do not hold Christ to be free of all taint, merely because he was born of a woman unconnected with a man, but because he was sanctified by the Spirit.[43]

Calvin continued to say that the sanctifying work of the Spirit did not apply to Christ's divine nature, but only to his human nature.[44] In other words, though Calvin did not fuse the two natures of Christ, he argued that the Spirit imparts divine qualities to Christ's human nature in the same manner that he communicates divine blessings to all human beings. The only difference is that Christ receives the Spirit without limits so that he is exempt from corruptibility.[45] This communication of divine qualities, however, is not from Christ's divine nature to Christ's human nature, but from the *Logos* that conveys it through the Person of the Spirit to the human nature of Christ.[46] David Willis rightly notes that, according to Calvin, "Christ's human nature can develop in a special way without transgressing the bounds of genuine humanity because of the gifts that the *Logos* conveys to it by the Spirit."[47]

From the preceding discussion it is clear that Calvin's Christology is loaded with dialectical tension. Richard Muller summarizes Calvin's Christological approach well when he states that Calvin's "emphasis on the historical person of the Mediator and on the integrity of the natures united in the person, the *communicatio idiomatum in concreto*, the *aseitas* of Christ's divinity and the related concept of the *extra calvinisticum*" cannot be approached in "isolation" but should be viewed "as one aspect of a tension that pervades the entire Christological structure" of Calvin's thought.[48] Calvin utilized the *unitis non confusis* formula to hold together opposite

---

43. Calvin, *Institutes*, 2.13.4; *CO* 2.352: "Pueriliter autem nugantur: si ab omni macula immunis est Christus ac per arcanam spiritus operationem genitus fuit ex semine Mariae, non esse igitur impurum semen mulieris, sed viri duntaxat. Neque enim immunem ab omni labe facimus Christum, quia tantum ex matre sit genitus absque viri concubitu, sed quia sanctificatus est a spiritu." Also see Calvin's Commentary on Hebrews 2:11 (*CO* 55.28).

44. Calvin, *Institutes*, 2.13.4; *CO* 2.352.

45. See Calvin, *Institutes*, 2.13.4; *CO* 2.352. Also see *CO* 45.15. See Fisk, "Calvin's Metaphysics," 322.

46. See *CO* 45.350 and *CO* 45.576. Also see the discussion of Willis, *Calvin's Catholic Christology*, 83–84.

47. Willis, *Calvin's Catholic Christology*, 6–7.

48. Muller, "Christ in the Eschaton," 33–34.

poles without compromising their integrity: the two natures of Christ are united in one Person. Each nature maintains its own integrity and distinctive properties. The two natures do not mix with each other or compromise each other's integrity by communicating their distinctive properties to each other. Instead, the properties of the two natures are predicated to the Person of Christ who is one acting Agent. Christ's actions as Mediator cannot be divided into human or divine actions; instead, they are inseparable in terms of the identity of the Source and their mediating effect.

The Cycle of Descent and Ascent and Union with Christ

Calvin utilized the theme of descent and ascent to integrate his Christology, soteriology and anthropology. The scheme of descent and ascent is, indeed, a fundamental feature in Calvin's theology and permeates his works from start to finish. It is characterized by a cycle of exchange: because of Christ's descent to earth we can ascend to heaven; through Christ's appropriation of mortality, we acquire immortality; and because of Christ's submission to weakness, we receive heavenly strength.[49] The descent-ascent theme is, of course, not exclusive to Calvin; he picks up on a Patristic and Scholastic topic. However, as Canlis rightly notes, there is a different emphasis in Calvin's construction. Whereas Augustine focuses on the soul's ascent and Aquinas on ascent through grace in an ontological sense, Calvin is concerned with Christ's ascent, specifically the way in which we ascend in him and through the Spirit to the Father.[50]

The Son not only descended to earth through his incarnation, but as the glorified Christ he continuously descends to humanity through his Spirit and Word, while acting as our Mediator before the Father. Through the Spirit, Christ enables believers to ascend to God, yet this ascent is not possible if they do not continuously descend into themselves through self-mortification and repentance in order to be vivified to a new life in true union with God.

Atonement

For Calvin the *telos* of human life is union with God through the communion that Christ makes possible as Redeemer. The fall, however, seriously endangers the human's created communion with God. After the disruption of the fall, union with God is only possible "if the Godhead himself

49. *CO* 2.1003.
50. Canlis, *Calvin's Ladder*, 43–44.

descends to us, it being impossible for us to ascend to God."[51] To restore communion between God and humanity, Christ descends to humanity in order to "raise" us again with him unto the Father.[52] Only this affective pull of God can draw us into communion with him:

> "And behold a ladder." It is Christ alone therefore, who connects heaven and earth: he is the only Mediator who reaches from heaven down to earth: he is the medium through which the fullness of all celestial blessings flows down to us, and through which we in turn, ascend to God.[53]

Christ descends to create a covenantal union between God and believers based on love.[54] The incarnated Christ displays the true image of God, since in him we come into contact with the glory of God.[55] We cannot have any knowledge of our salvation until "we behold God in Christ," nor can we truly understand what our image entails before we see the image in Christ.[56] Kehm[57] rightly notes that, in Calvin's thinking, our *telos* as images of God cannot be "discovered by an analysis of the immanent properties of man's soul and body, but [only] in the actual embodiment and revelation of it in Jesus Christ, the true man." Whereas creation and the human being can only mirror God's glory in a vague sense, Christ mirrors God's will in a direct and bright sense. Even the incarnation did not inhibit the majesty of God shining forth in Christ, but he displayed God's glory despite being surrounded by "the low condition of flesh."[58] Christ's imaging of God, after all, is not embodied in physical appearance, but is tied to his role in the Trinity

---

51. Calvin, *Institutes*, 2.12.1; *CO* 2.340: "Deplorata certe res erat, nisi maiestas ipsa Dei ad nos descenderet, quando ascendere nostrum non erat."

52. Calvin, *Catechism or Institution*, art. 20; *CO* 5.337; Calvin, *Institutes*, 1.13.26; *CO* 2.114: "Et certe ideo ad nos descendit Christus, ut, ad patrem attollendo, simul etiam ad se ipsum attolleret."

53. *CO* 23.390–91: "ecce scala . . . Solus ergo Christus est qui coelom terrae coniungit: hic solus est mediator, qui pertingit a coelo usque ad terram: ille idem est per quem omnium bonorum coelestium plenitudo deorsum ad nos fluit, nosque vicissim ad Deum conscendimus." The English translation is from Calvin, *Commentaries on Genesis*, 2:113.

54. See Fisk, "Calvin's Metaphysics," 312.

55. Calvin, *Sermons on Genesis 1–11*, 92; *SC* 11/1.55.

56. Calvin, *Institutes*, 2.6.4; *CO* 2.251: "nisi occurrat nobis Deus in Christo, non posse in salutem nobis innotescere."

57. Kehm, "Christ and Man," 202.

58. Calvin, *Commentary on John*, 1:47; *CO* 47.15: "Dei maiestatem non fuisse exinanitam, quamvis carne circumdata esset: latuit quidem sub carnis humilitate, sed ita tamen ut fulgorem suum emitteret."

as the Speech who not only reveals, but himself is the eternal Wisdom and Will of God.[59] As God's Speech, Christ reveals through his preaching the unique and hitherto unknown mystery of the Gospel of the Kingdom.[60] As God's Wisdom he reflects God's knowledge, purity, righteousness and true holiness.[61]

For Calvin, Jesus's sinless relationship with the Father reopens community between God and humanity. Because of his sinless nature Christ can act as the pledge through which the promises of God are sealed, because his coming confirms that the promises of the Law are fulfilled.[62] Christ alone can redeem humanity because he is the true image of God, untainted by sin, and therefore alone able to "wipe away our guilt" and "appease the anger of God."[63] Those who deviate from Christ have no other form of access to God, but are subject to God's wrath and judgement.[64] Calvin insisted that God loves no human being "outside Christ", since his love dwells in his Son, from whom it afterwards is extended to us.[65]

Christ's descent to earth culminates in his substitutionary work through which he makes possible the great exchange that brings us back into communion with God:

> This is the exchange which out of his measureless goodness he has made with us: that receiving our poverty unto himself, he has transferred his wealth to us; that taking our weakness upon himself, he has strengthened us by his power; that having received our mortality he has given us his immortality; that descending to earth, he has prepared an ascent to heaven for us; that becoming Son of man with us, he has made us sons of God with him.[66]

---

59. *CO* 47.1.
60. *CO* 2.311
61. *CO* 2.147.
62. *CO* 5.333; *CO* 2.312.
63. Calvin, *Institutes*, 2.12.3; *CO* 2.342: "carnem quam a nobis accepit, obtulisse in sacrificium, ut facta expiatione reatum nostrum deleret, et placaret iustam patris iram."
64. *CO* 2.645.
65. Calvin, *Institutes*, 3.2.32; *CO* 2.424, 425: "neminem a Deo extra Christum diligi."
66. Calvin, *Institutes of the Christian Religion 1536*, *CO* 1.119: "Haec est commutatio, qua immensa sua bonitate nobiscum usus est: quod nostram in se paupertatem recipiens, suam ad nos opulentiam transtulerit; quod suscepta nostra imbecillitate, sua virtute nos confirmaverit; quod accepta nostra mortalitate, sua nos immortalitate donaverit; quod in terras descendens, ascensum nobis in coelum straverit; quod filius hominis nobiscum factus, nos secum Dei filios fecerit."

Calvin understood the crucifixion as standing "at the nexus of descent and ascent."[67] Christ's death is a mysterious encounter between God's love and justice. In Christ, both God's love for humanity and his demand for justice are at work. God reconciles himself to us, because he has loved us since before the foundation of the world, yet his justice demands the punishment of sin.[68] Blochner[69] notes that Calvin mainly used two language sets when speaking about the atonement. One is the cultic language of sacrifice with terms such as expiation, curse, propitiation, uncleanness and purification through the shedding of blood. The other is forensic or judicial language such as guilt, imputation, judgement, penalty and remission. Calvin, seemingly, regarded the sacrificial and legal images in Scripture "as the core" foundation of a doctrine of atonement.[70] Christ in his death was offered to the Father as a "propitiatory victim" so that expiation could be made by his sacrifice.[71] Through his expiatory work Christ appeases God's wrath on sin and reinstates God's favour to us.[72] The satisfaction that Christ brings is thus twofold: it is a satisfaction of the righteous demands of the law, and an acquittal of the penalty due to sin.[73] Being reconciled by the righteousness of Christ, God becomes instead of a Judge, a kind Father.[74]

The Spirit as Our Bond with Christ

The descent of Christ to crucifixion and death is directed at bringing humanity up to the Father.[75] The resurrection and ascension of Christ is, according to Calvin, essential to the work of Christ, because his reign only truly commences when he lays aside the ignoble condition of a mortal life.[76] Yet his ascension does not create a void in the human-divine relationship, because Christ exercises his power on earth through the Spirit.[77]

- 67. Canlis, *Calvin's Ladder*, 93.
- 68. See *CO* 2.371.
- 69. Blochner, "Atonement in John Calvin's Theology," 283.
- 70. Vorster, "Nature of Christ's Atonement," 131.
- 71. Calvin, *Institutes*, 2.16.6; *CO* 2.373: "satisfactoriam peccati hostiam."
- 72. *CO* 2.366.
- 73. Cf. Vorster, "Nature of Christ's Atonement," 132; See *CO* 2.373–74.
- 74. *CO* 2.393.
- 75. Canlis, *Calvin's Ladder*, 126.

76. Calvin, *Institutes*, 2.16.14; *CO* 2.381: "Resurrectioni non abs re annectitur in coelum ascensus. Etsi enim gloriam virtutemque suam Christus resurgendo plenius illustrare coepit, deposita iam scilicet abiecta et ignobili conditione mortalis vitae et crucis ignominia."

77. By emphasizing the work of the Spirit in relation to Christ, Calvin presented a

The Holy Spirit is not merely the Spirit of Christ in Calvin's theology, but a Person distinguishable from the Father and the Son. Calvin's understanding of the divine person of the Holy Spirit is most vividly expressed in his 1537 reply to Pierre Caroli and in Book 1 of the *Institutes*. As noted earlier, Pierre Caroli charged Calvin, Viret and Farel of expounding an Arian doctrine of Trinity in their Genevan Confession of 1537. In his response to Caroli, Calvin depicted the Holy Spirit as one in essence with the Father and Son, but as distinguishable in terms of subsistence. Calvin utilized the same terminology in the *Institutes*. The unity of the triune God consists in them sharing the same divine essence (*essentia Dei*); while subsistence (*subsistentia*) denotes the distinctive incommunicable properties of the Father, Son and Spirit not shared by the Persons and not transferred from the one to the other.[78] According to Calvin, the words Father, Son and Holy Spirit denotes a real distinction in persons, still they indicate "distinction only, not division."[79] Calvin affirmed that "the Father Son and Spirit are one God and yet the Son is not the Father, nor the Spirit the Son, but that each has their own subsistence."[80] The Father is the Source and Origin of all things, the Son is the Wisdom that arranges and orders all things and the Spirit is the energy and efficacy of the Son's action.[81] When the Scriptures refers to the name God, the one essence of God is depicted; while the names Father, Son and Holy Spirit bring into view the relations of the three Persons within the one divine being.[82]

The peculiar properties of the Spirit consist in him quickening all things, sustaining life, preserving order, regenerating believers, dwelling in believers, sanctifying the elect and resurrecting and glorifying those destined for immortality.[83] Calvin, in fact, described the work of the Holy Spirit as a threefold activity. First, there is the cosmic activity of the Spirit that animates, sustains and invigorates all creatures; second, the donative actions

---

model of the Trinity that focuses on the modes of the relationships within the Godhead. He did not regard the Spirit as a spiritual extension of Christ, but as a Person in whom we have access to Christ. Medieval theology, in contrast, was largely occupied with the shared substance within the Godhead. For a discussion of the issue see Canlis, *Calvin's Ladder*, 96–97.

78. CO 2.90; CO 2.94

79. Calvin, *Institutes*, 1.13.17; CO 2.104: "distinctionem non divisionem."

80. Calvin, *Institutes*, 3.1.3.5; CO 2.91: "patrem, et filium, et spiritum esse unum Deum; nec tamen aut filium esse paterm, aut spiritum filium, sed proprietate quadam esse distinctos."

81. CO 2.105.

82. CO 2.106.

83. CO 2.101–2.

of the Spirit that are peculiar to humanity and act upon human morality and history, and lastly, the regenerative work of the Spirit which is limited to the regenerate children of God. John Bolt[84] remarks that Calvin's distinction between the threefold work of the Spirit corresponds with his understanding of the three modes of life in creation, namely universal life that consists in motion and sense, human life that all the children of Adam possess, and supernatural life that only the elected and regenerate obtain.

The Spirit is the connection between us and Christ, uniting us with Christ and bestowing upon us "everything that Christ has."[85] The purpose of the Spirit's enlightenment is not to bring us to an intellectualist contemplation of the divine, but to energize us into living in communion with God. Just as the sun's rays "generate, cherish and invigorate its offspring," the radiance of the Spirit transfuses to us the communion of Christ's flesh and blood.[86] By emphasizing the work of the Spirit, Calvin deliberately moved away from scholasticism's ontological notions of gradation of being to avoid the possible conflation of divine and human essences. Instead, the Holy Spirit makes it possible for human nature to participate in divine nature without assimilating the two natures.

Calvin used the term "indwelling" (habitat in nobis) rather than "incarnation" (incarnatio) to describe the Spirit's presence in the believer.[87] The indwelling of the Spirit connotes a spiritual union, whereas incarnation signifies a hypostatic union. The Holy Spirit does not assume human flesh nor does he become us, but he enters into a spiritual union with us that is mystical in nature. Calvin stated it as follows in the *Institutes*:

> Therefore to that union of the head and members, the residence of Christ in our hearts, in fine, the mystical union, we assign the highest rank, Christ when he becomes ours making us partners with him in the gifts with which he was endued.[88]

Calvin immediately proceeded in the same passage to indicate that this mystical union does not amount to a "gross mixture of Christ with believers"

---

84. Bolt, "Spiritus Creator," 19.

85. Calvin, *Institutes*, 4.17.12; *CO* 2.1011: "Ut totum Christum possideamus et habemus in nobis manentem."

86. Calvin, *Institutes*, 4.17.12; *CO* 2.1010: "Nam si solem conspicimus radiis in terram emicantem, ad generandos, fovendos, vegetandos eius foetus suam quodammodo substantiam ad eam traiicere: cur inferior spiritus Christi esset irradiatio, ad communionem carnis et sanguinis eius in nos traducendam?"

87. Calvin, *Institutes*, 3.11.10; *CO* 2.540.

88. Calvin, *Institutes*, 3.11.10; *CO* 2.540: "Coniuntio igitur illa capitis et membrorum, habitation Christi in cordibus nostris, mystica denique uino a nobis in summon gradu statuitur."

(*crassam mixturam Christi*) as taught by those who hold a substantial view of the Supper or Osiander who entertained an essential understanding of righteousness.[89] Indwelling entails a spiritual union of faith from which flows the *extra nobis* benefit of the imputation of the Christ's righteousness and the *in nobis* benefit of the renewal and renovation of our actions through the Spirit that governs our wills.

In his 1555 letter to Vermigli, Calvin attempted to define the essence of our spiritual communion with Christ. Van't Spijker notes that Calvin stayed clear of any reference to incarnation, but utilized the Greek term *koinonia* which he translated into Latin with *sacra unitas* rather than *societas*.[90] The *unitas* is brought about by faith and consists in the communication of Christ's righteousness to us through the Spirit, not a mingling of substance.[91] Van't Spijker rightly observes:

> When Calvin speaks about *unio mystica,* this does not entail any actual unification, nor any equality in essence. Rather it is a mystical union which wants to be nothing but faith communion.[92]

Calvin regarded redemption as the fruit of the perichoretic cooperation between the Father, Son and Spirit. The Father's love is the efficient cause, the Son's obedience is the material cause and the Holy Spirit's illuminative work is the instrumental cause in God's salvational work.[93] The illuminative work of the Spirit consists of him working faith in the hearts of the elect, which raises them to heaven and makes them partakers in divine life.[94] By faith, believers ascend to God so that they are born again into a new divine life. The noetic orientation of Calvin's theology is quite evident here: just as sin primarily has a noetic effect on the human being, God's restoration of the believer through the Spirit is first and foremost illumination, that is, an "opening of our intellectual eyes."[95] Calvin therefore often refers to the Spirit as the Spirit of truth and understanding.[96]

True to the noetic orientation of his theology, Calvin related the work of the Spirit closely to the Word. Through the Word the Spirit descends to us to reveal God's will in a language that accommodates our weakness.

89. Calvin, *Institutes*, 3.10.11; *CO* 2.541.
90. Van't Spijker, "Calvin in a Pneumatological Light," 48.
91. Van't Spijker, "Calvin in a Pneumatological Light," 49.
92. Van't Spijker, "Calvin in a Pneumatological Light," 50.
93. *CO* 2.578.
94. *CO* 5.334–35.
95. Calvin, *Institutes*, 3.1.4; *CO* 2.397: "spiritus ille intelligentiae aperiret mentis oculos."
96. *CO* 2.396.

The human mind is too blinded to ascend from itself to God, therefore, the Spirit must first descend to us through the means of the Word to enlighten our minds.[97] The Word is the instrument through which the Spirit calls us, works faith in us and strengthens our faith. Calvin regarded the Word as the "outward" working of the Spirit, because through the Word the Spirit calls all people. Yet, this "outward" working of the Spirit must be accompanied by the "inward" working of the Spirit that consists of him illuminating the minds of the elect.[98] The external manifestation of the Word ought to be enough to bring us to faith, but due to human blindness the Word has no effect without the illumination of the Spirit.[99]

On various occasions, Calvin described the work of the Spirit as consisting in testimony. Closer inspection reveals that Calvin understood the Spirit's testimony to be a form of inner authentication. The Spirit authenticates the Word of God by affirming the promises of Scripture in the hearts of believers. In his Commentary on Romans 8:16 Calvin depicted the testimony of the Spirit as a confirmation of our adoption as children of God.[100]

Calvin also employed the notion of illumination that signifies an inward working of the Spirit as opposed to the outward working of the Word.[101] The Spirit works faith in the believer through the illumination of the human mind and by sealing God's promises in their hearts.[102] Illumination, hence, entails for Calvin a form of recognition that raises the mind above itself to know something that she cannot comprehend by nature.[103]

> Knowing that our minds are heavy and grovel on earth, he (God's Spirit) raises us above the world that he may shrug of our sluggishness and inactivity.[104]

As human beings cannot measure God's immensity, this illuminary recognition coincides with a persuasion and assurance that function on the relational level of experience rather than the epistemological sphere of analytical knowledge.[105] The regenerative work of the Spirit consists in him regulating

---

97. *CO* 2.403.
98. Calvin, *Institutes*, 2.5.5; *CO* 2.233.
99. Calvin, *Institutes*, 3.2.33; *CO* 2.425.
100. Calvin, *Romans*, 1:301; *CO* 49.150.
101. Calvin, *Institutes*, 2.5.5; *CO* 2.233.
102. Calvin, *Institutes*, 2.5.5; *CO* 2.233.
103. Raitt, "Saving Work," 13.
104. Calvin, *Institutes*, 1.13.1; *CO* 2.87: "Scite sibi unus ex veteribus dicere visus est Deum esse quidquid videmus et quidquid non videmus."
105. *CO* 2.87.

(*corrigat*), reforming (*reformet*) and renewing (*renovet*) the human will.[106] Calvin described the regenerative work of the Spirit as an "intrinsic energy" (*proprio vigore*) that the Spirit exerts in us.[107]

The result is that the human will is renewed to such a degree that his nature is changed to doing what the Spirit does in us.[108] Yet, Calvin must not be misunderstood as intimating that the human will is coerced by the Spirit. The Spirit transforms human nature, but does not obliterate human agency. For Calvin, faith is properly called ours, yet it is derived from God. This assertion might seem contradictory, but Calvin justified his view by using the two-causes argument—we act only after being acted upon. Thus, though the Spirit works faith in us, faith is properly an act of ours because the Spirit does not circumvent the human faculties while working faith in us.

Justification and Sanctification[109]

Recent Calvin scholarship has been characterized by intense debate on the relationship between justification and sanctification in Calvin's soteriology. Some scholars assert that Calvin prioritized justification to avoid a fusion between justification and regeneration and to emphasize that we are saved through God's unmerited grace alone.[110] These scholars posit that Calvin regarded justification as a forensic event that precedes regeneration both in a logical and chronological sense, while the sanctifying process of regeneration occurs as a result of justification.[111] Other scholars maintain that such an interpretation casts Calvin's soteriology in a legal framework, thereby underplaying the variety of other elements involved in his understanding of our personal union with Christ. Marcus Johnson, Cornelis Venema, Mark Garcia, Todd Billings and Lane Tipton[112] all share the view that there is no chronological or causal relationship between justification and regeneration in Calvin's theology; instead, these two forms of grace are distinguishable,

---

106. Calvin, *Institutes*, 2.5.15; *CO* 2.243.

107. Calvin, *Institutes*, 1.13.14; *CO* 2.102

108. *CO* 2.243.

109. Calvin used the terms sanctification, regeneration, and repentance interchangeably. See Venema, "Calvin's Understanding," 67–105.

110. See Canlis, "Beyond Tearing One Another," 79–88; Wenger, "New Perspective on Calvin," 311–28; Johnson, "New or Nuanced Perspective," 543–58; Evans, "Déjà Vu," 135–51.

111. See Wenger, "New Perspective on Calvin," 325.

112. Johnson, "Luther and Calvin," 73; Garcia, "Imputation as Attribution," 423; Billings, "Multifaceted 'Sum' of the Gospel," 428; Tipton, "Union with Christ," 19; Venema, "Calvin's Understanding," 78.

yet inseparable elements of our union with Christ. Attention to Calvin's application of the Christological *united but not mingled* formula to his soteriology might elucidate the matter.

In Book 3 of his *Institutes*, Calvin described the relation between faith and repentance (*poenitentia*) as a unity without mingling. He states that "as there is no faith without hope, and yet faith and hope are different, so repentance and faith, though constantly linked together, are only to be united, not confounded (*coniungi volunt quam confundi*)."[113]

In his Commentary on Jeremiah 26:17–19, Calvin made the same point when he described faith and repentance as "things wholly distinct and yet not contrary" [*sunt quidem res distinctiae, sed tamen non diversiae, nec separari debent*].[114]

The abovementioned passages resemble the *united but not mingled* (*unitis non confusis*) logic that Calvin applied in his doctrine on the two natures of Christ. In doing so, he made two important assertions. First, faith and repentance are inseparably connected because the one cannot exist without the other.[115] A faith without repentance does not exist, nor a repentance that exhibits no faith. Secondly, faith and repentance are different theological categories and their theological content should not be confounded by mixing the properties of the two categories. Faith consists of the knowledge of God's will as expressed in Christ and his Word,[116] an enlightenment brought about by the Spirit,[117] a trust in the truth of the Gospel, and a certainty of being adopted as a child of God.[118] Repentance, on the other hand, is a conversion proceeding from a fear of God that is displayed in the mortification of sins and a new vivified life.[119]

Calvin's theological point was that faith precedes repentance in a *logical but not chronological sense*. In logical terms, faith is a precondition for repentance, because repentance flows logically from faith. Yet, in a chronological sense, faith and repentance are *united* because they emanate from an act of God's Spirit that illuminates our mind and quickens our wills. The one category naturally flows into the other so that we cannot make a temporal distinction between the two categories. A distinction in terms of time would

---

113. Calvin, *Institutes*, 3.3.5; *CO* 2.437: "Quemadmodum sine spe fide non est et tamen fides ac spes varia sunt, ita poenitentia et fides, quanquam perpetuo inter se vincula cohaerent, magi stamen coniungi volunt quam confundi."

114. *CO* 38.532. See Venema, "Calvin's Understanding," 81.

115. *CO* 2.437.

116. *CO* 2.435.

117. *CO* 2.404.

118. *CO* 2.392.

119. *CO* 2.400–401.

mean that faith can exist without repentance. Calvin stated that "those who think that repentance precedes faith instead of flowing from, or being produced by it, as the fruit by the tree, have never understood its nature, and are moved to adopt that view on very insufficient grounds."[120]

Calvin also applied the united but not mingled logic to the relation between justification and regeneration. He described the connection between justification and regeneration as inseparable but distinct (*non separari... licet res sint distinctiae*). Again the phrase seems to convey a similar logic as *unitis non confusis* and *coniunctis non confundis*. This can be deduced, not only from the immediate context in which the term is used; but also from Calvin explicitly modelling the relation between justification and regeneration on the unity of Christ's Person since "as Christ cannot be divided into parts, so the two things justification and sanctification (regeneration), which we perceive to be united in him, are inseparable."[121]

We can safely assume that Calvin used the phrase *non separari... licet res sint distinctae* to construct the same kind of argument made earlier in *Institutes*, 3.3.5, with regard to the relation between faith and repentance. Justification and regeneration are inseparable in a chronological sense because the one category naturally flows into the other, and they are inseparable in terms of effect because a union with Christ is only possible if we are both justified and sanctified. Yet, justification and regeneration differ with regard to theological content and ought not to be confounded with each other on a conceptual level. Justification is the first grace and regeneration is the second grace (*secunda gratia est*).[122]

Calvin explained the mutual connectedness of the two categories but difference in conceptual content with the simile of the sun. Justification and regeneration flow from our union with Christ, just as heat and brightness come from the sun. As the brightness and the heat of the sun cannot be separated, justification and regeneration are inextricably connected in terms of origin and effect. Yet, as the brightness and heat of the sun have their own peculiar properties, we should distinguish between the conceptual content of justification and regeneration.[123]

---

120. Calvin, *Institutes*, 3.3.1; *CO* 2.434-35: "Quibus autem videtur fidem potius praecedere poenitentia quam ab ipsa manare, vel proferri languam fructus ab arbore nunquam vis eius fuit cognita, et nimium levi argumento ad id sentiendum moventur."

121. Calvin, *Institutes*, 3.11.6; *CO* 2.537: "Sicut non potest discerpi Christus in partes, ita inseparabilia esse haec duo, quae simul coniunctim in ipso percipimus, iustitiam et sanctificationem."

122. Calvin, *Institutes*, 3.11.1; *CO* 2.533.

123. *CO* 2.537-38.

In Book 3 of the *Institutes*, Calvin refuted the errors of Osiander by explaining in detail the logical difference between justification and regeneration. Osiander mixed the respective categories by holding to a notion of essential righteousness. According to Osiander, God transfuses his divine essence into the human being through the Spirit, hence, confounding the essence of Christ with that of the believer.[124] Since the human is justified by the transfused essence of God, justification does not denote a "free imputation" of God's grace based on the sacrifice of Christ, but signifies a process of regeneration inspired by the essence of God implanted in us. Calvin, in contrast, argued that the difference between justification and regeneration ought to be maintained because the righteous, even after being justified, are still sinful. If justification and regeneration are equated on a logical level, we can have no confidence in appearing before God's judgement seat. Our adoption as children of God will then depend on the holiness of our works, not God's free grace.[125]

In contrast to Osiander and the Council of Trent (1545), Calvin described justification as a forensic act of acquittal:

> We simply interpret justification as the acceptance with which God receives us into his favor as if we were righteous, and we say that this justification consists in the forgiveness of sins and imputation of the righteousness of Christ.[126]

Imputation means that we are not justified based on our own holiness, but based on Christ's righteousness.[127] When God justifies us through the intercession of Christ, he does not acquit us on the basis of our own innocence; but he attributes Christ's righteousness to us so that "though not righteous in ourselves, and strictly deserving of punishment, we are deemed righteous in Christ."[128] Garcia rightly asserts that imputation entails for Calvin that the "distinctive righteousness of Christ, which is proper to him alone, is attributed to believers only within and because of the reality of their union

---

124. *CO* 2.536.

125. See *CO* 2.542.

126. Calvin, *Institutes*, 3.11.2; *CO* 2.534: "Ita nos iustificationem simpliciter interpretamur acceptionem qua nos Deus in gratiam receptos pro iustis habet. Eamque in peccatorum remissione ac iustitiae Christi imputatione positam esse dicimus."

127. Calvin, *Institutes*, 3.11.2; *CO* 2.533–34.

128. Calvin, *Institutes*, 3.11.3; *CO* 2.535: "Quum itaque nos Christi intercessione iustificet Deus, non propriae innocentiae approbatione, sed iustitiae imputatione nos absolvit, ut pro iustis in Christo censeamur, qui in nobis non sumus."

with him."¹²⁹ Justification is thus wholly an act of God alone, no human works are able to acquire God's justification.

Regeneration, on the other hand, brings the life of the believer in harmony with the righteousness of God, thereby confirming our adoption as children of God. While justification signifies our status as adopted children of God, sanctification denotes a process of renewal according to our new status before God. Though Calvin regarded justification and sanctification as interconnected and temporally inseparable, he consistently held that to be justified is logically different from being made a new creature.

> But as it is too well-known by experience, that the remains of sin always exists in the righteous, it is necessary that justification should be something very different from reformation to newness of life.¹³⁰

For Calvin justification is a prerequisite for sanctification, whereas sanctification denotes a gradual and incremental process of inner moral renewal brought about by the regenerative work of the Holy Spirit:

The *united but not mingled* logic underlying Calvin's understanding of the twofold grace of God is quite clear. The peculiar properties of the one category cannot be dissolved into the other, yet both categories are inseparable effects of our one union with Christ.

The inseparability of justification and sanctification consists in them being a "double grace" that flows from our union with Christ.¹³¹ Salvation does not depend on justification alone, but on justification and sanctification together.¹³² For Calvin, imputation is part and parcel of our participation in Christ. Righteousness entails more than a forensic acquittal, but also a communication and transfusion of the righteousness of Christ to the believer, who is engrafted in him:

> Our righteousness is not in ourselves, but in Christ; that is the only way in which we become possessed of it is by being made partakers with Christ . . . Our Lord Jesus Christ communicates his righteousness to us, and so by some wondrous way, insofar as it pertains to the justice of God, transfuses its power into us.¹³³

---

129. Garcia, "Imputation as Attribution," 419.

130. Calvin, *Institutes*, 3.11.11; *CO* 2.542: "Sed quia experiential plus satis notumest, manere semper in iustis reliquias peccati, necesse est longe aliter iustificari quam reformantur in vitae novitatem."

131. Billings, "Multifaceted 'Sum' of the Gospel," 440.

132. Billings, "Multifaceted 'Sum' of the Gospel," 446.

133. Calvin, *Institutes*, 3.11.23; *CO* 2.552: "Vides non in nobis, sed in Christo esse iustitiam nostram; nobis tantum eo iure competere quia Christi sumus participes . . . Eo

Being illuminated through faith, believers are justified and engrafted[134] into Christ; resulting in the faithful obtaining the right to be adopted as "sons of God."[135] Through adoption, the believer receives "both the legal declaration of becoming a child of God" and the gift of the Spirit who conforms us further to the image of Christ.[136] The child metaphor is especially important in Calvin's doctrine on sanctification. Childship denotes God's goodness and love and inspires in us moral agency. Canlis[137] notes that Calvin used the notion of adoption to "highlight a radical participation in the divine that simultaneously secures creaturehood." It affirms that the believer truly is an "heir of heaven, a partaker of righteousness, a possessor of life" and receives all the merits of Christ, but his sonship is an acquired sonship, not a divinization of human nature.[138] This honour of adoption belongs to the faithful solely on the basis of Christ's merits. Faith is not a human achievement with which believers raise themselves up to God, but is a gracious gift of the Spirit through which believers "receive Christ" and become inheritors of all his blessings.

Mortification and Vivification

The Spirit who dwells in the believer is the agent that makes possible her union with Christ. The *telos* of the sanctification that the Spirit brings about in the believer is a restoration into the image of God as exhibited by Christ. Actually, the regeneration of the believers is "nothing else than the formation anew of the image of God in them."[139] The restoration of the *imago Dei* occurs through repentance, which "consists of two parts: namely mortification of the flesh and vivification of the spirit."[140] Contra Roman Catholicism, Calvin was adamant that reconciliation with God is not possible through

---

enim iure communicat nobiscum Dominus Christus suam iustitiam, ut mirabili quodam modo, quantum pertinet ad Dei iudicium, vim eius in nos transfundat."

134. According to Canlis, the metaphor of "engrafting" (insero) is used by Calvin to decenter the human. By using this term, he highlights the human-in-Christ. Canlis, *Calvin's Ladder*, 146.

135. Calvin, *Commentary on John*, 42; Calvin, *Catechism*, art. 20; CO 5.337.

136. Billings, "Multifaceted 'Sum' of the Gospel," 429.

137. Canlis, *Calvin's Ladder*, 138, 237.

138. Calvin, *Institutes*, 3.15.6; CO 2.584: "coelorum haeres, iustitiae particeps, vitae possessor."

139. Calvin, *Galatians and Ephesians*, 296; CO 51.208: "Nec sane aliud est regeneratio piorum, quam reformatio imaginis Dei in illis."

140. Calvin, *Institutes*, 3.3.8; CO 2.439: "quod dicimus poenitentiam duabus partibus constare: mortificatione scilicet carnis et spiritus vivificatione."

penitence and contrition. Fear of God cannot transform moral agency, but God's love enables transformation.

Repentance entails that the human being must descend into himself and contrast his conduct with the righteousness of the Law, which reveals to us how far we are from living according to God's will. The result ought to be that we develop a distrust in our own ability and seek our salvation outside ourselves in Christ.[141] For Calvin, true knowledge is not knowledge of our excellence, but of our destitution and inherent depravity because of sin.[142] The human being, thus, must respond to Christ's descent with a descent of his own. When we deny ourselves by being aware of our sins, we make the remarkable discovery of apprehending the immensity of God's grace and kindness in Christ. The result of our union with Christ is that Christ's death and resurrection becomes the life pattern of the believer in the sense that "the transition in Christ from humiliation to exaltation, suffering to glory, cross to resurrection and obedience to eschatological life (becomes) the historical location of the believer's present life in Christ."[143] Calvin explained in his commentary on 1 Peter 4:1 what conformity to the death of Christ entails for the believer:

> Scripture recommends to us a twofold likeness to the death of Christ: that we are conformed to Him in reproaches and troubles (Phil 3:6), and also that the old man being dead and extinct in us, we are to be renewed to a spiritual life (Rom 6:4). Yet, Christ is not simply to be viewed as our example when we speak of the mortification of the flesh; but it is by His Spirit that we are really made conformable to His death, so that it becomes effectual in us to the crucifixion of our flesh.[144]

Conformity to the death of Christ thus consists of an ongoing process of turning away from the self towards God. Self-renunciation and mortification, implying an uprooting of all ambition and cravings for glory and a dying of the self, is the precondition for a genuine love towards the neighbour

---

141. Calvin, *Institutes*, 2.8.3; CO 2.268.
142. See Zachmann, "Deny Yourself," 467.
143. Garcia, "Imputation as Attribution," 426.
144. John Calvin, *Commentaries on the Catholic Epistles*, 120; CO 55.270: "Duplicem hanc mortis Christi similitudinem scriptura nobis commendat: nempe ut illi configuremur in probris et aerumnis: deinde ut nobis mortui, et extincto veteri homine, renovemur in spiritualem vitam. Tametsi non simpliciter considerandis est nobis Christus tanquam exemplum, ubi de carnis mortificatione agitur: sed spiritu eius vere inserimur in eius mortem, ut ipsa in nobis sit efficax ad crucifigendam carnem nostram."

and God.¹⁴⁵ True human existence is only possible in a decentered existence that finds its goal and destiny in God.

Communion with the resurrection of Christ, conversely, entails for Calvin a raising up of the Christian mind to the resurrected and exalted Christ:

> Ascension follows resurrection: hence, if we are members of Christ we must ascend into Heaven, because He, on being raised up from the dead was received up into Heaven that he might draw us with Him.¹⁴⁶

This "raising up" leads to a Christian life embedded in a practical conformity to the image of Christ, which exhibits the supernatural gifts that the human person lost because of the fall. By reflecting the supernatural virtues of uprightness, knowledge, purity, righteousness and true holiness, the believer conforms to the image of Christ and becomes *filii Dei*.¹⁴⁷ Though believers are able to reflect God's attributes, Christ alone can reveal God's attributes perfectly because he is the infinite God, whereas humans as finite beings are only capable of reflecting God's attributes in a limited measure.¹⁴⁸ The human's restored image is the result of an imputed, transfused and communicated righteousness that reflects some attributes of God, but not God's essence. Yet, the imputed righteousness that the believer receives is an admirable gift, because through their restoration the faithful enjoys so much of "the good things which they lost in Adam" that it ought to fill them with wonder about the grace that God bestows on them.¹⁴⁹ Despite the miracle of God's grace, Calvin was realistic about the effects of our sanctification. He avoided the notion of realized sanctification by emphasizing the need for continuous self-mortification.¹⁵⁰ God's grace ends the "reign" of sin in us, but sin still "dwells" in believers. Christ's image is therefore only "partly" seen in the elect, insofar as they are regenerated by the Spirit.¹⁵¹ The effects of the fall still linger in the elect, because there always remains in us vestiges

---

145. Senior, "Cruciform Pilgrims," 126.

146. Calvin, *Colossians*, 205; *CO* 52.117: "Ascensio resurrectionem comitatur. Ergo si Christi membra sumus, in coelum conscendere nos oportet: quia excitatus a mortuis in coelum receptus est, ut secum nos traheret."

147. *CO* 49.47; Calvin, *Institutes*, 1.15.4; *CO* 2.138. Van Vliet, *Children of God*, 77.

148. Ibid., 87.

149. *CO* 31.95: "residua bonorum, quibus in Adam spoliati fuerant, parte sic potiri, ut ampla illis admirationis materia suppetat, quod tam benigne ab eo tractentur." The English translation is from Calvin, *The Book of Psalms*, vol. 1, 108.

150. See Murphy, "Reformed Theosis?," 201.

151. Calvin, *Institutes*, 1.15.4; *CO* 2.138.

of fleshly corruptions.[152] Since sanctification is a gradual process of transformation, not a once-off event, we have to struggle throughout our entire lives against our fleshly desires.[153]

The Christ-like life amounts, according to Calvin, to self-denial, cross-bearing and meditation on the future life.[154] Calvin's emphasis on self-denial is not surprising since he regarded the human being's blind self-love as the main consequence of sin. Calvin repeatedly emphasized that "we are not our own" and the opposite, "we are God's."[155] Self-denial includes both mortification and vivification. On the one hand it denotes the abandonment of our selfish desires, conversely love of God and our neighbour.[156] Calvin distinguished between three branches of self-denial, namely self-denial with respect to God, the self-denial that we owe our neighbours and self-denial that consists in bearing our cross.

For Calvin, self-denial is never self-centered but always God-centered.[157] It entails that we replace our sinful self-love with a love for God that reorients our lives towards God.[158] The believer must renounce whatever his reason and will dictate and direct his whole mind to God. Resigning ourselves to God involves that we abandon all the sinful vices that emanate from our blind self-love such as pride, ambition and arrogance and that we accept that we are not our own.[159] It entails that we surrender our worldly ambitions, longing for earthly wealth and human honour and that we accept that God alone is the Ruler of our fortunes and that our course of life is at God's disposal.[160] We never have the right to murmur against God because of our destiny but must find our solace in God's providential reign.[161] Most importantly, self-denial entails that, in contrast to the philosophers, we submit our human reason to the guidance of God's Spirit so that we are reduced to nothing while Christ lives and reigns in us.[162] Our natural reason is after

---

152. SC 11/1.328.
153. SC 11/1.328.
154. Leith, *John Calvin's Doctrine of the Christian Life*, 38.
155. See Sytsma, "Calvin's Loci on the Christian Life," 270.
156. Leith, *John Calvin's Doctrine of the Christian Life*, 77.
157. See Beeke, "Calvin's Piety," 59.
158. Beeke, "Calvin's Piety," 59.
159. CO 2.502–503.
160. Ibid., 506.
161. Ibid., 514.
162. Calvin, *Institutes*, 3.7.8; CO 2.512; CO 45.481.

all inclined to "carnal" reasoning and needs to be dethroned so that God's wisdom can enter our lives.[163]

Self-denial also pertains to our relation with fellow human beings. The believer needs to have a humble opinion of himself and to have respect for others.[164] We overcome our natural inclination to blind self-love by transferring the hatred we feel for others to ourselves.[165] Calvin's call to self-hatred seems at first sight very harsh, but it is part of his rhetorical style to make abrasive statements just to follow it up with directly opposite and equally strong statements in other passages that highlight the other side of the story. Calvin's intention was clearly that the believers need to examine themselves, to understand and hate their own sinful nature before judging others. While repressing our own natural inclination to self-love, we need to behold and respect the gifts that God endowed our neighbours with. In essence, this entails that we attend to the image of God that exists in all human beings and to which we owe honour.[166] Self-denial also requires that we devote ourselves to our neighbours by serving them with the gifts which God bestowed to us:

> All the endowments which we possess are divine deposits entrusted to us for the very purpose of being distributed for our neighbor.[167]

The gifts God bestows on us are not for the sake of our own advancement, but should be used in the service of the church and community.[168] The right administration thereof is always determined by love and charity. This love extends even to our enemy.[169] Calvin's notion of enemy love is closely related to his view that humanity is in essence one flesh and that we see an image of ourselves even in our enemies.[170] Self-denial requires that we act against our nature by loving those who hate us, rendering good for evil, and blessing those who curse us. This is only possible when we look beyond their faults to observe the image of God in them that compels us to love them.[171] In his exposition of the sixth commandment, Calvin stated that our love

---

163. *CO* 49.348.
164. *CO* 2.509.
165. *CO* 31.62.
166. *CO* 2.509–510.
167. Calvin, *Institutes*, 3.7.5; *CO* 2.509: "omnes quibus pollemus dotes, Dei esse deposita, ea lega fidei nostrae commissa, ut in proximorum bonum dispensentur."
168. See Zachmann, "Deny Yourself," 472.
169. *CO* 45.188.
170. *CO* 37.330.
171. *CO* 37.330.

for God necessarily ought to emanate in an unconditional love for all of humankind. The first step to such an all-embracing love is not to turn our eye to the faults of our fellow human beings, but to God. We ought to love our neighbor, because God loves our neighbor.[172] To despise others is not only the greatest form of inhumanity but in a sense also a betrayal of God who bestows his love on us despite our own perversity.[173] We show ourselves to be true children of God when we love our enemy in the same manner that God loves us in Christ.[174]

Cross-bearing is the main feature in Christ's life to which believers must conform.[175] It entails partaking in the suffering of Christ by bearing our own cross when confronted by the tribulations and afflictions of earthly life.[176] Leith rightly notes that Calvin speaks of cross-bearing in terms of discipline, chastisement and persecution.[177]

Cross-bearing is first of all part of a disciplinary process of being conformed to the image of Christ.[178] Through affliction God tries our patience and trains us in obedience and endurance.[179] When afflicted by adversity we experience closer fellowship with Christ. By learning to follow Christ's example of patience amidst affliction and to trust on God alone, our assurance of salvation is greatly enhanced.[180] In the process of cross-bearing, God rids us of our blind self-love and our natural inclination to trust ourselves. Instead, we learn to distrust ourselves and transfer our confidence to God.[181] Whereas the Stoics learned that the wise person overcomes the tribulations of human life by transcending emotional passions, Calvin regarded emotions as natural, but called upon believers to overcome their feelings of bitterness and hardship by resigning and surrendering themselves to God.[182]

Cross-bearing also serves the purpose of chastisement. God's chastisement is in essence driven by God's love. God will doom us to destruction if he does not correct our ways through chastisement.[183] Whereas non-

172. *CO* 2.306.
173. *CO* 45.187.
174. *CO* 45.188.
175. *CO* 46.451.
176. *CO* 2.515.
177. Leith, *John Calvin's Doctrine of the Christian Life*, 78.
178. Leith, *John Calvin's Doctrine of the Christian Life*, 515.
179. Leith, *John Calvin's Doctrine of the Christian Life*, 515.
180. Leith, *John Calvin's Doctrine of the Christian Life*, 516–17.
181. Leith, *John Calvin's Doctrine of the Christian Life*, 516–17.
182. See Zachmann, "Deny Yourself," 476. See Leithart, "Stoic Elements," 60.
183. Zachmann, "Deny Yourself," 476.

believers are only hardened by afflictions, believers are turned through misfortunes towards repentance.[184]

Lastly, Calvin identified persecution for the sake of righteousness as part of the faithful's cross-bearing. When we are forced to maintain the truth of God against the lies of Satan or to defend the innocent against the bad, we incur the hatred and offence of the world.[185] However, the believer will experience the joy of suffering for God and will attain assurance of eternal life.[186]

Meditation on the future life is the third feature of a Christ-like life. Some have interpreted Calvin's call to meditation of the future life as an effort to affirm "a world-denying otherworldliness."[187] Such an interpretation is understandable, since Calvin used very strong words to express the penultimate nature of the present and the attitude that Christians ought to display towards the present. He described the present as "uncertain, fleeting, vain and vitiated with an admixture of evil" (*incerta fluida, vana, multisque admixtis ma lis vitiata esse*) and he exhorted Christians to "despise the present" (*preasentis contemptu*).[188] A closer reading, however, reveals that Calvin's intention was not to devalue the present, but rather to warn against an idolatrous and obsessive attachment to the present that seeks its happiness in earthly things rather than in God. Calvin, after all, resisted the world-denying practises of his day such as monasticism and celibacy because these practises endeavoured to attain righteousness by abstaining from God's gifts.[189] Beeke rightly notes that Calvin typically used the *complexio oppositorum* here; a rhetorical style that presents opposites to find a middle way.[190] Calvin's purpose was clearly to state that humans are by nature inclined to a "slavish love" of this world, but they must resist this natural desire by not seeking their happiness in worldly things. Instead, believers ought to aspire to the future heavenly life.[191] God safeguards us against an obsessive love for this world by bringing miseries over us that remind us of the "vanity of the present life" (*de preasentis vitae vanitate*).[192]

---

184. Zachmann, "Deny Yourself," 476.
185. Zachmann, "Deny Yourself," 476.
186. Zachmann, "Deny Yourself," 476.
187. See Leith, *John Calvin's Doctrine of the Christian Life*, 80.
188. Calvin, *Institutes*, 3.9.1; CO 2.523–24.
189. CO 52.294.
190. Beeke, "Calvin's Piety," 61.
191. Calvin, *Institutes*, 3.9.1; CO 2.523: "in belluinum mundi huius amorem simus natura inclinati."
192. Calvin, *Institutes*, 3.9.1; CO 2.523.

Despite the strong rhetoric that he employed, Calvin conversely emphasized that our attitude towards the present should not beget a hatred towards the present or ingratitude towards God. Human life remains a blessing from God and should not be despised in itself but we ought to rejoice in its blessings.[193] In the present we already experience a foretaste of God's eternal goodness.[194] The new future begins in the present, because Christ's death and resurrection is the ultimate turning point in history at which the renewal of the world commences.[195]

The fundamental premise of Calvin's eschatology was that the coming age does not transcend or suspend the creational order; instead, it gradually restores and completes God's original creation.[196] Despite sin, God still maintains his creation and endows human beings with his blessings and gifts. The future life is thus intimately connected to the present life in that it sustains and preserves God's creation.[197] Leith rightly notes that, for Calvin, the meditation of the future life is closely tied to a participation in the fruits of the eternal life here on earth:

> The point Calvin is endeavoring to make is that the Christian life is life in fellowship with God, not life in the things of the earth. This is not world denying, as Calvinism subsequently proved.[198]

The Christian life consists for Calvin in a correct disposition towards both the present and the future. Calvin regarded earthly life as a pilgrimage to eternal life that consists in a continuous mortification of our fleshly desires and a proper use of God's earthly blessings.[199] As stewards of God, we must give account of our use of creation to the Creator himself. We ought to use the gifts of God according to the purpose they were created for. The natural qualities of things demonstrate to which end God created them and to which degree it can legitimately enjoyed.[200] God's gifts may never be used contrary to law, in service of license, or in a superfluous abundance that amounts to excessive luxury.[201] Instead, moderation, temperance and frugality are, for Calvin, the key principles that regulate a proper use of God's

---

193. *CO* 2.526; *CO* 49.692.
194. *CO* 49.692.
195. See Holwerda, "Eschatology and History," 122.
196. See Bolt, "Eschatological Hermeneutics and Women's Ordination," 385.
197. Bolt, "Eschatological Hermeneutics and Women's Ordination," 385.
198. Leith, *John Calvin's Doctrine of the Christian Life*, 82.
199. *CO* 2.528.
200. *CO* 2.530.
201. *CO* 2.531.

gifts. The believer always needs to use God's natural gifts for the edification and well-being of his neighbour.[202]

While our disposition to earthly life is characterized by self-mortification and cross-bearing, our attitude towards future life is enthused by a vivification that rests in the resurrection motif. Wallace rightly notes that, for Calvin, we "find the commencement of our salvation in the death of Christ and the consummation in the Resurrection".[203] It is through communion with Christ's death that sin is subdued in us, and it is through communion with Christ's resurrection that we already experience the new life in us.[204] Our aspiration for the future is inspired by our own resurrection:

> No man has made much progress in the school of Christ who does not look forward with joy to the day of death and final resurrection.[205]

The resurrection motif encourages believers to raise their minds to heaven, to rise above present affairs and to order their actions according to their divine callings.[206] The meditation on the future is thus fundamentally a communion with God that orders the Christians' actions and relationships in the temporal realm.

Prayer and the Use of the Sacraments

For Calvin, partaking in the divine nature entails that we experience the "quickening energy" of the Spirit in us.[207] His emphasis on the work of the Spirit served as a safeguard against any notion of substantial participation that might threaten either God's divinity or the human's creatureliness. The Scholastics employed the Platonic notion of *methexis,* which amounts to a participation in eternal realities based on a substantialist ontology. Calvin, instead, understood participation as a sharing in personal relationships; his anthropology is bound up in a participation in Christ, and not an innate Godward movement of the soul that presupposes continuity between nature and divine reality. Though being "one with Christ" is a transfusion of

---

202. *CO* 2.531.
203. Wallace, *Calvin's Doctrine of the Christian Life,* 78.
204. Wallace, *Calvin's Doctrine of the Christian Life,* 78.
205. Calvin, *Institutes,* 3.9.5; *CO* 2.527: "Hoc tamen habeamus constitutum, neminem bene in Christi schola profecisse, nisi qui et mortis et ultimae resurrectionis diemcum gaudio exspectet."
206. *CO* 2.528; *CO* 2.532.
207. Calvin, *Institutes,* 1.13.14; *CO* 2.102: "vigere . . . spiritus virtute."

divine communion, not substance, this transfusion is as powerful as any unity in substance could be, because it invigorates, sustains and preserves us.[208] That is why prayer is of such crucial importance in Calvin's theology. Through prayer the believer enters the "upper sanctuary of God, he appears before Him and appeals to his promises."[209] An impersonal faith that is not accompanied by prayer is not genuine.[210] In his *Institutes*, Calvin described prayer as the "chief exercise of faith" (praecipuum est fidei).[211] He identified six uses of prayer: namely, to bring our needs before God, to prepare us to receive God's gifts with a humble attitude, to meditate on God's kindness, to experience the delight of God's answers, and to confirm God's promises.[212] Calvin regarded prayer as primarily not for God but for us. It is a "Spirit-enabled activity" in which the Spirit raises believers up to pray to God so that the believer can be sustained by God.[213] Prayer cannot change God's will but it contributes to and strengthens the major attribute of the Christian life, which is faith.[214] Discipline of prayer is, consequently, essential to sustain our communion with God.

Besides prayer, the sacraments are the main instruments through which believers enter into communion with Christ. In Calvin's thoughts the sacraments are institutions of God, not the church. The ministering of the sacraments exemplified for Calvin the descent of God to raise us up to him through the Spirit of Christ. Our union with Christ entails that the faithful receive the gifts of the Spirit, which enable them to have fellowship with him and to share in his righteousness.[215]

The dual function of the sacraments is to affirm our union, while also "being the means of participation" in divine reality.[216] They are aids through which we are engrafted in the body of Christ or, if already engrafted, become more and more united with him.[217] The corporeal signs of the sacraments represent God's invisible promises in a manner adapted to our weak

---

208. Calvin, *Institutes*, 4.17.18; *CO* 2.1007.

209. Calvin, *Institutes*, 3.20.2; *CO* 2.625–26: "Est enim quaedam hominum cum Deo communicatio, qua sanctuarum coeli ingressi de suis promissis illium coram appellant."

210. Calvin, *Institutes*, 3.20.1; *CO* 2.625.

211. Calvin, *Institutes*, 3.20.1; *CO* 2.625.

212. *CO* 2.626–27.

213. Billings, "Multifaceted 'Sum' of the Gospel," 437.

214. Kelsay, "Prayer and Ethics," 172, 174.

215. *CO* 2.540.

216. Canlis, *Calvin's Ladder*, 164.

217. Calvin, *Institutes*, 3.11.10; *CO* 2.540.

capacity, while we in turn exhibit our faithful acceptance.[218] They only perform their office when accompanied by the Spirit, who alone can work faith in us. Without him the sacraments are of no avail, since the office of the sacraments is purely to make the Spirit's promises visible to our eyes.[219] Against both Roman Catholicism and Lutheranism, Calvin maintained that there is no latent virtue inherent in the sacraments themselves. They do not bestow grace by being performed, but their efficacy is produced by being believed.[220]

Baptism signifies, according to Calvin, that we are washed and purified and that we have been acquited of the condemnation imputed to us and the penalty brought about by original sin.[221] It is the initiatory sign by which the believers are admitted to the *koinonia* of the Church, "engrafted into Christ," and counted as children of God.[222] As such, it signifies that we are "united to Christ himself as to be partakers of all his blessings."[223] Those who receive baptism "therefore experience the efficacy of Christ's death in the mortification of their flesh, and the efficacy of his resurrection in the quickening of the Spirit."[224]

Calvin regarded the Supper as the celebration of our redemption and union with Christ.[225] During the Supper Christ descends to believers in the Spirit by means of visible elements, while at the same time drawing the church into a heavenly worship of the Father in the Spirit through the mediation of the ascended Christ.[226] The Supper seals the sacred communion through Christ, transfuses his life into us, and denotes the *koinonia* of the believers with God and each other.[227] Through the Supper we are enjoined to take and eat the body of Christ so that we can experience the efficacy of his death for us.[228] As bread nourishes and sustains us, so the body of Christ keeps our soul alive through the Spirit.[229] In contrast to Zwingli, Calvin did

218. *CO* 2.942.
219. *CO* 2.947, 949.
220. *CO* 2.954. See Murphy, "Reformed Theosis," 208.
221. *CO* 2.958; *CO* 2.967.
222. Calvin, *Institutes*, 4.15.1; *CO* 2.962: "Christo insiti."
223. Calvin, *Institutes*, 4.15.6; *CO* 2.965: "non modo in mortem et vitam Christi nos insitos esse, sed sic ipsi Christo unitos ut omnium eius bonorum participes simus."
224. Calvin, *Institutes*, 4.15.5; *CO* 2.965: "vere efficiam mortis Christis sentiunt, in mortificatione carnis suae; simul etiam resurrectionis, in vivificatione spiritus."
225. Calvin, *Institutes*, 4.14.22; *CO* 2.958.
226. Butin, *Revelation, Redemption and Response*, 118.
227. *CO* 2.1009; *CO* 2.663.
228. *CO* 2.1002.
229. *CO* 2.1003.

not understand the Supper to be merely symbolic in nature, nor a mere imitation of Christ or a partaking in his benefits; but a true communion with Christ, who is present in the Supper through his Spirit.[230] We truly eat the body and drink the blood of Christ through the mouth of faith.[231] Christ, afterall, can exert his energy wherever he wants. He is present within us, sustains, confirms and invigorates us just as if he were with us in the body.[232]

The Resurrection of the Human Body

The ascent of believers culminates in the resurrection when the believers will become "partakers of divine nature" so that Christ will be all in all.[233]

Even though Calvin regarded the body as an accessory to the soul, he did not exclude the human body from God's salvational work. The body as "tabernacle" (tabernaculum) of the soul is the home of the quickening Spirit that dwells in us so that God's life flows into us and vivifies the body.[234] The Spirit sanctifies every part of the body and enjoins the various parts of the body to praise and glorify God.[235] This vivifying work of the Spirit becomes particularly evident in the sacrament of the Supper when the believer partakes in Christ.[236]

Whereas the immortal soul needs no resurrection, but—retaining its own essence– "migrates" after death from its tabernacle, the body will be the special object of God's resurrecting power.[237] The resurrection entails that the "Lord will then revive us from mortality into immortality and receive us glorified both in body and in soul into blessedness that will last forever."[238] Christ's own resurrection serves as warrant that the believer's body will be resurrected and eternally changed from a "vile body" to a "glorious body."[239]

230. Calvin, *Institutes*, 4.14.17; *CO* 2.954. Also see Billings, "United to God through Christ," 315–34.

231. *CO* 2.1005.

232. *CO* 2.1016.

233. Calvin, *Institutes*, 3.25.10; *CO* 2.742: "ut divinae fiant consortes naturae."

234. *CO* 5.339.

235. *CO* 2.736.

236. *CO* 2.1010–11.

237. *CO* 2.1010–11.

238. Calvin, *Catechism*, art. 20, ix; *CO* 5.342: "ut tum nos Dominus ex corruptione in incorruptionem, ex mortalitate in immortalitatem suscitabit, corporeque et anima glorificatos in beatitudinem recipiat, sine fine perstaturam, extra omnem mutationis aut corruptionis sortem."

239. Calvin, *Institutes*, 3.25.3; *CO* 2.731: "ut corpus nostrum humile et abiectum configuret corpori suo gloriose."

Calvin insisted that the believer does not receive a new body with the resurrection, but receives a revived body. To suggest that the believer receives a new body amounts to a denigration of the earthly body. The earthly body is, after all, a temple of God and God will not allow his temples to fall into corruption without hope of resurrection.[240] For Calvin, the immortality of our earthly body is the culmination of the gradual process of our restoration in the image of Christ.[241] If we receive a substituted body, the connection between the body of Christ and our earthly bodies will be broken. Christ did not receive a new body, because this would have meant that that which he had offered as expiatory sacrifice had been destroyed. The same principle applies to believers. Believers will receive their earthly bodies—not substitute bodies—at the Consummation, because they will be resurrected in the same manner as Christ was.[242]

Evaluation and Reflection

Our discussion has revealed that Calvin's understanding of our union with Christ is characterized by two important analytical tools, namely the *united but not mingled* understanding of the relationship between divine and human realities; and the scheme of descent and ascent.

Calvin utilised the *united but not mingled* logic to resist forms of monism that could confuse the divine and human realms or dissolve them into each other. He rejected Scholastic realism; the Lutheran notion of ubiquity; the Manichean and Servetean mixing of divine and human substances; and the Osiandrian concept of essential righteousness. Since God and human beings exist on different ontological planes, the peculiar integrity of both divine and human natures ought to be guarded. Equally, against the dichotomous tendencies in Marcionism and Nestorianism, Calvin upheld the "unity in distinction" of the divine-human realms. Calvin affirmed God's sovereignty over all things and the absolute dependence of human reality on divine reality.[243] Human reality cannot exist on its own independent from God, but is sustained by God's blessings through the sacrifice of Christ, the Word, the sanctifying work of the Holy Spirit, and God's covenantal and providential grace. Since human reality is sustained by God's glorious grace,

---

240. *CO* 2.736.
241. See Engel, *John Calvin's Perspectival Anthropology*, 177.
242. *CO* 2.738.
243. See for instance *CO* 45.20; *CO* 55.190.

Calvin was able to speak of both creation and human beings as "mirrors of God's glory."[244]

Calvin's *united but not mingled* logic is theologically important because it articulates a basic ontological supposition in his theology that is paradigmatic of his view of reality, namely that the human and divine realms are closely related to each other, yet they are distinct and separate. Calvin's ontology and robust pneumatology provides Reformed Theology with promising tools to develop a doctrine of *theosis* that relate the divine-human realms without dissolving them into each other.[245]

Reformed Theology can, in my view, embrace the notion of *theosis* as long as *theosis* is understood as God's Spirit imparting God's power or energy to human nature without confusing divine and human essences.[246] Calvin referred repeatedly to the Spirit as the energy, efficacy and power of the Son's actions.[247] He depicted the Spirit's energy as *virtute*, his power as *potentia* and his efficacy as *efficacia*. *Virtute* connotes a radiating power, *potentia* a causating power and *efficacia* an effecting power. All three terms denote actions that proceed from a single origin and are mediated by the Spirit. Calvin's theological anthropology, moreover, contained a robust pneumatological orientation in that God's Spirit, who invigorates all of creaturely life, literally breathes life into human beings and vivifies believers.[248] Notions such as the Spirit's impartation of immortality to believers; his illumination, quickening and vivification of believers; and believers sharing and partaking in Christ's life through the power the Spirit infuses in them; are abundantly present in Calvin's theology.[249] Muller rightly notes that Calvin's "ontological distinction of divine from human is by no means a rigid separation."[250]

244. See CO 23.23; CO 5.325; CO 31.92.

245. Calvin's doctrine on union with Christ is a much debated topic in contemporary Reformed theology. Recently some Calvin scholars have argued that elements of *theosis* can be found in Calvin's soteriology which are reminiscent of the Greek Patristic and Byzantine approach. The patristic fathers held that God's energies radiate from his essence; infusing human beings with his power without absorbing human nature into divine essence. Reactions to this thesis have ranged from enthusiastic support and qualified interest to outright rejection. See Mosser, "Greatest Possible Blessing," 36–57; Murphy, "Reformed Theosis," 191–212; Ollerton, "*Quasi Deificari*," 237–54; Slater, "Salvation as Participation," 41, 53; Garcia, *Life in Christ*, 257–58; McCormack, "Union with Christ," 512–16.

246. See Horton, "Union and Communion," 398–414, 406.

247. See for instance CO 2.105; CO 2.131.

248. CO 5.221; Calvin, *Institutes*, 1.13.4; CO 2.92; Calvin, *Institutes*, 1.15.3; CO 2.137.

249. See CO 55.446; CO 2.31; CO 2.137; CO 2.541.

250. Muller, "Christ in the Eschaton," 50.

For Calvin, our union with Christ involved more than a mere extrinsic or moral relationship; it is mystical in nature. Mystical communion, however, is not necessarily ontological in nature.[251] In Calvin's thought Christ stands in a mystical relationship with us by exerting his effectual divine power and energy in us without confounding divine and human essence. Calvin understood the Spirit's power not as something that circumvents, replaces, or takes over our human faculties; but as a power that acts upon the human will and faculties; transforming, correcting and renovating our lives.[252] This inworking of the Spirit is vivifying and nutritious. Muller aptly captures this nuance in Calvin's approach:

> The union with believers is genuine, true, spiritual and perhaps even "substantial" in Calvin's non-ontological eucharistic senses of the term as indicating something fully bestowed and "nourishing." The basic issue, for both Calvin and Vermigli, is that the personal union of divinity and humanity in Christ provides the foundation for the further, spiritual or mystical union that is best explained in the metaphor of Christ as the head and believers as members of his body.[253]

Whereas the *united but not mingled* approach largely functions on a presuppositional level in Calvin's theology, the descent-ascent is a constructive tool that pervades his theology quite explicitly and enables him to develop a highly dynamic notion of our union with Christ. Seven features of this construction justifies serious consideration.

First, as noted earlier, the cycle of descent and ascent in Calvin's theology is essentially a divine movement. This marks Calvin's soteriology as theocentric in nature. Humans are not the prime agents in the mystical union with Christ. Instead, our ascent to God depends on Christ first descending to us and then enabling us to ascend with him to the Father through the work of the Spirit. Through the divinely activated cycle of descent and ascent that is mediated by the Spirit, Calvin avoided the extremes of anthropocentrism and deism in favour of a reciprocal relationship between God and believers that exists in a cycle of gift and return. Yet since the gratitude that believers return to God is always asymmetrical in relation to the grace of God and is itself inspired by the Spirit, the cycle of gift and return has a divine rather than human etiology.

---

251. Muller rightly notes in response to Evans that ontological communion is not the only alternative to an extrinsic relationship. See Muller, *Calvin and the Reformed Tradition*, 216.

252. *CO* 2.243.

253. Muller, *Calvin and the Reformed Tradition*, 216–17.

Secondly, Calvin utilized and transformed a patristic and scholastic theme to develop a soteriology with a strong pneumatological emphasis. The Spirit, not a creational ontology that emphasizes innately created capacities in the human being, acts as the connection and bridge between God and human beings. This pneumatological emphasis allowed Calvin to differentiate between Creator and creature, whilst also relating them. Moreover, Calvin's emphasis on the Spirit as enabling our ascension provided his theology with a dynamic quality that medieval theology lacked.

Thirdly, Calvin's use of the theme of descent and ascent allowed him to weave together the juridical and mystical categories of our union with Christ. In Calvin we do not find juridical and participationist models that compete with each other, but he succeeded in integrating the two aspects of Christian soteriology without absorbing the one category into the other. Through Christ's descent we are forensically acquitted and justified, while through the descent of the Spirit to earth and our spiritual ascent to heaven mediated by the regenerative work of the Spirit, we are mystically united with Christ. The process of acquittal and mystical union is part of the same cycle and this cycle cannot come to fruition without the one or the other. Yet, there is a logical difference between the two.

Fourthly, Calvin used the schema of descent and ascent to denote the relationship between God and the believer as a personal relationship grounded in a covenantal union based on love. Calvin avoided theological abstraction by locating the believer's union with Christ in the concrete historical particularity and the story of the person of Jesus Christ and the work of the Spirit that communicates the effects of the historical Jesus's atoning work to us. Hereby Calvin provided an alternative to ontological participation theories that regarded God's work in the human being as indirect and intermediate in nature. Instead, he emphasized Christ's personal activity in the mystical union between God and believers that allows for an I-Thou relationship that neither consists of a fusion of divine and human essences, nor a mere moral relationship, but of an authentic communion that actualizes the human being without erasing our creaturely status. Calvin's emphasis on the I-Thou personal relationship between God and human, however, must not be misconstrued as a justification for individualism. His understanding of participation, as reflected by his doctrine on the Supper, contained a strong communal motive. The people of God are the body of Christ and ascend as one body to God through the Spirit.

Fifthly, the descent-ascent construction enabled Calvin to develop a concrete ethic for Christian life modeled on the example of Jesus Christ. The Spirit of God descends to us to reinvigorate us with the power and grace of Christ and to keep our union with Christ alive. In doing so, he raises us up to Christ to follow the example of Christ who is the true image of God. As the believer grows in his spiritual union with Christ through the continuous process of self-mortification and vivification enabled by the Spirit, his moral ability to replicate the impeccable nature of Christ increases.[254] By developing a doctrine of union with Christ that is based on Christ as model and that asserts the indwelling of the Spirit into us, which reinvigorates us, Calvin developed a dynamic ethical model that asks for the continuous renovation, sanctification and reformation of Christian life and society. The dynamism of Calvin's ethical construction, however, did not function at the expense of human security, because the Spirit ensures that our union with Christ is inseverable.[255] Calvin also did not fall into the trap of utopianism, but he exhibited a remarkable realism as far as the Christian vocation and the sanctification of human life is concerned. He warned against a misdirected obsession with the earthly that can only result in idolatry and urged Christians to perform their duty, while realizing that sanctification can never be fully realized during our existence on earth.

Sixth, through the cycle of descent and ascent, Calvin supplied us with a valuable model to construe the relation between transcendent and immanent reality. As noted earlier, Calvin understood salvation in a comprehensive cosmological sense. The divinely activated cycle of descent and ascent indicates that immanent reality cannot sustain itself without participating in transcendent reality. Without the descent of Christ and the Spirit, immanent reality cannot maintain itself, but is destined to descend into the abyss of sin and chaos. However, in Christ and through the mediation of the Spirit, immanent reality is able to "raise" itself to God. This "rise" to transcendent reality allows immanent reality to endure, subsist and persist. However, the participation of immanent reality in transcendent reality does not consist in an ontological union or a fusion of the substance of the two realities, but is actualized through the Spirit of God that sustains and preserves creation. This allowed Calvin to develop a participation model that related immanent and transcendent reality to each other, while at the same time preserving the integrity of both by not positioning the immanent and transcendent on the same ontological levels. Participation in God does not dissolve human creatureliness nor compromise the "otherness" of God.

Lastly, Calvin's descent-ascent construction provided a strong eschatological orientation to his soteriology in the sense that the believer who is bound up in the ascended and exalted Christ is in a continuous process of being "raised up." Calvin consistently linked union with God to both our

---

254. See Fisk, "Calvin's Metaphysics," 319.
255. Fisk, "Calvin's Metaphysics," 323.

past createdness in the image of God and to the future resurrection and consummation of the believer.[256] Christ liberates us from a perverse love of this world and turns our eyes to the "power of the resurrection" so that we will long for the life to come.[257] This expectation nourishes the believer in his existence and enables him to carry his cross with joy.

Conclusion

Calvin's doctrine on the believer's union with Christ is characterized by a united but not mingled ontological approach and the scheme of descent-ascent as constructive and integrative tool. He used the united but not mingled logic to explain, in the best possible terms, the ontological principle that the divine and human realms are united, but distinct. He applied this logic through the use of various formulae in strategically important passages of his works to explain the relationship between the two natures of Christ and the twofold grace of God. Calvin furthermore used the theme of a divinely activated cycle of ascent and descent to integrate the various themes of his soteriology. Calvin employed it in order to weave together the juridical and mystical categories in his soteriology without postulating an ontological unity between God and human. This descent-ascent schema furthermore strengthened the theocentric and pneumatological character, eschatological outlook and personal dynamism of his anthropology and assisted him in devising a concrete ethical framework located in the life of the historical Christ and the work of the Spirit. Most importantly, the descent-ascent construction enabled Calvin to relate the immanent and transcendent realities to each other in a manner that avoided the abstraction of realism.

---

256. Horton, "Union and Communion," 403.

257. Calvin, *Institutes*, 3.9.6; *CO* 2.528: "si oculi in resurrectionis potentiam convertuntur."

4

The Boundaries of Human Knowledge[1]

Introduction

CALVIN FRAMED HIS THEOLOGY against the background of sixteenth-century scholasticism that exhibited optimism in the ability of the human to know things as they really are. Roman Catholic theology subscribed to the Aristotelian/Scholastic notion that the order of things are intelligible because meaning is embedded in the structure of things through the existence of ideal patterns or forms that serve as archetypes for individual phenomena. Thomas Aquinas's teleological ethics, in particular, dominated Catholic thinking in the Late Medieval Ages. He utilized Aristotle's notion of potency and act to argue that all human beings possess an innate capacity to understand their *telos*. Central to Aquinas's thought was the idea that human beings are moved by habits that are in essence dispositions towards good and evil.[2] Bad habits lead humans astray from God, whereas good habits enhance human actions by directing human passions within a specific context towards a good end.[3] By nurturing good habits and disciplining passions, the human can be assisted in comprehending his *telos*. However, the various habits need to be informed by the spiritual dispositions of faith (habit of intellect) and *caritas* (habit of will) that gives all "virtuous behaviour its life and existence" by directing human beings towards a love for God and each other.[4]

According to Aquinas, natural habits infused by *caritas* make a social ethics possible because *caritas* integrates all the various habits and directs

---

1. This chapter is a modified and extended version of a published article by Nico Vorster entitled "Calvin on Human Reason" in *In Luce Verbi* 48.1 (2014) 1–9. AOSIS Publishers allows for the re-use of journal material published by them under a CC-BY license. See https://creativecommons.org/licenses/by/4.0/.

2. Aquinas, *Summa Theologiae*, Ia-IIae.49.4.

3. Aquinas, *Questions on the Virtues*, 14.

4. Aquinas, *Questions on the Virtues*, 249; Aquinas, *Summa Theologia*, IIa-IIae.23.8.

them towards the ultimate goal of serving God and our fellow human beings.[5] When our natural habits are utilized to acquire virtue and the goals of society are made compatible with the ultimate goal of *caritas*, true tranquillity and peace becomes possible.[6] Though Aquinas did not deny the importance of grace for attaining true knowledge, he regarded reality as fundamentally intelligible and accessible to human reason. His premise was that sin affects the human's desires, but does not have a decisive influence on reason. This limited approach to sin allowed him to construct a teleological ethics that was informed by a positive affirmation of reason. Aquinas's rationalism found in the sixteenth century an extreme expression in the Sorbonne, who held that sin did not affect the mind, only the lower faculties that are related to human desires.

Various developments in the sixteenth century would, however, inaugurate an intellectual revolution that threatened the stable worldview of scholasticism. The natural scientific discoveries of Galileo, Copernicus, and Kepler challenged Aristotelian physics profoundly and caused the downfall of the Ptolemaic worldview. The fear of disturbing the universal patterns inherent in "being" resided, while the scope of natural philosophy was no longer restricted to the discovery of the patterns and forms underlying the essence of things. Instead, instrumental forms of rationality that left thinkers prepared to experiment with and reconstruct reality, replaced scholasticism's contemplative kind of natural philosophy. The Renaissance humanists attempted to reconstruct society by cultivating a sense of virtuosity, self-control, and sound etiquette in society. The realist worldview of scholasticism was seen as too sterile for such a reconstruction of society. The Renaissance movement rejected scholasticisms' dependence on logic and the organization of truths in rationally intelligible systems, instead turning to rhetoric and practical knowledge.[7] In their search for practical wisdom, they rediscovered the importance of classical sources and the philological study of classical languages. The Scholastic attempt to preserve the ideal of a static order that is intelligible was eroding and was in danger of being replaced by the ideal of a dynamic order that can be reconstructed through instrumental rationality.[8]

---

5. Aquinas, *Summa Theologia*, IIa-IIae.23.7.

6. Cf. Aquinas, *Questions on the Virtues*, 266; Aquinas, *Summa Theologia*, IIa-IIae.23.8.

7. Bouwsma, *John Calvin*, 114.

8. Vorster, "Die Westerse Mens en Betekenisverlies," 35.

Calvin's epistemological reflections were inextricably linked to these developments. He took note of developments within the natural sciences[9] and utilized the hermeneutical and philological methods of the Renaissance to understand Scripture. True to the scholarly tenets of Renaissance humanism, he rejected pure objectivism by relating knowledge to an understanding of the predicament of the self. He also abandoned the speculative and theoretical approach of scholasticism in favour of an instrumental and empirical approach to knowledge that engaged with Scripture as God's revealed Word and creation as a theatre of God's works.[10] Perhaps the most pervasive humanist element in his thinking was the profound practical nature of his theology. The fundamental interest of Calvin's theology was not to contemplate God's being intellectually, but to understand the communion between God and human beings in Christ and the practical implications of this for all spheres of life.

This chapter commences by discussing Calvin's understanding of reason as endowment, while the next section studies his stance on the effects of sin on reason. The third part probes his view on the relation between grace and reason; whereafter the relevance of Calvin's epistemology for modern theology is examined.

Human Knowledge as Endowment of God

Calvin used various terms when addressing the theme of faith and reason. The term he employed most frequently was *sapientia* (wisdom), but he also made use of the terms *ratio* (reason), *cognitio* (knowledge), *fides* (faith) and *entendement* (understanding).[11] Though he utilized these terms mostly as synonyms, his frequent use of *sapientia*, most notably in the first sentence of his 1539 and 1559 *Institutes*, is noteworthy. Engel[12] rightly states that Calvin utilized *sapientia* as a "comprehensive term for his religious epistemology." Through *sapientia* he expressed his belief that faith and knowledge are inextricably linked to each other. Muller also draws attention to Calvin's integrated approach to knowledge which he ascribes to Calvin's encounter with Romans. Calvin regarded both the intellect and will as rational and as together with the heart as the seat of our emotions involved in all our

---

9. See in this regard his commentary on Genesis, where he explicitly refers to developments within astrology (Calvin, *Commentaries on Genesis*, 1:86; *CO* 23.45).
10. See Edgar, "Calvin and the Natural Order," 3.
11. Engel, *John Calvin's Perspectival Anthropology*, 73.
12. Engel, *John Calvin's Perspectival Anthropology*, 73.

cognitive acts.[13] Including all these faculties in cognition, enabled Calvin to relate faith and its positive impacts on the human person to both "intellective knowledge" and "affective knowledge."[14] Muller proceeds to state:

> Unlike Aquinas Calvin does not lodge faith in the intellect and place only the capability of choice in the will. Faith, for Calvin, is a matter of intellect and will in conjunction.[15]

Calvin's doctrine of knowledge[16] was characterized by a twofold movement that is simultaneous and complimentary in nature. When we contemplate "the face of God" by raising our thoughts to God and perceiving his glory, we cannot avoid becoming displeased with ourselves.[17] Similarly, when we descend into ourselves and observe our own misery and depravity we cannot help but to realize that we are unable to live detached from God. Looking into the outer mirror of God's greatness and the inner mirror of our own misery have the same effect: We become displeased with ourselves and long for communion with God.

Calvin held that we are capable of contemplating God, because we are created with the ability to observe God's works that are revealed in creation and scripture. Knowledge of God first of all shines forth in his fashioning of the universe. Calvin often depicted the created order as a theatre of God's glorious works.[18] The created order reminds us that we

---

13. Muller, *Unaccommodated Calvin*, 165.
14. Muller, *Unaccommodated Calvin*, 169-70.
15. Muller, *Unaccommodated Calvin*, 171.
16. van den Brink and van der Kooi argue that Calvin's doctrine on the origin of true knowledge exhibited some influence of the humanist climate of the Renaissance. Though Calvin maintained that true knowledge is not attainable without knowledge of God, he did not want to speculate on which type of knowledge come first: knowledge of ourselves or of God. According to them, Calvin's approach signified a shift from a premise that examined the human being purely from the perspective of God to a method that considers knowledge from a subjective anthropological angle as well. This assessment might be worth pursuing, but the gist of Calvin's central argument, in my view, was still profoundly theocentric and far removed from the optimistic anthropologies of the Enlightenment. See van den Brink and van der Kooi, *Christelijke Dogmatiek*, 234.
17. Calvin, *Institutes*, 1.1.2; CO 2.32: "Rursum, hominem in puram sui notitiam nunquam pervenire constat, nisi prius Dei faciem sit contemplatus, atque ex illius intuitu ad se ipsum inspiciendum descendat." Also see Calvin, *Institutes*, 1.15.2; CO 2.135.
18. Cf. SC 11/1.15. See Calvin, *Institutes*, 1.14.8; CO 2.123: "Sed quia maior pars erroribus suis imbuta, in tam illustri theatro caecutit, exclamat rarae et singularis esse sapientiae, prudenter expendere haec Dei opera, quorum aspectu nihil proficiunt qui alioqui videntur esse acutissimi."

are the "workmanship" of God and that God is the "origin and fountain of all goodness."[19] Calvin also used the metaphor of creation as a "mirror" in which we may behold God, who is otherwise invisible.[20] We cannot open our eyes without being compelled to behold God.[21] The heavens and earth presents us with "innumerable proofs" of God's majesty that force themselves even on the most illiterate.[22] In the works of God the "perfections of God are delineated as in a picture" and the whole of the human race is lured to attain knowledge of God.[23] Scripture provides an even more splendid revelation of God's works than the created universe, because it reveals God's redeeming action in Christ. We cannot know the "mystery" of Christ or enter into a relationship with God without the knowledge that the Gospel provides us.[24] The authority of Scripture rests upon God being its Author and the Holy Spirit being the *Guarantor* of its truth.[25] Calvin emphatically stressed that the authority of Scripture is not derived from human beings, but only from the Spirit.[26] Its authority cannot be proved through rational arguments, nor does it depend on the decisions of councils. Only faith can attest to the authority of Scripture.

> The testimony of the Spirit is superior to reason. For as God alone can properly bear witness to his own words, so these words will not obtain full credit in the hearts of men, until they are sealed by the inward testimony of the Spirit.[27]

19. Calvin, *Institutes*, 1.2.2; CO 2.35: "figmentum illius ... Rursum nec ad liquidum perspicere ipsum potes, nisi ut bonorum omnium fontem esse et originem agnoscas."

20. Calvin, *Institutes*, 1.5.1; CO 2.42: "Quare eleganter autor epistolae ad Hebraeos (11, 3) saecula nuncupat invisibilium rerum spectacula; quod nobis vice speculi sit tam concinna mundi positio, in quo invisibilem alioqui Deum contemplari liceat."

21. Calvin, *Institutes*, 1.5.1; CO 2.41.

22. Calvin, *Institutes*, 1.5.2; CO 2.42: "Mirificam eius sapientiam quae testentur, innumera sunt tum in coelo, tum in terris documenta: non illa modo reconditiora, quibus propius observandis astrologia, medicina, et tota physica scientia destinata est; sed quae rudissimi cuiusque idiotae aspectui se ingerunt, ut aperiri oculi nequeant quin eoru cogantur esse testes."

23. Calvin, *Institutes*, 1.5.2; CO 2.48: "Fatendum est igitur, in singulis Dei operibus, praesertim autem in ipsorum universitate, non secus atque in tabulis, depictas esse Dei virtutes; quibus in eius agnitionem, et ab ipsa in veram plenamque felicitatem invitatur atque illicitur universum hominum genus."

24. CO 2.310.

25. CO 2.310.

26. Calvin, *Institutes*, 1.6.4; CO 2.56.

27. Calvin, *Institutes*, 1.7.4; CO 2.59: "Atqui testimonium Spiritus omni ratione praestantius esse respondeo. Nam sicuti Deus solus de se idoneus est testis in suo sermone, ita etiam non ante fidem reperiet sermo in hominum cordibus quam inferiore spiritus testimonio obsignetur."

Whereas the universe forms the macrocosm of God's works, the human person constitutes a "microcosm" of God's works in the sense that he is the brightest mirror of God's glory.[28] Calvin describes the human being as "a rare specimen of divine power, wisdom and goodness."[29] The difference between the human and other creatures is that the human is created after the image of God and possesses the "light of understanding. Having "been endued with reason" humans rank higher than all other creatures in the creaturely realm because they are able to acknowledge God and stand in a relationship with him.[30] Hence, though Calvin reacted against Scholastic forms of extreme rationalism, he did not reject the importance of rational reflection. Calvin was no fideist or irrationalist, but he regarded reason and understanding as a special and defining endowment of God that separates the human being from the rest of creation and connects him to God. His recognition of the importance of reason and will is closely connected to the relational nature of his theology. Unlike the Schoolmen who portrayed the relationship between God and human beings as existing in a gradation of being, Calvin emphasized the direct personal relationship between God and the human being. The faculties of reason and play an important role in enabling our relationship with God.

As noted already, Calvin regarded the human soul as "immortal essence," which not only has the ability to transcend the body, but also has the innate capacity to conceive of God. He ascribed this ability of the soul to God engraving a sense of the divine in the human mind:

> That there exists in the human minds and indeed by natural instinct, some sense of deity, we hold to be beyond dispute, since God Himself, to prevent any man from pretending ignorance, has endued all men with some idea of his Godhead.[31]

The human being is thus more than a living body, he is a living soul that has a mind in order to meditate on the heavenly life in which he finds the true destiny of his being in the image of God.[32] By depositing the seed of religion

---

28. *CO* 2.43; Calvin, *Book of Psalms*, 1:93; *CO* 31.88.

29. Calvin, *Institutes*, 1.5.3; *CO* 2.43: "rarum sit potentiae, bonitatis et sapientiae Dei specimen."

30. Calvin, *Commentary on John*, 1:32; *CO* 47.4.

31. Calvin, *Institutes*, 1.3.1; *CO* 2.36: "Quemdam inesse humanae menti, et quidem nuturali instinctu, divinitatis sensum, extra controversiam ponimus; si quidem, ne quis ad ignorantiae praetextum confugeret, quamdam sui numinis intelligentiam universis Deus ipse indidit."

32. Torrance, *Calvin's Doctrine of Man*, 31.

on our minds God shows his felicity towards all people and provides us with the capacity to discern his creative wisdom.[33]

Human Knowledge and Sin

Calvin described self-knowledge as consisting of two parts, namely knowledge of the gifts with which the human being was originally endowed, and knowledge of the "miserable ruin into which the revolt of the first man has plunged us."[34] Whereas Augustine located the first sin in pride, Calvin ascribed it to the human's longing for illicit knowledge.[35] Sin is essentially a failure to know God and the self. True knowledge is not possible, because sin defects the very origin of true knowledge: our relation with God. Since the human is no longer capable of knowing God, he is not able to know himself either. The metaphor that Calvin repeatedly utilized is that of *blindness*. The mind's corruption exists in a fundamental religious blindness; the human being is plunged into darkness:

> Men are now widely distant from that perfectly holy nature with which they were originally endued; because their understanding, which ought to have shed light in every direction, has been plunged in darkness, and is wretchedly blinded.[36]

The effects of this blindness are radically incisive and wide-ranging. No person is able to penetrate into the "kingdom of God" through his own sagacity.[37] In his Commentary on 1 Corinthians 2:10 Calvin stated that God has "shut up all mankind in blindness" by taking "away from the human intellect the power of attaining a knowledge of God by its own resources."[38]

Knowledge of God is out of reach of all human beings, because the human mind "has become a kind of labyrinth."[39] No longer able to "ascend" to

---

33. Calvin, *Institutes*, 1.14.1; CO 2.41–42.

34. Calvin, *Institutes*, 1.1.1; CO 2.31: "Praesertim miserabilis haec ruina, in quam nos deiecit primi hominis defectio."

35. CO 23.60.

36. Calvin, *Commentary on John*, 33; CO 47.6: "Nam multum distare, nunc homines dicit ab integra illa natura, qua initio praediti fuerant: mentem enim eorum, quae lucida omni ex parte esse debebat, tenebris immersam misere caecutire."

37. Cf. Calvin, *Commentary on John*, 38; CO 47.9.

38. Calvin, *Corinthians*, 1:110; CO 49.340–341: "Postquam conclusit universos homines sub caecitate, et humanae menti hoc ademit ne possit ad Deum proprio marte conscendere."

39. Calvin, *Institutes*, 1.5.12; CO 2.49: "Suum enim cuique ingenium instar labyrinthi est."

God, the human being is engulfed in darkness. Though the manifestation of God's works are as bright as ever, the human "has no eyes to perceive it."[40] The range of this blindness becomes clear when we "test our reason by the divine Law, which is a perfect standard of righteousness."[41]

As noted earlier, Calvin ascribed the spread of this blindness from the first human beings to the rest of humanity to a "hereditary corruption."[42] Adam was not merely a "progenitor," but "a root" whose corruption penetrated the whole human race in the same way that corrupt branches proceed from a corrupt root.[43] Sin is, therefore, systemic in nature; when Adam sinned he "transmitted the contagion to all his posterity." Adam's posterity is punishable, not because Adam's sin pertains to them, but because they are infected by the same corruption.

The "blindness" under which human beings labour is according to Calvin almost invariably accompanied by vain, pride and stubbornness.[44] Since the human being is no longer able to "ascend" to God and observe his holiness and perfection, he is not able to understand his own deformity either and therefore becomes self-inflated. Cut off from its source of knowledge and deprived of the light of God, the human being becomes "carnally" minded.[45] Calvin states it thus:

> the mind is so entirely alienated from the righteousness of God that he cannot conceive, desire, or design anything but what is wicket, distorted, foul, impure and iniquitous; that his heart is so thoroughly envenomed by sin that it can breathe out nothing but corruption and rottenness; that if some men occasionally make a show of goodness, their mind is ever interwoven with hypocrisy and deceit, their souls inwardly bound with the fetters of wickedness.[46]

40. Calvin, *Institutes*, 1.5.14; *CO* 2.52: "sed ad illam perspiciendam non esse nobis oculos."

41. Calvin, *Institutes*, 2.2.24; *CO* 2.205: "Et si rationem nostram volumus ad Dei legem exigere, quae perfectae est iustitiae exemplar, comperiemus quam multis partibus caecutiat."

42. Calvin, *Institutes*, 2.1.5; *CO* 2.179.

43. Calvin *Institutes*, 2.1.6; *CO* 2.180: "Ita certe habendum est: fuisse Adamum humanae naturae non progenitorem modo, sed quasi radicem."

44. Calvin, *Institutes*, 1.4.1; *CO* 2.38: "ergo se corrupit Adam, ut ai eo transierit in totam sobolem contagio."

45. Calvin, *Institutes*, 2.3.1; *CO* 2.209.

46. Calvin, *Institutes*, 2.5.19; *CO* 2.247: "mentem hominis sic alienatam prorsus a Dei iustitia, ut nihil non impium, contortum, foedum, impurum, flagitiosum concipiat, concupiscat, moliatur; cor peccati veneno ita penitus delibutum, ut nihil quam corruptum foetorem efflare queat. Quod si quidpiam interdum boni in speciem ostentant,

Not only does the "blindness" that sin bring pervert the human mind, but it also leads to the creation and veneration of idols in the place of God.[47] Scarcely a person can be found who does not "fashion for himself an idol or spectre in place of God."[48] In fact, reason itself becomes an idol. No longer is the human being willing to consult God's will and to confine his reason to the boundaries of God's will, but reason itself is placed higher than God.[49] This sinful inclination to devise shapes of deity "is diametrically opposed to the divine nature" and corrupts and adulterates true religion.[50] For Calvin, the human's pride and self-adoration is the exact opposite of the image of God that is directed at reflecting God's virtues and heightening God's glory. Instead the human person steals "divine glory for himself."[51]

As discussed in chapter 2, Calvin modified his initial position that the fall destroyed the *imago Dei* to one that posits the total depravity of the image. Total depravity denotes that there is no part in the human being that is not vitiated by sin and that is blameless. Even the best works of the human person are corrupted by sin. Yet, this does not mean that the human person bears no capacity for the good.[52]

As noted earlier, Calvin distinguished between the supernatural and natural gifts of the human being. The supernatural gifts such as faith, charity, holiness and uprightness that enable the human to attain the heavenly life were totally destroyed by the fall, so that no human being can ascent to God. Yet some vestiges of the natural gifts remain that enable the human person to have a sense of right and wrong.[53] These natural remnants of the *imago Dei* are not sufficient to attain salvation and amount to nothing with regard to our relationship with God, but they do make it possible for human beings to act morally:

> In this corrupted and degenerate nature light has been turned into darkness. And yet he (John) affirms that the light of understanding is not wholly extinguished; for amidst the darkness of

mentem tamen semper hypocrisi et fallaci obliquitate involutam, animum interiori perversitate illigatum manere."

47. CO 2.50.

48. Calvin, *Institutes*, 1.5.12; CO 2.49: "vix unus unquam repertus est qui non sibi idolum vel spectrum Dei loco fabricaret."

49. Cf. CO 2.117.

50. Calvin *Institutes*, 2.8.17; CO 2.279: "Ac iam . . . satis aperte docuimus, quascunque excogitat homo visibiles Dei formas, pugnare ex diametro cum eius natura, ideoque, simulac in medium prodeunt idola, corrumpi veram réligionem et adulterari."

51. Waugh, "Calvin's Understanding of Human Reason," 14.

52. Bouwsma, *Sixteenth Century Portrait*, 139.

53. Calvin, *Institutes*, 2.2.11; CO 2.195.

the human mind, some remaining sparks of the brightness still shines ... natural reason will never direct men to Christ; and as their being endued with prudence for regulating their lives, or born to cultivate the liberal arts and sciences, all this passes away without yielding any advantage.[54]

The survival of the remnants are not attributable to any indestructible characteristic of the human being, but is solely the result of God's common grace[55] that preserves humanity from descending into chaos.[56] In *Bondage and Liberation of the Will*, Calvin stated the difference between God's common grace and special grace as follows:

> We exist and move in one sense as human beings and in another as the sons of God. The former grace is the possession of everyone, but the latter is granted specially to the elect. The former is in a certain way implanted in our nature, but the latter is given to man as a supernatural gift.[57]

Common grace entails that though the Spirit does not work faith in the reprobate, he is still present in their lives since all things are filled and moved by the Spirit. Behind every distinguished act there is the inspiration of the Spirit.[58]

Calvin regarded the divinely preserved faculties of reason and will, albeit only in part, as the two most important remnants of the *imago Dei*. If God had not preserved reason and will, human nature itself would have been destroyed.[59]

The question is: In what sense are reason and the will corrupted by sin? Calvin addressed the issue by distinguishing between heavenly and earthly

---

54. Calvin, *Commentary on John*, 33–34; *CO* 47.6–7: "quia in hac vitiata et degenere natura lux in tenebras versa fuerit. Interea tamen negat prorsus exstinctam esse intelligentiae lucem: quia in obscura humanae mentis caligine adhuc quaedam fulgoris scintillae emicant ... In summa, nunquam naturalis ratio homines ad Christum diriget. Iam quod prudentia ad regendam vitam instructi sunt, quod ad praeclaras artes ac disciplinas nati, id quoque totum sine fructu evanescit."

55. Calvin never uses the words "common grace," but the idea is prevalent in his works.

56. Cf. Calvin, *Institutes*, 2.2.14; *CO* 2.198.

57. Calvin, *Bondage and Liberation*, 167; *CO* 6.347: "Atqui alio modo sumus et movemur, ut homines: alio, ut filii Dei. Communis omnium est ilia gratia, haec electis peculiariter confertur, ilia naturae quodammodo insita est, haec praeter naturam homini datur."

58. *CO* 2.199–200.

59. Calvin, *Institutes*, 2.2.17; *CO* 2.199: "nisi nobis pepercisset, totius naturae interitum secum traxisset defectio."

knowledge. Heavenly knowledge pertains to "true knowledge of God, the method of righteousness and the mysteries of the kingdom."[60] Natural knowledge consists in the human person possessing some "seed of religion" and being able to distinguish between good and evil.[61] It entails a kind of universal reason naturally implanted in human beings that relate to matters of policy, economy, mechanical arts and liberal studies.[62] As far as heavenly things are concerned, the human being is totally blind;[63] he cannot ascent to God without the guidance of the Spirit.[64] Yet, in earthly matters the minds of all people "have impressions of civil order and honesty." All societies need to be governed by rules and all human beings are able to comprehend these rules.[65] Calvin[66] not only stated that "in regard to the constitution of the present life no man is devoid of reason," but he also displayed a positive attitude towards the achievements of human culture and regarded it as emanating from the Holy Spirit that bestows his gifts on humanity despite sin:

> The human mind, however much fallen and perverted from its original integrity, is still adorned and invested with admirable gifts from its Creator. If we reflect that the Spirit of God is the only fountain of truth, we will be careful, as we would avoid offering insult to him, not to reject or condemn truth wherever it appears.[67]

60. Calvin, *Institutes*, 2.2.13; CO 2.197: "Res coelestes [voco], puram Dei notitiam, verae iustitiae rationem, ac regni coelestis mysteria."

61. Calvin, *Commentary on John*, 34; CO 47.7.

62. Calvin, *Institutes*, 2.2.13; CO 2.197: "In priore genere sunt politia, oeconomia, artes omnes mechanicae, disciplinaeque liberales . . . quia insita sunt universis, absque magistro legislatore, ipsarum semina."

63. Human beings have the seed of religion implanted in them, but this is not sufficient to enter in communion with the true God. See CO 31.91.

64. Calvin disassociated himself from the teachings of Rome that held that the human being was only corrupted with regard to his sensual desires, while the faculties of reason remained undamaged. Instead he maintained that the mind itself must be renewed because there is no part in the human being that is not perverted or corrupted. Cf. Torrance, *Calvin's Doctrine of Man*, 90; Calvin, *Institutes*, 2.2.3; CO 2.209–210.

65. Calvin, *Institutes*, 2.2.13; CO 2.197: "civilis cuiusdam et honestatis."

66. Calvin, *Institutes*, 2.2.13; CO 2.197: "Atque hoc amplum argumentum est, in huius vitae constitutione nullum destitui luce rationis hominem."

67. Calvin, *Institutes*, 2.2.15; CO 2.198: "Quoties ergo in profanos scriptores incidimus, ilia quae admirabilis in iis affulget veritatis luce admoneamur, mentem hominis, quantumlibet ab integritate sua collapsam et perversam, eximiis tamen etiamnum Dei donis vestitam esse et exornatam. Si unicum veritatis fontem Dei spiritum esse reputamus, veritatem ipsam neque respuemus, neque contemnemus, ubicunque apparebit, nisi velimus in spiritum Dei contumeliosi esse; non enim dona spiritus, sine ipsius contemptu et opprobrio, vilipenduntur."

Calvin proceeded to deduce from our possession of natural knowledge the existence of a natural law that functions within the ambit of God's common grace. Even gentiles have a sense of righteousness because God has engraved his natural law on our minds. Natural law is naturally engraved in all people, works through the human conscience, is discernible by all people and provides a right course for conduct.[68] In contrast to some natural philosophers of his time, Calvin did not regard the natural law as a perpetual law that functions on its own; rather it is sustained by God himself who reigns providentially over all things.[69] Natural knowledge is thus not a feature of nature, but a special gift of God.[70] In fact, God governs the wills of men and the course of history exactly according to the course he has destined.[71]

The above discussion indicates that Calvin regarded a shared social ethos as possible, not because rules are imposed unilaterally by divinely appointed governments on people, but because human beings are innately "social animals" with a sense of justice.[72] This natural sense of justice is not isolated to an ability to adhere to rules, but all human beings are capable of virtuous behaviour by following the course of natural law:

> If the gentiles have the righteousness of the law naturally engraved on their minds, we certainly cannot say that they are altogether blind as to the rule of life. Nothing, indeed, is more common, than for man to be sufficiently instructed in a right course of conduct by natural law.[73]

Calvin pointed to the fact that there have been through the ages many persons who guided by nature strived towards virtue. Through their zeal and honesty they provided proof that there was some purity in their lives.[74] This is due to the work of the Holy Spirit who is present in the lives of all people, even the reprobate. His presence in the lives of unbelievers consists of him bestowing virtues as gifts.[75] To say that a person is depraved does not mean

---

68. *CO* 2.203.

69. *CO* 2.203.

70. *CO* 2.203.

71. *CO* 2.203.

72. Calvin, *Institutes*, 2.2.12; *CO* 2.197: "homo animale est natura sociale."

73. Calvin, *Institutes*, 2.2.22; *CO* 2.203: "Si gentes naturaliter legis iustitiam habent mentibus suis insculptam, certe non dicemus eas in vitae ratione prorsus caecutire. Et nihil est vulgatius, quam lege naturali . . . hominem sufficienter ad rectam vitae normam institui."

74. *CO* 1.292–94.

75. *CO* 1.292–94.

that such a person is morally considered bad[76] or incapable of virtue.[77] In fact, Calvin expressed appreciation for profane authors that produce works of "admirable light of truth," and men with "excellent "gifts that use them to the "common benefit of all mankind."[78] Calvin also regarded the arts and sciences not only as legitimate, but as essential aids for the common life.

> But if the Lord has been pleased to assist us by the work and ministry of the ungodly in physics, dialectics, mathematics and other similar sciences, let us avail ourselves of it, lest by neglecting the gifts of God spontaneously offered to us, we be justly punished for our sloth.[79]

Yet, while Calvin showed admiration for the natural gifts of the human person, maintained that the human person's natural knowledge was not destroyed by sin, and believed that God's common grace makes a social ethics possible, he nevertheless consistently reminded his readers of the corruption of our natural knowledge and the boundaries of natural reason. The "common light of reason" that God implanted in human persons is far inferior to faith and cannot penetrate into the kingdom of God.[80] The human person is thus not able to worship God truthfully through the means of natural law.[81] Every attempt to understand God through natural reason

---

76. It is important to note that Calvin did not equate virtuous moral acts and good works with each other. Calvin defined good works in a very narrow sense. Good works aim at glorifying God. Beneficial acts for humanitarian ends might be commendable and regarded as virtuous, but if they are driven by wrong inner intentions they are not blameless. Only deeds that emanate from a gratitude for God's grace can be regarded as "good" in the soteriological sense of the word. Human virtue thus, though possible to exercise through the light of natural reason, amounts to little if not directed at serving God. See Calvin, *Institutes*, 3.14.2; CO 2.565. Also see CO 2.193.

77. Gerrish, "Mirror of God's Goodness," 220.

78. Calvin, *Institutes*, 2.2.15; CO 2.198–99: "Quoties ergo in profanos scriptores incidimus, ilia quae admirabilis in iis affulget veritatis luce admoneamur . . . eximiis tamen etiamnum Dei donis vestitam esse et exornatam . . . Neque tamen interim obliviscamur haec praestantissima divini spiritus esse bona, quae in publicum generis humani bonum, quibus yult, dispensat."

79. Calvin, *Institutes*, 2.2.16; CO 2.199: "Quod si nos Dominus impiorum opera et ministerio, in physicis, dialecticis, mathematicis et reliquis id genus voluit adiutos, ea utamur; ne si Dei dona ultro in ipsis oblata negligamus, demus iustas ignaviae nostrae poenas."

80. Calvin, *Commentary on John*, 38; CO 47.9.

81. Calvin, *Institutes*, 2.8.1; CO 2.267.

leads to perversion and alienates the human person only more from God.[82] Calvin stated it as follows:[83]

> Natural reason never will direct men to Christ; and as to their being endued with prudence for regulating their lives, or born to cultivate the liberal arts and sciences, all this passes away without yielding any advantage.

From the perspective of God all earthly knowledge detached from heavenly knowledge is vain and fleeting. Engel[84] rightly notes that Calvin considered earthly knowledge as having a "relative though positive value." It contributes to our understanding of earthly reality, but it is of no use for understanding eternal reality. To understand the eternal things we need grace.

Grace and Knowledge

In Calvin's thought knowledge of God can only be acquired through an act of God's grace that goes "beyond the natural capacity of the human mind."[85] Humans cannot ascend to God through natural reason, because natural knowledge tends to descend into superstition. In order for us to ascend to God, God first needs to descend to us. Only the affective pull of God can draw us into communion with God. This descent takes place through Christ that becomes flesh and dies for our sins on the cross, God accommodating himself to our capacity in his Word, and the Spirit that dwells in us.

To acquire heavenly knowledge we first of all need to be illuminated by the Spirit of God.[86] The Spirit opens our eyes for our sins, state of disgrace and spiritual nakedness before God through the mirror of the Word. The Word is the instrument whereby the Spirit calls us, works faith in us and sanctifies us. Calvin therefore called the Word our "eyeglasses" that "dissipates the darkness and shows us the true God clearly."[87] Through these metaphors he conveyed that we can only know God through his revelation. No knowledge of God is possible "apart from the gracious will of God to

---

82. Cf. Torrance, *Calvin's Doctrine of Man*, 150.

83. Calvin, *Commentary on John*, 34; CO 47.5: Postquam ergo generalem gratiae Christi considerationem evangelista proposuit, ut homines propius ad eam reputandam adducat, ostendit quid ipsis peculiariter datum fuerit."

84. Engel, *Calvin's Perspectival Anthropology*, 91.

85. Torrance, *Calvin's Doctrine of Man*, 129.

86. Torrance, *Calvin's Doctrine of Man*, 129.

87. SC 11/1.2; Calvin, *Institutes*, 1.6.1; CO 2.53: "specillis autem interpositis adiuti distincte legere incipient: ita scriptura confusam alioqui Dei notitiam in mentibus nostris colligens, discussa caligine liquido nobis verum Deum ostendit."

reveal himself to us."[88] God reveals himself to us through comparisons that we know, in order to accommodate our limited capacity.[89] This means that our knowledge of God is essentially analogical, not in the sense of *analogia entis*, but in the form of an "*analogia fidei* which is subject to God's word."[90] Nothing in human nature itself, such as an analogy of being or a remnant of the image, can prepare us for grace.[91] Only through the Spirit and Word are our minds raised up to know God:

> It is only when the human intellect is irradiated by the light of the Holy Spirit that it begins to have a taste of those things which pertain to the kingdom of God.[92]

The illumination of the Spirit is not merely a rekindling of the mind, but especially of the heart, which is the seat of our affections.[93] Knowledge is, after all, for Calvin about attaining a wisdom that is practical and relational in nature, not theoretical and speculative. The result of the Spirit's illumination is that we progress in the knowledge of ourselves and that we long for God's mercy.[94] In doing so the Spirit directs us to Christ, because God can only be known in Christ who is the brightest image of God. No knowledge of God is effectual without knowledge of the atoning work of Jesus Christ who restored through his death and resurrection the perverted created order.[95]

The Spirit connects us to our Saviour by working in us a faith in Christ that is a "firm and sure knowledge" of God's favour towards us.[96] Faith is a gift of God since God invites and rouses the elect by "forming, bending and directing our hearts to believe."[97] It is not a "bare or cold knowledge," that asks for "proofs or probabilities on which to rest our judgment," but

---

88. Torrance, *Calvin's Doctrine of Man*, 178.

89. *CO* 50.47.

90. Torrance, *Calvin's Doctrine of Man*, 128, 149.

91. Torrance, *Calvin's Doctrine of Man*, 134.

92. Calvin, *Institutes*, 3.2.34; *CO* 2.427: "Atque ita quidem spiritus sancti lumine irradiatus hominis intellectus tum vere demum ea quae ad regnum Dei pertinent gustare incipit, antea prorsus ad ea delibanda fatuus et insipidus."

93. Calvin, *Institutes*, 3.2.8; *CO* 2.404.

94. Calvin, *Institutes*, 2.2.11; *CO* 2.194–95.

95. Calvin, *Institutes*, 2.6.1; *CO* 2.247–48; Torrance, *Calvin's Doctrine of Man*, 169.

96. Calvin, *Institutes*, 3.2.7; *CO* 2.403: "Nunc iusta fidei definitio nobis constabit, si dicamus esse divinae erga nos benevolentiae firmam certamque cognitionem."

97. Calvin, *Bondage and Liberation*, 204; *CO* 6.374: "corda nostra formando, flectendo, dirigendo in iustitiam."

it subjects the intellect to God's transcendent revelation.[98] Faith is about "certainty" rather than "discernment."[99] Calvin therefore stated:

> The first step in true knowledge is taken, when we reverently embrace the testimony which God has been pleased therein to give of himself.[100]

Since faith is part of our regeneration, it gives us entrance into the kingdom of God and puts us into possession of God's blessings as adopted children of God.[101]

Flowing from our justification, Christ sanctifies us through his Spirit.[102] The noetic element in Calvin's understanding of sanctification is quite noticeable. No person will ever know Christ "aright without at the same time receiving the sanctification of the Spirit."[103] Sanctification entails that our knowledge is renewed by the Holy Spirit, not merely in the sense that the mind is enlightened, but the whole of the human person is transformed so that the believer is able to shine forth the glory of God.[104] Sanctified reason is characterized by a denial of the self and submission to the Spirit that illuminates us through his Word.[105] The contradictions between depraved reason and sanctified reason in Calvin's thought is clear: Whereas depraved reason posits its own autonomy, sanctified reason decenteres the human being and submits the human person to the Word of God; while depraved reason is characterized by self-affirmation, sanctified reason is characterized by self-emptying; where depraved reason is prone to superstition, sanctified reason is able to acquire true knowledge of the heavenly things; while depraved reason seeks after the glorification of the self, sanctified reason seeks the glory of God.

---

98. Calvin, *Institutes*, 1.7.5; *CO* 2.60; Calvin, *Commentary on John*, 44; *CO* 47.13: "Non argumenta, non verisimilitudines quaerimus quibus iudicium nostrum incumbat."

99. Calvin, *Institutes*, 3.2.14; *CO* 2.410: "Unde statuimus fidei notitiam certitudine magis quam apprehensione contineri."

100. Calvin, *Institutes*, 1.6.2; *CO* 2.54: "Unde etiam emergit verae intelligentiae principium, ubi reverenter amplectimur quod de se illic testari Deus voluit."

101. Calvin, *Commentary on John*, 44; *CO* 47.13.

102. Calvin, *Institutes*, 3.2.9; *CO* 2.403–404; Calvin, *Commentary on John*, 44; *CO* 47.13.

103. Calvin, *Institutes*, *CO* 2.404: "eum haud dubie rite cognoscere nunquam poterit quin sanctificationem spiritus simul apprehendat."

104. Calvin, *Philippians, Colossians and Thessalonians*, 211–12; *CO* 52.121–22.

105. Waugh, "Calvin's Understanding of Human Reason," 13.

Canlis[106] rightly notes that Calvin regarded sanctification as an "entire reorientation from the autonomous self to the self-in relationship." The fundamental premise of Calvin's soteriology is that the human cannot exist on his own, but finds his destiny by being engrafted in Christ. When we live in Christ his "wisdom" and "will" rule all our actions.[107] True knowledge is only possible through Christ who is the light of all truth. Calvin therefore admonished natural philosophers that reason needs to give way and submit to the Holy Spirit so that the man himself no longer lives, but Christ lives and reigns in him.[108] As long as humanity maintains the autonomy of reason it is on a self-destructive course of alienation from God, because the true identity of the human person does not lie within herself, but in her bond with Christ through the Spirit.

The sanctification of reason, though, is in Calvin's thought an ongoing process because as long as we are in the "prison of our body" we constantly struggle against our fleshly desires and natural inclinations that also affect reason.[109] The Spirit's work in us is not coercive,[110] nor instantaneous in nature, but he gradually transforms us by increasing our faith and knowledge of God.[111] Once reason finds its orientation in faith it "knows that the knowledge of God exceeds the natural capacity of man." Faithfull reason strives to grow in the knowledge of God, the knowledge of his favour towards us and how to regulate our conduct in accordance with God's will.[112] Yet our knowledge of God will always be "obscure and slender" in the present. Sanctification does not mean that the human can attain perfect heavenly knowledge.

---

106. Canlis, *Calvin's Ladder*, 247.

107. Calvin, *Institutes*, 3.7.1; *CO* 2.505.

108. Calvin, *Institutes*, 3.7.1; *CO* 2.506: "ut homo iam non ipse vivat, sed Christum in se ferat viventem ac regnantem (Gal. 2, 20)."

109. Calvin, *Institutes*, 3.3.20; *CO* 2.450: "Proinde, donec in carcere corporis nostri habitamus, assidue nobis cum naturae nostrae corruptae vitiis luctandum est, adeoque cum naturali nostra anima."

110. Calvin held that the human faculties act when acted upon by the Spirit. Thus, though the Spirit works faith in us, he does not bring it about through coercion. Faith is properly an act of ours because the Spirit does not circumvent the human faculties while working faith in us.

111. Cf. *CO* 2.426; *CO* 50.47.

112. Cf. Torrance, *Calvin's Doctrine of Man*, 146; *CO* 2.200.

Evaluation and Reflection

Calvin's scepticism of the powers of human reason is highly relevant for the practise of theology in a postmodern era. In contrast to the realist theologians of his time who regarded reality as intelligible and accessible to human beings and who viewed reason as innately able to comprehend the human telos through a process of habituation and self-disciplining, Calvin, related the attainability of knowledge to the predicament of the self.[113] True knowledge depends on a knowledge of God and the self and cannot be attained as long as human beings live in a state of sin detached from God.[114] He therefore did not regard reason as a trustworthy guide for morality, because detached from God reason is always in danger of idolising itself or creating all kinds of spectres in the place of God.[115] For Calvin sinful actions entail more than merely wilful intent, but they are underlined by a structural noetic incapacity and inability. This makes sin a power that cannot be conquered by human ingenuity.

Calvin's scepticism of reason is relevant in various ways. First he demythologized the notion of pure intellect. We need to acknowledge that there exists no such thing as a pure uncompromised rationality devoid of emotive influences, sinful desires, unaffected by interests or the prospect of choices that have to be made. The whole person is involved in cognitive acts and a whole range of very complex cross pressures ranging from worldviews, historical backgrounds, emotions, subconscious counter-reactions, anxieties and various interests are at play in human decision-making. Universalist discourses that present themselves as neutral, objective and universally applicable should be approached with great caution. Human knowledge systems always contain some fighting creed. Wisdom and integrity demands that we ought to be conscious of the creeds that orient our lives, apply self-critisism and be willing to state our vantage point and interests openly to bystanders.

A second important feature of Calvin's critique of human knowledge, is the propensity of human knowledge systems to create distorted idols. Detached from God, human reason is inclined to seek replacements for God, either by venerating the power of rationality itself or creating distorted ideologies that absolutize aspects of creation rather than the Creator. In history we have seen such distortions too often: the veneration of enlightened reason, science, the race, nation, people or ideal political and economic systems.

---

113. See Gregory, *Unintended Reformation*, 207.
114. *CO* 2.32.
115. *CO* 2.49.

Depraved reason indeed posits its own autonomy, centers human existence in the human being or in a collection of people, seeks self-affirmation and self-glory and is prone to superstition. The end result is distorted personal identities that lead to a self-centered rather than eccentric existence. Though Calvin did not regard natural knowledge as destroyed by sin, natural reason stays corrupted and limited to certain boundaries and destined to apply itself to wrong ends.[116] This reality necessitates a continuous deconstructive critique of human thinking, the power structures that underlie human reason, and the idols it creates. Theology can, and indeed, should endeavour to identify the idols that underlie much of human thinking. This includes a continuous self-critique in the spirit of *semper Reformanda*. Christians, themselves, ought to be conscious of their own capacity to create idolatrous systems in the name of God. Slavery, Colonial Imperialism, Nazi Theology and Apartheid are vivid reminders of the potential ways in which the Christian faith can be misused to justify oppression.

Thirdly, Calvin provided insight into the preliminary nature of human knowledge. Humans are inclined to "misunderstand." Not only do they sin voluntarily, but they often sin inevitably because of their epistemic shortcomings. Reason has limits; it can act as a guide, but only up to a point. The ecological disaster that humanity faces, for instance, is not merely the result of unlimited economic expansion and consumerism, but also emanates from a historical inability to understand the sensitive interrelated effects of ecosystems and the effects of emission gasses on the planet. Many conflicts on a micro, meso and macro level are caused by misconceptions and misunderstanding of situations, moral misjudgements and a lack of full understanding of complex situations. This underlines the fallen state of human nature even further. Reason and knowledge are gifts of God, but these faculties are also relative and preliminary in nature, prone to mistakes and misjudgements and therefore should not be absolutized.

Christian theologians and philosophers often err by attempting to develop highly idealistic all-encompassing Christian worldviews that provide intricate details on the composition of reality and the ideal structures that human societies should enact. Examples are the Kuyperian and Neo-Calvinist Christian paradigms that attempted to transform and Christianise culture by explicating the created norms applicable to every sphere of life; creationism that endeavors to provide a biblical based natural-scientific explanation of human origins; and the Corpus Christianum ideal that attempted to subject all spheres of society to the power of the Church. The weakness of these neat rational systems not only consist in them lacking

---

116. SC 11/1.326.

humility but also underestimating the complexity of life and the rapid changing nature of human situations. When preconceived rational systems are enforced on societies in order to "transform culture," unintended consequences might ensue. South Africa is a good example of a scenario where the enforcement of transformationist Christian ideals on society went horribly wrong and emanated in large scale oppression. Calvin rightly attempted to avoid the neat highly rational and philosophical approach of scholasticism in favour of a practical approach to knowledge. He realised that authentic faith seek practical wisdom by following the example of Christ and discerning the signs of the times through the Spirit. Authentic faith does not seek after political power, neither does it attempt to replace the penultimate with the ultimate through coercive social action, nor should it attempt to present "objective" all-encompassing theoretical systems of knowledge. Instead, Christian faith ought to recognise the penultimate and preliminary nature of human knowledge and pursue a practical wisdom that enacts the ethos of Christ in life by searching after justice, truth and mercy in the world.

This statement should not be misinterpreted as an attempt to insulate the Christian tradition from intellectual or rational debates or to seek escape in irrationalism. The intention, rather, is too caution Christian traditions against bold attempts to explain "everything" or to enter theoretical discussions that extend beyond the competency of the church, the witness of Scripture and the core confessions of the Christians faith. At the same time Reformed Christians should always be willing to revisit their doctrines and creeds in the spirit of *semper Reformanda*. Though the church is a confessing and witnessing community, she should avoid the pitfall of degenerating into a *confessionalist* community that evade difficult theological questions and much needed self-reflection by awarding her confessions an axiomatic sacral status that cannot be responsibly challenged, either in theory or practise, by church members, ministers or theologians. Confessionalism ought to be rejected because it amounts to a form of ecclesiastical power abuse that closes of debate, protects special interests, intentionally stifles theological reflection, and endangers the vibrant and living nature of the Christian tradition.

A last notable feature of Calvin's epistemology, is that he maintained that reason cannot function adequately without faith. Without faith reason becomes "carnally minded." Faith binds the believer to the source of true Wisdom and reorients the believer's focus and direction in life. Faith reminds us that we are not alone, that our existence is theocentrically determined and eccentrically directed. By grounding our identity in God and correlating our God-relationship with a love for our neighbours, faith safeguards us from distorted identities that degenerate into idolatrous forms of "carnal mindedness."

Conclusion

Calvin's epistemology is characterized by a concurrent twofold movement that achieve a similar effect. When we look into the mirror of God glory as revealed in scripture and creation, we are overwhelmed by God's majesty and inevitably become displeased with ourselves. At the same time, when we do introspection we are confronted by our shortcomings and develop a desire for God's grace. Calvin resisted systematic scholastic approaches to rationality and had little appetite for speculative theology. Instead, the concern of Christian knowledge is practical wisdom (sapientia), having communion with God and imitating the example of Christ in life. Calvin displayed a scepticism in the powers of human reason and maintained that knowledge and faith are inseparable. Without faith knowledge tends to become carnal minded and destined to construct idols in the place of God. The chapter argued that Calvin's critique of reason is highly relevant in postmodern times. Calvin reminds us that the ideal of a pure, unadulterated rationality is a myth, that knowledge systems have a propensity to create idols, that human knowledge ought to be regarded as preliminary in nature, and that reason cannot function properly without faith and divine revelation.

5

The Anthropological Roots of Society[1]

Introduction

THERE IS CONFUSION AMONG scholars on the exact nature and structure of Calvin's societal doctrine. Some believe that Calvin's theology and societal doctrine is determined by a sharp dualistic distinction between the spiritual and material realms. Brian Edgar[2] argues that the structure of Calvin's theology is characterized by an anthropological dualism and a "fundamental dualism of grace" that "reflects a broader dualism of the physical and spiritual realms."[3] This leads to a theology that is incapable of integrating the spiritual and material realms.[4] David VanDrunen,[5] in a similar vein, states that Calvin does not regard the kingdom of Christ as having anything to do with the earthly realm:

> For Calvin Christ's kingship is spiritual, pertaining not to things earthly or of this world, but to things heavenly and of the future life... For Calvin, the kingdom of Christ has nothing to do with human conditions and earthly laws. This truth, he explained, is rooted in the fact of the twofold government in man.

Because of God's "twofold government of man," the Christian does not need to organize the civil kingdom in a specific form to enable the spiritual

---

1. This chapter contains amended and extended versions of articles that were published in the *Journal of Church and State* and *Dialog: A Journal of Theology*. The full references are Nico Vorster, "'United but Not Confused': Calvin's Anthropology as Hermeneutical Key to Understanding his Societal Doctrine" in the *Journal of Church and State* 58.1 (2016) 117–42; Nico Vorster, "John Calvin on the Christian's Social Responsibility: Cultural Activist or Modest Social Reformer?," 56.4 (2018) 441–48. Permission for re-use was obtained from Oxford University Press Academic and Wiley Periodicals.
2. Edgar, "Calvin and the Natural Order," 1–15.
3. Edgar, "Calvin and the Natural Order," 9, 12.
4. Edgar, "Calvin and the Natural Order," 14.
5. David VanDrunen, "Context of Natural Law," 515.

kingdom to flourish.[6] According to VanDrunen, Calvin viewed the civil kingdom as grounded in the created order, not in the redemptive spiritual order. This led him to "a very modest view of social reform."[7] VanDrunen asserts that, in contrast to later Calvinist transformationists, Calvin "strictly prohibits Christians from treating the civil realm as an aspect of the kingdom of Christ."[8] On the question of how this interpretation of Calvin's two kingdoms doctrine corresponds with the jurisdiction that the Consistory in Geneva possessed, VanDrunen states that Calvin was inconsistent in his application of the doctrine:

> the fact that the Consistory as an ecclesiastical body was given jurisdiction over all residents of Geneva is difficult to reconcile with Calvin's two kingdoms' theology, for it gives the church jurisdiction over those who are not members of the church, a spiritual jurisdiction over those outside of the spiritual kingdom.[9]

A second group of scholars take an opposite stance. They depict Calvin's societal doctrine as transformationist and integrated in nature. Hans-Helmut Esser[10] argues that Calvin's allowance for state intervention in religious affairs was "still ensnared in medieval *corpus Christianum* thinking." Calvin's political theory assigned governors the role of executing their tasks according to both tables of the Decalogue. This included the duty of worship and the protection of the true religion. Witte, correspondingly, states that as his theology matured, Calvin increasingly thought in "integrated" and "institutional" terms. He "blurred the lines between spiritual and political life, law and liberty."[11] Gatis[12] posits that Calvin envisaged a theocratic and theonomic religious republic where all laws are derived from God's law, and "life, law and politics are pervaded by religion." Leith[13] interprets Calvin's belief that God's claim on human life is absolute and that the goal of the Christian life is *Soli Deo Gloria*, as being infused by an "aggressive spirit" towards social action:

> Calvin's interpretation of the Christian life inspired a vigorous and aggressive spirit. On the human level it involved a real

---

6. VanDrunen, "Context of Natural Law," 515.
7. VanDrunen, "Two Kingdoms: A Reassessment," 249.
8. VanDrunen, "Two Kingdoms: A Reassessment," 260.
9. VanDrunen, *Natural Law and the Two Kingdoms*, 87.
10. Esser, "Contemporary Relevance," 375–76.
11. Witte, "Moderate Religious Liberty," 375.
12. Gatis, "Political Theory of John Calvin," 452, 467.
13. Leith, *John Calvin's Doctrine of the Christian Life*, 163.

conquest of evil. In its relation to God it had no less incentive than his glory. It followed naturally for the Calvinist to exhibit an unusual aggressiveness in history. Calvin himself described the Christian life in terms of progress, conquest, and heroism.

A third group of scholars describe Calvin's social thought as ambiguous. Bouwsma[14] suggests that Calvin's thought on social polity was characterized by a tension between his theological understanding of the existence of two realms of governance and his inner urge for order, while Graham[15] claims that there is a discontinuity between Calvin's theoretical understanding of the existence of two kingdoms and his practical political convictions. Jeon[16] asserts that Calvin was inconsistent in his application of the two kingdoms doctrine. Calvin gave the state enough power to intervene in religious affairs to give his followers the impetus to develop theocratic ideals.

The question this chapter probes is: How does Calvin's anthropology influence the structure and nature of his doctrine on society? In addressing this question it is important to take account of contextual considerations which shaped Calvin's societal doctrine. Calvin defied the theocratic imperialism that the Roman Catholic Church imposed on society; he reacted against Swiss and English Erastianism that subjected the church to the authority of the state in matters of faith, doctrine and discipline; and he attempted to distinguish himself from the voluntarism of the Anabaptists who insisted on a radical separation of church and state. While following the two kingdoms doctrine of Luther, his thought was molded by his practical political experiences in Geneva that often required an institutional overlap between church and state. Lastly Calvin experienced severe opposition from the followers of Ami Perrin in the Consistory of Geneva who expounded Libertinist doctrines.

Though all these experiences contributed to his understanding of the relation between the two kingdoms, this chapter argues that Calvin's thought was mainly inspired by the fundamental tenets of his theology. Calvin's doctrine of society is decisevely informed by his theological anthropology, which portrays the human being as a microcosm of the macrocosmic reality. Calvin grounded the roots of society in his theological anthropology and modeled the relation between the heavenly and civil kingdoms on the relation between the human's body and soul which, in turn, exemplifies the two natures of Christ. These hermeneutical keys help us to understand that Calvin entertains a societal doctrine of differentiation and relation.

14. Bouwsma, *Sixteenth Century Portrait*, 210–11.
15. Graham, *Constructive Revolutionary*, 158.
16. Jeon, "Calvin and the Two Kingdoms," 300, 316, 319.

The Human Person as Microcosmic Model of Reality

Calvin regarded communion with the Trinitarian God as the *telos* of human life.[17] The fundamental motive of his theological anthropology was to explain how the human is united with God in Christ through the work of the Holy Spirit. Since the human being is created to ascend to God and because she possesses immortal essence, she is the "brightest mirror" of God's works.[18] Calvin depicted the human as a microcosm of God's works:

> Hence the philosophers have not improperly called man a microcosm (miniature world), as being a rare specimen of divine power, wisdom, and goodness, and containing within himself wonders sufficient to occupy our minds, if we are willing so to employ them.[19]

Here we find an early indicator of the close relation between Calvin's anthropology and cosmology. As microcosm of God's works the created structure of the human being depicts the overall macrocosmic structure of reality. Anthropology is, after all, for Calvin "woven into the context of knowledge of God."[20] Calvin's theological anthropology contains three microcosmic features that influences his societal doctrine; namely the relation between body and soul, the createdness of the human being as male and female and the effects of sin and grace on the human being.

Soul and Body as Microcosmic Model

Bouwsma[21] notes that Calvin understood the created structure of the human as consisting of soul and body, which corresponded with his understanding of the cosmos as existing of a superior and inferior realm. Moreover, the structure of the human being as soul and body serves in his thought as a microcosmic example of the structure of the broader societal realm. Calvin differentiated between the human's internal and external existence, the

---

17. Billings, "United to God through Christ," 324.
18. Calvin, *Institutes*, 1.5.3; *CO* 2.43: "clarum operum Dei speculum."
19. Calvin, *Institutes*, 1.5.3; *CO* 2.43: "Ac proinde quidam ex philosophis olim hominem non immerito vocarunt mikrókosmon, quia rarum sit potentiae, bonitatis et sapientiae Dei specimen, satisque miraculorum in se contineat occupandis nostris mentibus." For similar references see Calvin, *Book of Psalms*, 1:99; *CO* 31.91; Calvin, *Commentaries on Genesis*, 1:9; *CO* 23.25–26.
20. Edgar, "Calvin and the Natural Order," 10. See Balserak, "Accommodating Act Par Excellence," 413.
21. Bouwsma, *Sixteenth Century Portrait*, 79.

future and present life, supernatural and natural realms, heavenly kingdom and civil kingdom and church and state. The internal, future, supernatural, heavenly and churchly domains correspond with the soul and the external, present, natural, civil and governmental realms with the body.[22]

As noted earlier, Calvin regards the soul as the "nobler" part of the human and the seat of the *imago Dei*.[23] Whereas the body is "motion devoid of essence," the soul is spirit, have intellect that enables it to conceive of God, possesses conscience, and has the ability to rise higher than the world.[24] All these relational capacities are specific to the soul; the body in contrast is a "tabernacle," "house of clay," "prison" that habituates the soul, but possesses no spirit.[25]

We noted in chapter 3 that Calvin related the body and soul in an analogous sense to the two natures of Christ. In the case of Jesus Christ, the divinity was "conjoined" and "united" with the humanity in a manner that maintained the full properties of both, and yet the "two natures constitute only one Christ."[26] Similarly, the human being consists of two substances, neither of which is intermingled with the other but together they form one human person.

When we apply Calvin's doctrine on the two natures of Christ to the relationship between the human body and soul, it becomes clear that Calvin differentiates between the soul and body to relate them. The term "united but not mingled" denotes, in Wendel's words, that the human is a "composition of body and soul" and that "the two parts of a whole could perfectly well preserve the properties peculiar to them."[27] Yet, the human soul and body cannot be separated in an absolute sense because their properties form one human person. The properties of the body, though, does not determine the essence of the soul, nor can the properties of the soul change the composition of the body.

From the discussions in chapter 3, it should be clear that a fundamental reason for Calvin's partitioning of the human into a body and soul was his belief that the heavenly and earthly realms should be *kept* apart. Once

---

22. Calvin, *Institutes*, 3.19.15; CO 2.622–23.

23. Calvin, *Institutes*, 1.15.2; CO 2.135: "nobilior eius pars est."

24. Calvin, *Institutes*, 1.15.2, 7–8; CO 2.135, 2.142, 2.148; Calvin, *Sermons on Genesis 1–11*, 94; SC 11/1.56.

25. CO 2.135; 2.141; CO 23.3; CO 5.178.

26. Calvin, *Institutes*, 2.14.1; CO 2.353: "Si quid in rebus humanis tanto mysterio simile potest reperiri, hominis similitudo appositissima videtur, quem ex duabus substantiis conspicimus constare; quarum neutra tamen sic alteri permixta est, ut non retineat naturae suae proprietatem. Neque enim aut anima corpus aut corpus anima est."

27. Wendel, *Calvin*, 221.

the heavenly and earthly is confused the critical distance between God and creation is breached and the spiritual is subsumed by the temporal. For the soul to be immortal its powers and faculties need to be not so entrenched in the body that it cannot exist apart from it.

For the purposes of this chapter it is important to note that Calvin employed the soul-body distinction to elucidate the relation between the spiritual and civil governments of God:

> Let us observe that in man government is twofold: the one spiritual, by which the conscience is trained to piety and divine worship, the other civil by which the individual is instructed in those duties which, as men and citizens, we are boldly to perform. To these two forms are commonly given the not inappropriate names of spiritual and temporal jurisdiction, intimating that the former species has reference to the life of the soul, while the latter relates to matters of the present life ... For there exists in man a kind of two worlds, over which different kings and laws preside.[28]

From the abovementioned passage it is clear that Calvin explicitly related spiritual affairs to the realm of the soul, and external issues to the physical and material realm. Calvin regarded the soul/body relationship as not merely of anthropological import, but as indicative of the ontological makeup of reality.

Male and Female

Calvin considered the human being's createdness as male and female as another microcosmic model for the broader structure of reality and society. Human gender indicates that "man was formed to be a social animal."[29] In his sermon on Genesis 2:18–21 Calvin stated that God created Eve from the substance of Adam so that there would be a "holy communion" between the

---

28. Calvin, *Institutes*, 3.19.15; *CO* 2.622–23: "Ad eum ergo lapidem ne quis impingat, primum animadvertamus duplex esse in homine regimen: alterum spirituale, quo conscientia ad pietatem et ad cultum Dei instituitur; alterum politicum, quo ad humanitatis et civilitatis officia, quae inter homines servanda sunt, homo eruditur. Vulgo appellari solent iurisdictio spiritualis et temporalis, non impropriis nominibus. Quibus significatur, priorem illam regiminis speciem ad animae vitam pertinere, hanc autem in his quae praesentis vitae sunt versari ... Sunt enim in homine veluti mundi duo, quibus et varii reges et variae leges praeesse possunt." For a similar reference see 4.20.1; *CO* 2.1092.

29. Calvin, *Commentaries on Genesis*, 1:128; *CO* 23.46 "Principium ergo generale est, conditum esse hominem, ut sit sociale animal. Iam non poterat exstare hominum genus sine muliere."

human race.[30] All people are derived from one single source, consequently every individual is connected to his neighbours.[31] Calvin stated it thus:

> He (God) immediately implemented a procedure which the creation of Eve informs us of: that since we are all formed in the likeness of Adam and begotten of his seed, we must be truly one, and everyone must individually recognize his own flesh and bones, his own substance, in his neighbors.[32]

Calvin regarded this human sociability as part of the created order and as established for our well-being and advantage.[33] Because we are all "one flesh" (une chair), each of us has to serve our neighbour since the human race is "one body" (qu'un corps).[34]

He identified marriage as the most basic social union that God uses to maintain the human race:

> Marriage would be the means for maintaining the human race in its condition, with a man having an individual helpmate and the woman also having the companionship of her husband. In that way, everyone, by and large would tend toward unity because there are, as it were, two parts of the human race, one for the guidance of the other and one for mutual help.[35]

Interestingly, Calvin portrayed the order of marriage as an order of nature that serves as an exemplar for the order of society as a whole.[36] He described the institution of marriage as "the first step of human society."[37] Marriage is

---

30. Calvin, *Sermons on Genesis 1–11*, 180; SC 11/1.125: "conjonction saincte."

31. SC 11/1.125

32. Calvin, *Sermons on Genesis 1–11*, 181; SC 11/1.126: "voire et l'ordre a esté quant et quant estably en sorte que nous sommes admonestez par la creation d' Eve, qu'estans ainsi tous formez de nostre pere Adam et procreez de sa semence, il faut que nous soions vraiement un, et que chascun congnoisse en ses prochains sa chair et ses os, et sa proper substance."

33. SC 11/1.127.

34. Calvin, *Sermons on Genesis 1–11*, 182; SC 11/1.127.

35. Calvin, *Sermons on Genesis 1–11*, 191; SC 11/1.133: "Et en cecy voions nous qu'il y a eu un don singulier en Adam, qu'estant creé soudain, il distinque en telle varieté de bestes et leur aproprie á chascune son nom. Ill failloit bien qu'il y eust autre esprit qu'aujourduy il ne nous reste. Et ainsi congnoissons tousjours que si nous sommes grossiers et que nous ne sachions discerner souvent entre le blanc et le noir". Also see Calvin, *Commentaries on Genesis*, 1:136; CO 23.50.

36. Calvin, *Sermons on Genesis 1–11*, 180; SC 11/1.125.

37. Calvin, *Commentaries on Genesis*, 1:128; CO 23.46: "Quoniam viro non expedit esse soli, creanda est uxor quasit illi adiutrix. Ego tamen ita accipio: quod Deus a primo quidem gradu incipiat humanae societatis."

an inviolable union, a covenant that implies mutual duties and rights. When Calvin reflected on human associations, the same "covenantal" perspective surfaces. In his Commentary on Genesis 2:18, Calvin described all human community as a "reflection of the sacred bond in which two people become one body and one soul."[38] Just as husband and wife have mutual obligations to assist each other, the members of a society have obligations towards each other. In fact, every human being is "obligated to associate with his neighbours" and must realise that we "exist mutually through one another' in a "mutual bond of love."[39] This natural order cannot be reversed and every attempt to withdraw ourselves from our neighbors should be regarded as evil.[40]

Witte[41] notes that Calvin often referred to the "common rights of mankind," "the rights of a common nature" and the "equal rights and liberties of all." This terminology of rights and duties depicted his understanding of the nature of social communities, beginning with marriage as the most sacred union. Calvin's extension of the covenantal nature of the marriage bond to all social bonds had a significant impact on the social thought of the seventeenth century. Johannes Althusius, for instance, developed his theory of federal and symbiotic politics on the basis of the Calvinist understanding of marriage as an exemplary union that depicts the neighborly nature of the human being. Althusius posited that all human associations are constituted by pacts, reminiscent of the sacral bond that exists between husband and wife. The various social spheres are therefore sovereign in nature and ought to be allowed to govern themselves without external interference insofar as they respect other spheres.[42]

General and Special Grace

A third "microcosmic" feature of Calvin's anthropology that influenced his societal doctrine was his understanding of sin and the distinctions he made between the human being's supernatural and natural gifts; and God's general and special grace. As noted in chapter 2 Calvin posited that sin destroys the supernatural gifts of the human person, but not his natural gifts. Total

---

38. Calvin, *Commentaries on Genesis*, 1:128; CO 23.46: "adeoque in coniunctione hominum praecipue eminet sanctius illud vinculum, quo maritus et uxor in unum corpus unamque animam coalescunt."

39. Calvin, *Sermons on Genesis 1–11*, 180, 191, 193; SC 11/1.125, 132, 135.

40. SC 11/1.132.

41. Witte, *Reformation of Rights*, 55.

42. See Althusius, *Politica*, 28, 31.

depravity entails that the whole human being is vitiated by sin, even his best works. However, this does not mean that the human is by nature "evil" and that he bears no capacity for good.[43] Calvin stated it thus in a sermon on Genesis 9:3–7:

> Although that image is almost completely destroyed in us, we see clearly how God still shows it in our neighbours and distinguishes them from the brute beasts and demonstrates they possess a nobility and dignity above all other creatures.[44]

Again, the divide between the spiritual and temporal, supernatural and natural, comes into play. The human being is despoiled of those supernatural gifts that enabled him to ascend to God, such as faith, holiness and righteousness.[45] The natural gifts, in contrast, are corrupted, but not destroyed. If they were destroyed the human being would no longer be human. Though weak and immersed in darkness, the human faculties of reason and will still possess a residue of sound judgment and discernment:

> In the perverted and degenerate nature of man there are still some sparks which show that he is a rational animal, and differs from the brutes, inasmuch he is endued with intelligence.[46]

The residue of the remaining natural gifts is not sufficient to attain salvation, cannot direct us to Christ and do not enable us to develop a natural theology, but they do provide human beings with enough prudence to act morally.[47] In his commentary on Psalm 8 Calvin identified the residues of natural gifts as the ability to distinguish between good and evil, our natural sense of God, our ability to marry and preserve this sacred bond, the sense of shame and guilt and the ability to subject ourselves to civil laws.[48] The excellence of these gifts must not be denied because the Spirit dispenses it "to whom he will for the common benefit of humankind," thereby preventing the destruction of human nature.[49] Gerrish rightly notes that Calvin "builds

---

43. Bouwsma, *Calvin*, 139.

44. Calvin, *Sermons on Genesis 1–11*, 745; SC 11/1.485: "Et combine que ceste image là soit quasi du tout aneantie en nous, si est ce que nous vioons bien comme Dieu la represente encores en nos prochains, et qu'il monster qu'il les a distinguez a d'avec les bestes brutes, et qu'il y a quelque noblesse et dignité par dessus toutes autres creatures; nous voions cela."

45. CO 2.196.

46. Torrance, *Calvin's Doctrine of Man*, 92.

47. Calvin, *Commentary on John*, 33–34; CO 47.6–7. See Steinmetz, "Theology of John Calvin," 121.

48. CO 31.91.

49. Calvin, *Institutes*, 2.2.16–17; CO 2.199–200: "haec praestantissima divini spiritus esse bona, quae in publicum generis humani bonum, quibus vult, dispensat."

his social ethics partly on the endurance of the divine image even in fallen man."[50] Society, social order and social cohesion is possible despite sin, because the human being is a "social animal" who is by nature disposed towards "cherishing and preserving" society. "Every individual" understands that society must be regulated by laws and are capable of comprehending the principles of those laws.[51]

Calvin's distinction between the human's natural and supernatural gifts inevitably brought another category into play, namely the differentiation between God's special grace (*specialis Dei gratia*) and general grace (*generalem Dei gratiam*). If God bestows the elect with supernatural gifts but denudes others from possessing such gifts, it follows that different kinds of grace are at work in God's providential reign over the human being. In *Bondage and Liberation of the Will*,[52] Calvin stated the difference between the two forms of God's grace as one pertaining to our lives as human beings and the other to our lives as children of God. The former is a natural form of grace, while the latter is supernatural in nature.

Based on exegesis of Romans 2 Calvin posited the existence of a natural law that is "engraved" on the minds of all people and is displayed by the ability of even Gentiles to distinguish between good and evil and to maintain "some integrity among themselves."[53] In fact, the "minds of all men have impressions of civil order and honesty."[54]

These natural moral abilities bear no relation to justification and sanctification in Christ, but are special gifts from God that serve the preservation of the earthly realm, the "common benefit of humankind"[55] and prevents

---

50. Gerrish, "Mirror of God's Goodness," 213.

51. Calvin, *Institutes*, 2.2.13; CO 2.197: "Hinc fit ut nemo reperiatur qui non intelligat."

52. Calvin, *Bondage and Liberation*, 167: "We exist and move in one sense as human beings and in another as the sons of God. The former grace is the possession of everyone, but the latter is granted specially to the elect. The former is in a certain way implanted in our nature, but the latter is given to man as a supernatural gift." CO 6.347: "Atqui alio modo sumus et movemur, ut homines: alio, ut filii Dei. Communis omnium est ilia gratia, haec electis peculiariter confertur, ilia naturae quodammodo insita est, haec praeter naturam homini datur, ut quod erat esse desinat, et esse incipiat quod nondum erat."

53. Calvin, *Institutes*, 2.2.22; CO 2.203. Calvin, *Sermons on Genesis 1–11*, 745; SC 11/1.485.

54. Calvin, *Institutes*, 2.2.13; CO 2.197: "ideoque civilis cuiusdam et bonestatis et ordinis universales impressiones inesse omnium bominum animis conspicimus."

55. Calvin, *Institutes*, 2.2.16; CO 2.197: "Neque tamen interim obliviscamur haec praestantissima divini spiritus esse bona, quae in publicum generis humani bonum, quibus vult, dispensat."

"the entire destruction of nature."[56] However corrupted the human being might be, God still keeps in mind his original intent with creation.[57] Yet, God willed that the human will never be able to penetrate into the mysteries of God's kingdom through the means of the "common light of nature." The Spirit alone opens "the gate of heaven to the elect."[58]

God's special grace, in contrast, restores the relation between God and the believer by uniting the believer with Christ through the work of the Spirit. Even though Calvin was adamant that the supernatural gifts are destroyed by sin, they are not totally irretrievable, but can be recovered through the regenerative work of the Spirit. The bestowal of supernatural gifts to some is a supernatural event, a special gift of God's grace, limited to the elect.[59] It consists of regeneration and justification and allows the believer to ascend to God through the illumination of the Spirit.

Calvin's understanding of the "united but not mingled" relation between the body and soul filters through to his soteriology. Lief[60] rightly notes that Calvin did not only regard the human mind as quickened by the Spirit of God, but also the human body as vivified. Just as Calvin understood the body/soul relationship as two parts of the one created nature of the human person, "so too redemption in Jesus Christ is not just the salvation of the soul but affects the entire person."[61] Lief,[62] furthermore, notes that the human's person's justification and regeneration is correspondingly for Calvin "inseparable parts of a unified whole." The "spiritual benefit" of Christ's work not only restores our spiritual relationship with God, but also manifests itself in our temporal existence as we love our neighbors. This indicates that Calvin clearly understood the spiritual and temporal dimensions of the human being as closely connected.

Yet, the recovery of the supernatural gifts is not a once-off event, but a gradual process of transformation. As long as the human being is prisoner of the body, he will be prone to the desires of the flesh.[63] For Calvin, no social utopia is possible on earth. The effects of sin, even on believers, are too wide-ranging, penetrative and total to make an ideal society possible.

56. CO 2.197: "quia nisi nobis pepercisset, totius naturae interitum secum traxisset defectio."

57. CO 35.147.

58. Calvin, *Commentary on John*, 38; CO 47.9: "solus est spiritus Christi, qui ianuam coelorum electis aperit."

59. Cf. CO 2.196.

60. Lief, "Is Neo-Calvinism Calvinist," 4.

61. Lief, "Is Neo-Calvinism Calvinist," 4.

62. Lief, "Is Neo-Calvinism Calvinist," 4.

63. SC 11/1.328; CO 2.409, 504.

This, nonetheless, does not mean that the Christian has no social calling. As will be discussed later, the notion of vocation was integral to Calvin's societal doctrine.

The Structure of Calvin's Societal Doctrine

From the preceding discussion it should be clear that Calvin's understanding of the microcosmic features of the human being formed the theological background for his societal doctrine. Calvin grounded the roots of society in the *imago Dei*, the createdness of the human being as male and female, God's infusion of general and special grace in humanity, and the survival of natural gifts in the human after the fall. His two kingdoms theory and understanding of the relation between church and state, accordingly, was based on the cosmological distinction between a supernatural and natural realm that is exemplified by the relation between the human's body and soul. We now turn to Calvin's understanding of the structural makeup of society.

Society as Neighborhood

Oberman[64] rightly states that Calvin thrusted God's rule "beyond the heart of the justified sinner and beyond the boundaries of the Church, to encompass the State, Society and whole created order." Calvin viewed common humanity as residing in our createdness in the image of God, which establishes the "common dignity" of human nature.[65] Despite its corruption, the *imago Dei* binds the whole human race without exception into one body.[66] Calvin stated it thus:

> But I say that the whole human race, without exception, are to be embraced by one feeling of charity: that there is no distinction of Greek or Barbarian, worthy or unworthy, friend or foe, since all are to be viewed not in themselves, but in God.[67]

---

64. Oberman, *Dawn of the Reformation*, 257.

65. Calvin, *Commentaries on Genesis*, 1:129; CO 23.46: "communem totius naturae dignitatem."

66. SC 11/1.57.

67. Calvin, *Institutes*, 2.8.55; CO 2.306: "Sed dico, Universum hominum genus, nulla exceptione, uno caritatis affectu esse amplexandum: nullum hie esse discrimen barbari aut Graeci, digni vel indigni, amici vel inimici; quoniam in Deo, non in se ipsis considerandi sunt."

Calvin grounded our duty to extend charity towards all people not in the inherent merits of the human, but in God who created the human being.[68] The human possesses dignity because he is a creature of God who mirrors him. God therefore prohibits the destruction of the image through violence and cruelty and expects us to "aid and support our neighbors."[69] When the dignity of humans is violated, not only God himself is injured, but also ourselves, because we are mirrored in the flesh of our neighbors.[70] Calvin emphatically rejected the notion that the *imago Dei* was destroyed by the fall and that the human therefore possesses no dignity. Firstly, some remnant of the image still exists that accords the human with considerable dignity, and secondly, God keeps his original intention with creation in mind.[71]

The human being's createdness as male and female indicates, according to Calvin, that the human is a communal being that desire relationships. The natural gift of reason that survived in the human after the fall as a result of God's common grace, enables humans to be sociable and provides them with an inherent sense of community and civil order:

> Since man is by nature a social animal, he is disposed from natural instinct to cherish and preserve society; and accordingly we see that the minds of all people have impressions of civil order and honesty. Hence it is that every individual understands how human societies must be regulated by laws, and also is able to comprehend the principles of those laws.[72]

Calvin regarded the family, polity and church as the three most important social institutions. Besides these, Calvin also recognized labor, economic, educational and scientific communities,[73] because God makes forms of social activity possible by bestowing his blessings and natural gifts on people to assist society and to preserve the good order of the world.[74] Through the various forms of social activities humanity exhibits its God given dominion

---

68. CO 2.510.
69. Calvin, *Sermons on Genesis 1–11*, 741; SC 11/1.476.
70. CO 23.146–47.
71. CO 23.147.
72. Calvin, *Institutes*, 2.2.13; CO 2.197: "quoniam homo animal est natura sociale, naturali quoque instinctu, ad fovendam conservandamque eam societatem propendet; ideoque civilis cuiusdam et honestatis et ordinis universales impressiones inesse omnium hominum animis conspicimus. Hinc fit ut nemo reperiatur qui non intelligat, oportere quosvis hominum coetus legibus contineri, quique non earum legum principia mente complectatur."
73. CO 51.222; CO 2.199.
74. CO 2.34, 199.

over the rest of creation, while God uses them to preserve order until the whole creation can be redeemed in Christ.[75]

Also fundamental to Calvin's social thought and congruent with his understanding of marriage and covenantal theology, was his understanding of community as a relationship of "neighbourhood" based on mutual obligation. In his commentary on Ephesians 5:22 Calvin defined society as consisting of groups of people who are like "yokes" in which there is a "mutual obligation" between parties.[76] Community is made possible by human interdependence and the diversity of natural gifts that the various members of a society possess.[77] Since society is a neighborhood individuals ought to serve each other within different vocational contexts through their gifts.[78] Every person has received a divine calling to exercise a distinct duty that pertain to a certain mode of life.[79] This calling gives direction to a person's life, places limits to personal ambition and prevents his or her life from descending into meaninglessness.[80] Vocation infuses our daily work with meaning, and even though our work might be inconvenient in nature, we have the consolation that in following our proper calling our work have value in the eyes of God.[81] Moreover, our vocation determines the ethical appropriateness of our actions. The call of the Lord is the "foundation and beginning of right action" (principium ac fundamentum).[82]

Christian vocation is in Calvin's theology closely related to his doctrine of *munex triplex*. Every believer has a religious calling to be a king, prophet and priest that "exhorts, ministers and rules" in his community.[83] Believers act in everything they do in the capacity of priests offering themselves as a sacrifice to God.[84] Faith, therefore, determines all ethics, also social ethics, because the Lordship of Christ demands that believers be socially responsible.[85] Calvin in fact went so far as to state that "there is no part of our life, and no action so minute that it not to be directed towards the glory of

---

75. Cf. Torrance, *Calvin's Doctrine of Man*, 48–49.
76. Cf. Calvin, *Galatians and Ephesians*, 317; CO 51.222.
77. CO 2.509; 2.306.
78. CO 49.415.
79. CO 2.532.
80. CO 2.532.
81. CO 2.532.
82. CO 2.532.
83. See Witte, "Law, Religion and Human Rights," 260.
84. Wallace, *Calvin's Doctrine on the Christian Life*, 29
85. Leith, *John Calvin's Doctrine of the Christian Life*, 188

God."[86] Not only does Calvin end his discussion of the Christian life in the *Institutes* with the remark that believers ought to order their lives according to their particular vocations,[87] but he wrote a lot about the various vocations of the believers with regard to the stewardship of earthly goods, the dignity of labor and the rights of working people.[88] This is a clear indication that his theology is not otherworldly in nature. In fact, Calvin's doctrine on vocation affirms that believers cannot separate the mundane aspects of present life from their Christian calling.[89]

A charismatic notion of vocation thus orders the individual's responsibility in various contexts. Since the universe should manifest God's perfections, Christians have the task to demonstrate and heighten God's glory by fulfilling their vocation in society.[90] Lief[91] rightly notes that vocation becomes in Calvin's theology the "means by which believers fully engage the cultural life" by using their gifts to serve their neighbor. In order to execute his vocation the individual needs to renounce himself and focus on service rather than profit. In fact, self-renunciation is for Calvin the "precondition for genuine service and love to the neighbor."[92]

The Relation between the Penultimate and Ultimate

Despite Calvin's emphasis on the importance of vocation, he did not regard the future eschatological order as suspending the temporal order. Calvin viewed the creational order as good and thus did not see nature and grace as in opposition to each other or grace as a superadded gift.[93] In fact, Calvin believed in a fixed moral order as proclaimed in the Word and embedded in the natural order. The natural order requires a certain hierarchical ordering of human relationships, especially when it comes to male-female relations, husband-wife relationships, familial relationships and citizen-state relationships.[94] The Christian needs to obey these creational prescripts and may

---

86. *CO* 48.590: "Car tout ce que nous avons, voire iusquau bout des ongles mesmes, deveroit tendre là, que la gloire de Dieu apparust et relusist par tout."
87. *CO* 2.532.
88. See Beeke, "Twelve Reasons," 245.
89. Senior, "Cruciform Pilgrims," 127. *CO* 49.415.
90. *CO* 2.44.
91. Lief, "Is Neo-Calvinism Calvinist," 5.
92. See Senior, "Cruciform Pilgrims," 126.
93. See Leith, *John Calvin's Doctrine of the Christian Life*, 151.
94. *CO* 51.222.

not use eschatological arguments to subvert the natural and civil order. We, afterall, live in a penultimate age.

In his commentary on Matthew 6:10 Calvin closely associated the kingdom of God with the restoration of order on earth.[95] God's reign is not a purely trans-historical phenomenon, but it is manifested in and through history wherever the original created order of God is restored to its original intention. However, there is a difference between restoring God's original order and progressively realizing God's coming eschatological kingdom on earth through social action. The difference exists in Christians respecting the penultimate nature of the present dispensation. In his Commentary on John 12:31 Calvin makes it clear that God's eschatological reign cannot be established in the penultimate age because the kingdom of Satan must first be destroyed. This will only be realized with the Consummation.[96]

Calvin was careful not to widen the ambit of Christian liberty to such a degree that it allows for anarchy. Christian liberty is essentially a spiritual matter designed to liberate our consciences from fear, but when it comes to the civil and temporal order Christians are bound to human laws.[97]

Two examples that illustrate how Calvin inhibited the exercise of Christian liberty in the civil realm relate to gender relations and the attitude of Christians towards a tyrannical government. As will be discussed at length in the next chapter, Calvin posited that men and women are equals in the spiritual realm as far as sin and salvation are concerned. Yet, in the civil realm women need to submit to the authority of men, because the natural order commands it. The spiritual equality of men and women in Christ do not suspend the natural order, because we live in a penultimate age.[98] Concerning the issue of civil obedience to a tyrannical state Calvin held that Christians do not have the right to overthrow civil governments, even when they are oppressive, because governments are institutions set up by God. Christians have no right to use eschatological arguments to subvert the civil order, but they should accept oppressive governments as a yoke in God's hands.[99]

From the above it is clear that Calvin was cautious not to confuse the penultimate and the ultimate. Christ's reign is present in the sense that it inaugurates a process that restores the original natural and moral order as

---

95. *CO* 45.197.
96. *CO* 47.293.
97. *CO* 2.618, 623.
98. *CO* 23.27. See Thompson, *John Calvin and the Daughters*, 22.
99. *CO* 2.1112–13.

created by God, yet it is penultimate in that it does not replace the created order of things with an eschatological order.

The Two Kingdoms

Calvin based his two kingdoms doctrine on his cosmological understanding of the existence of a supernatural and natural realm. The earthly realm relates to all those things that are connected with the present life and are "confined within its boundaries," while the heavenly things pertain to the mysteries of God's heavenly kingdom.[100] The earthly realm involves matters of policy, economics, mechanical arts and liberal studies, while the heavenly realm includes our knowledge of God and the means of framing our lives according to God's will.[101]

The question is: What was Calvin's understanding of the relation between the two kingdoms? This chapter argues that Calvin did not sever the two, but in the same manner that he regarded soul and body as "united but not mingled," he related the two kingdoms too each other, while also differentiating between them.

As noted earlier, Calvin explicitly used the analogy of soul and body to explain the relation between the two kingdoms. In Book 3 of the 1559 *Institutes*, he described the heavenly kingdom as spiritual and as parallel to the life of the soul, while the earthly kingdom relates to the present life, which not only includes bodily issues such as eating and drinking but also civil government.[102] According to Calvin, the two kingdoms need to be viewed apart. Different kings and different laws preside over the two realms. Attending to this distinction will safeguard us from transferring spiritual issues to the civil realm. Yet, this does not mean that the spiritual has no effect, influence or significance for the civil realm. God's justice binds our consciences and is also applicable to the civil realm. The civil realm is not eternal, nor spiritual in nature; but this does not exempt it from God's reign and justice. God's commands us after all to submit to magistrates.[103]

In Book 4 of the 1559 *Institutes* Calvin again used the analogy of the body and soul, this time, relating the two kingdoms to the "twofold government in man." The one government pertains to the eternal life of the "soul" and "inward man," while the second relates to the regulation of the

---

100. Calvin, *Institutes*, 2.2.13; *CO* 2.197: "et quodammodo intra eius fines continentur."
101. *CO* 2.197.
102. *CO* 2.616.
103. *CO* 2.870.

external life.[104] Calvin emphatically states that the two kingdoms should not be mingled:

> [But he] He who knows to distinguish between the body and soul, between the present fleeting life and that which is future and eternal, will have no difficulty in understanding that the spiritual kingdom of Christ and civil government are things widely apart.[105]

Lief[106] rightly notes that Calvin's distinction between the two kingdoms is firmly rooted in his soteriology that maintains that redemptive grace are to be found in the spiritual realm and can never be "achieved" in the temporal realm.

There are also practical matters that informed Calvin's stance. He was concerned about a fusion of the two realms because if princes are not kept out of spiritual matters "the purity of faith will perish."[107] Magistrates are not competent to do what is done by the church. Conversely, civil servants are often usurped by church clerics, even though the church does not bear the power of the sword.[108] Calvin thus insisted on a distinction between the magistracy and consistory in Geneva.[109]

Despite this, Calvin proceeded to state that though the two kinds of government are distinct they are not adverse to each other.[110] Just as the human body is an interrelated union of body and soul, the two kingdoms are intimately connected with each other.[111] The two kingdoms do not stand in an antithetical relationship, but together they serve the reign of Christ. Just as the compounds of the body and soul jointly constitutes one person, the two realms establish the one reign of God. The spiritual kingdom contributes through the preaching of the word and the governance of the church, while the civil realm assist by way of civil government and the maintenance of law

---

104. Calvin, *Institutes*, 4.20.1; *CO* 2.1092: "quum duplex in homine regimen superius statuerimus, et de altero illo, quod est in anima, seu interiori homine positum."

105. *CO* 2.1092: "At vero qui inter corpus et animam, inter praesentem hanc fluxamque vitam et futuram illam aeternamque discernere noverit, neque difficile intelliget, spirituale Christi regnum et civilem ordinationem res esse plurimum sepositas."

106. Lief, "Is Neo-Calvinism Calvinist," 5.

107. Lief, "Is Neo-Calvinism Calvinist," 5.

108. *CO* 2.894–95.

109. Oberman, *Two Reformations*, 143.

110. Calvin, *Institutes*, 4.20.2; *CO* 2.1094: "Verum ut distinctum istud regiminis genus a spirituali illo et interno Christi regno nuper monuimus: ita nec quidquam pugnare sciendum est."

111. Cf. Lief, "Is Neo-Calvinism Calvinist," 3.

and order. Calvin, thus, was able to state that the civil kingdom, in a sense, "begins the heavenly life in us" by nurturing in us virtues that are required to enter the kingdom of God, while the spiritual kingdom conversely forms our manners in such a way that we become better citizens.[112] Calvin, hence, insisted that there is a clear distinction, but also a relation between the two kingdoms. The heavenly and earthly kingdoms are united in the sense that they relate to and complement each other and are both subject to God's reign, but they should not be mingled with each other. Civil government cannot make laws that reach to the internal government of the soul; its jurisdiction pertains to the external conduct of people. Conversely, civil laws cannot be seen in isolation from our service to God, because God asks us to observe civil laws out of respect for him. The church, on the other hand, belongs to the spiritual realm. Its jurisdiction is "nothing but the order provided for the preservation of the spiritual polity."[113] It may not "impede" or "impair" civil government.[114] Yet, the church also "aids" and "promotes" the civil kingdom by "conciliating us to each other," by "adapting our conduct to society" and by cherishing "common peace and tranquility."[115]

Though Calvin distinguished between the heavenly and earthly kingdoms, he clearly did not erect a wall of separation between the two kingdoms as some scholars suggest. Such a notion would deny the sovereignty of God. Since God reigns over all things, Calvin held that believers should not only be concerned about religious reform, but also social reform. In his commentary on Matthew 12:7 Calvin stated that believers have not completed their task until all the world is reformed, while in his commentary on Psalm 82:1 he noted that Christ's glory is reflected in the world when legitimate government flourishes.[116] In Calvin's thought believers are citizens of both kingdoms and though the civil kingdom should not be conjoined with the heavenly kingdom, it must also be reformed to demonstrate God's glory. The language of the two kingdoms does not imply that God reigns over the one but not the other, neither that Christians live in the one but not the

---

112. Lief, "Is Neo-Calvinism Calvinist," 3. Calvin also grounds the relation between the two kingdoms in the fact that the kingdom of heaven was erected on earth, see Calvin, *Institutes*, 2.9.4; CO 2.312.

113. Calvin, *Institutes*, 4.11.1; CO 2.891: "Ista igitur iurisdictionis potestas nihil aliud erit in summa quam ordo comparatus ad spiritualis politiae conservationem."

114. CO 2.891: "quae tamen a civili prorsus distincta est, eamque adeo nihil impedit aut imminuit, ut potius multum iuvet ac promoveat."

115. Calvin, *Institutes*, 4.20.2, 4.11.1; CO 2.1094, 891: "ad civilem iustitiam mores nostros formare, nos inter nos conciliare, communem pacem ac tranquillitatem alere."

116. CO 44.325; CO 31.768.

other, nor that God is glorified in the one, but not the other. It simply means that God governs the two kingdoms differently.[117]

Church and State

The modern concept of political life as consisting of various modalities of political agency was not entertained in Calvin's times.[118] Calvin understood civil government as working concertedly with the church to promote public morals and godliness. Heiko Oberman[119] states that in Calvin's thought God's concern was not only the rule of the faithful, but the rule of the "whole earth." Through the state God "advances" and makes his kingdom "grow." Civil authority thus serves the common dignity of humankind by preserving the wellbeing of humankind and its common peace and tranquility.[120] Since the human person is prone to evil and egoism he needs the restraint of law.[121] The task of civil authority is to uphold justice, i.e. "protect, vindicate and free the innocent" and to punish evil and misdeeds.[122] It needs to treat all people just, because the sacred bond of humanity establishes the equality of all people before the law. It also needs to take care that the "public form of religion stay uncorrupted."[123]

Calvin did not accord civil authority with absolute power. Rulers may only execute their powers to serve the well-being of their subjects and the common good and are accountable to God in the exercise of their power.[124] In doing so, government should respect the natural rights and freedoms of its subjects by protecting the equity of all citizens.[125] Authorities, furthermore, may not use laws to bind the consciences of believers by imposing laws for the purpose of creating religious obligations or by regulating spiritual matters that "reach to the internal government of the soul."[126] Because

117. See Godfrey, "Kingdom and Kingdoms," 7.
118. Senior, "Cruciform Pilgrims," 125.
119. Oberman, *Dawn of the Reformation*, 238.
120. *CO* 49.250; *CO* 2.1094.
121. Cf. Witte, "Law, Religion and Human Rights," 260.
122. Calvin, *Catechism*, art. 33; *CO* 5.354: "Iustitia quidem est innocentes in fidem suscipere, complecti, tueri, vindicare, liberare."
123. Calvin, *Catechism*, art. 33; *CO* 5.354: "ut publicam religionis formam impollutam conservent."
124. *CO* 49.251.
125. On Calvin's understanding of natural rights, see Little, "Calvin and Natural Rights," 411–30.
126. Calvin, *Institutes*, 4.10.5; *CO* 2.870: "ad interiorem animae gubernationem pertinere."

of the danger that an individual may usurp his power, Calvin preferred an aristocratic form of government mixed with democratic principles that embeds power in a few persons that "mutually, assist, instruct and admonish each other."[127]

Scholars such as Jeon and Bouwsma[128] depict Calvin's understanding of the relation between church and state as inconsistent, because he did not consistently delineate between the two. This supposedly leads to all sorts of ambiguities and opens the door to theocracy. My suggestion is that Calvin's understanding of the relation between church and state corresponds with his "united but not mingled" approach to the two kingdoms. This becomes clear when we analyze his understanding of the function of law in church and state. Though Calvin distinguished between God's natural and written law he did not dissect the two forms of law from each other. He regarded natural law as the most basic, eternal and unchanging law engraved on the minds of all people. All people have a created sense of justice and equity.[129] Though sin does not destroy our sense of natural law, it obscures it. God, therefore, gives us the written law that makes a "more lively and permanent impression on our minds."[130] The moral law does not contradict God's natural law, but is a fuller expression of the testimony of natural law.[131] Calvin viewed the moral laws of Scripture as an expression of natural law and as applicable to all human beings at all times.[132]

Though natural law cannot work in us a sufficient knowledge of God's being or salvation, it provides acceptable standards for the political and legal apparatus of a state. Calvin allowed space for states to enact laws of their choice that pertain to their context insofar they deem them as beneficial to their societies and as long as such laws express the requirements of natural law.[133] Yet since moral laws provided a clearer expression of God's natural

---

127. Calvin, *Institutes*, 4.20.8; CO 2.1098: "Facit ergo hominum vitium vel defectus, ut tutius sit ac magis tolerabile plures tenere gubemacula, ut alii aliis mutuo sint adiutores, doceant ac moneant alii alios, ac si quis plus aequo se efferat, plures sint ad cohibendam eius libidinem censores ac magistri."

128. Bouwsma, *Sixteenth Century Portrait*, 210-11; Jeon, "Calvin and the Two Kingdoms," 300, 316, 319.

129. CO 2.1106.

130. Calvin, *Institutes*, 2.8.1; CO 2.267: "Dominus legem scriptam nobis posuit: quae et certius testificaretur quod in lege naturali nimis obscurum erat, et mentem memoriamque nostram, excusso torpore, vividius feriret."

131. CO 2.1106.

132. CO 2.1505-6.

133. CO 2.640.

law, Calvin simultaneously demanded that laws be enacted in accordance with the moral laws of Scripture.[134]

In accordance with his "united but not mingled" doctrine Calvin did not disengage the church and civil government, but related them by giving the civil government some authority in preserving and protecting the true religion. He did not entertain the notion of a neutral or secular state, nor did he consider the possibility of a religious pluralist state, but in accordance with the notion of a Christian state he assigned authorities the task to govern according to both tables of the Decalogue.[135] Civil authorities have the task to protect the external worship of God through laws, edicts and ordinances and to defend true doctrine.[136] Defense of true doctrine entails that the government may not allow blasphemy against the name of God, the practice of idolatry or offense against religion.[137] However, it does not include the right to formulate spiritual doctrine. That is exclusively the task of the church. With respect to spiritual matters the civil government should respect the sovereignty of the church. The church has unlimited freedom to teach and alone has the power to determine the content of faith.[138] The church, conversely, may not interfere in political, civil and legal affairs.[139] Calvin depicted the different forms of authority at stake by distinguishing between the government's "power of the sword" that is coercive in nature, as opposed to the Church's "power of the Word" which is spiritual in nature.[140] This application of the two kingdoms doctrine agrees with Calvin's "united but not mingled" Christological doctrine that permeates his anthropology and societal doctrine. The two kingdoms are united in that they achieve a singular effect. Christ reigns over both kingdoms, the supernatural morals of the heavenly kingdom can be applied to the civil kingdom, while the civil kingdom does provide believers with the security to practice their religion and does equip believers with social virtues that nurture their childship of God. At the same time the two kingdoms should not be mingled. The heavenly kingdom is spiritual, eschatological and eternal in nature, while the civil kingdom is external, temporal and provisional in nature. The heavenly kingdom is concerned with spiritual government that pertains to the life

---

134. *CO* 2.1104. Calvin regarded the moral laws of Scripture as eternally binding, while the ceremonial and judicial laws of Scripture are not relevant to a commonwealth, because they were abrogated after the coming of Christ.

135. See Vorster, "Calvin and Human Rights," 217.

136. *CO* 2.1094.

137. *CO* 2.1094.

138. Esser, "Contemporary Relevance," 379. See Senior, "Cruciform Pilgrims," 125.

139. *CO* 2.1092.

140. Calvin, *Institutes*, 4.11.3, 5; *CO* 2.894, 896: "ius gladii . . . verbi Dei potentia."

of the soul, whereas the civil kingdom has to do with the concerns of the present life that pertain to the arrangements of external affairs. Since these attributes are mutually exclusive, the two kingdoms cannot be confounded. While relating the two kingdoms, Calvin did not impose theocratic rule on society.

Evaluation and Reflection

Calvin did not develop a fully-fledged societal doctrine, but provided key theological and philosophical insights that were utilized by political, social, and legal philosophers such as John Althusius, Hugo Grotius, Groen van Prinsterer, Abraham Kuyper and Herman Dooyeweerd. Regrettably, Calvin's social insights have often been misunderstood, and sometimes, deliberately misappropriated to give legitimacy to certain social points of view. Transformationist, theocratic, liberal, and capitalist social theories have all been justified in the name of Calvin without exponents showing due regard for the historical accuracy of their claims.

Calvin's social insights developed in a pre-modern, pre-industrial, hierarchical and exclusively Christian social setting not yet confronted by the complex social processes of pluralization, stratification, differentiation, and secularization that we experience today. His modelling of the structure of society on the relationship between the soul and body or the inward and outward nature of human existence is too simplistic to be applied to plural modern societies and is, as noted before, based on outdated anthropological premises. The notion of a society governed by a church in the spiritual realm and a government in the material realm might make theological sense to some, but is implausible in highly diverse multi-faith societies.

Yet, Calvin's alignment of the *imago Dei* with God's providence to construct a societal doctrine contains profound insights that might be effectively utilized by modern theologians, especially public theologians, on the pre-condition that they do not invoke Calvin's name to present a supposedly pure Calvinist social theory, undiluted by modern considerations. Firstly, Calvin's notions of common grace, the survival of natural gifts despite sin, and the accessibility of natural law to all people, provides theology with avenues to recognize the total impact of sin, but at the same time to develop a global ethics that makes an overlapping consensus between various ethical discourses possible. Social cohesion is possible even in secular societies, because God infuses all people with a moral sense. The challenge for Christian social ethics is to translate Christian ethical principles into an overlapping moral discourse that can generate the minimal ethical consensus needed to safeguard social stability in diverse, plural societies.

Secondly, Calvin's two kingdoms doctrine warns us not to confuse the penultimate with the ultimate. Creaturely history and eschatological history overlap, but they are not identical, because eschatological history is promissory and not fully actualized in nature.[141] In reaction to the Anabaptists, Calvin warned that Christians need to refrain from imposing transformationist ideals on society as if heaven can be established on earth. Though the spiritual and civil kingdoms are related, they need to be kept apart.[142] The Apartheid system in South Africa (1948–1994) is probably the most vivid example of the dangers involved in employing Christian transformationist ideals to construct an ideal society. However, Calvin's insight also has a bearing on secular social metanarratives such as Marxism and Communism, as well as modern-day nation-building discourses. Though not eschatologically oriented, they often contain a totalising intent that inevitably leads to excessive social control. Inherent to these metanarratives are the idea that some kind of utopia or optimum society can be erected on earth through a radical transformation of society. From a Christian perspective, only God can consummate history. While obedience to God requires Christians to enact practices that address oppression and injustice; these practices should not be distorted by awarding them the ultimate status of goals-in-themselves. This happens when such enactments are no longer responses to the promissory nature of God's eschatological history; but are incorporated into a broader social metanarrative that has as its goal the creation of an optimum society.

Thirdly, in contrast with the highly individualist character of modern societies, Calvin provides us with a symbiotic approach to social ethics that correlate duties and rights closely to each other by grounding his view of society on a charismatic notion of vocation. Calvin depicted Christians as kings, priests and prophets who are called to respond to God's gift of salvation by acting responsibly. By being kings, prophets and priests, churches become communities of truth, justice and mercy. The royal dimension of the church is exhibited in its search for truth and justice and self-withdrawal for the sake of others; its priestly nature is displayed in its diaconal activities that entail self-sacrifice for the sake of others; whilst the prophetic dimension consists in the preaching of the Gospel, education and teaching.[143]

---

141. See Kelsey, *Eccentric Existence*, 452.

142. *CO* 2.192–93.

143. See Welker, *God the Revealed*. In this book, Welker applies Calvin's doctrine on the *munex triplex* to the role of the church in civil society.

For Calvin, the art of associating consisted in human beings recognizing their mutual and reciprocal dependency on each other and their common obligation to serve each other through their gifts to make social cohesion possible.[144] This attitude requires a sense of calling, self-renunciation, love of all human beings, and an attitude of service rather than self-profit.[145] To be sure, Calvin did not deny the need for asymmetrical forms of power in relations such as that between parents and children, rulers and followers. In fact, he regarded them as part of the established natural order. Yet, they are part of a cycle that Kelsey characterizes as "a pattern of reciprocal but differentiated dependency;" that is, a cycle of mutual dependency where the one needs the other to survive and attain goals.[146] This neighbourly attitude that Calvin encouraged stands in stark contrast to the dominant social and economic philosophy of Neo-Liberalism that regards self-realization, competition and profit-seeking as the basic principles that foster social and economic efficiency.[147] This maximal economic growth approach has had devastating effects on the ecology. It also tends to set individuals, communities, and sectors of society up against each other by encouraging an unhealthy kind of economic competition that negatively influences human welfare and social cohesion. Obviously, economic competition cannot be avoided and is part and parcel of a free society; yet the nurturing of a symbiotic spirit of mutual assistance rather than an emphasis on maximal profit might lessen the narcissistic and neurotic impulses of modern culture.

Conclusion

Calvin regarded the human being as a microcosm that reflects the dynamics of a larger macrocosm. It is therefore helpful to use Calvin's understanding of the microcosmic features of the human being as a tool to analyze his societal doctrine. This investigation revealed that the *imago Dei*, human createdness as male and female, the relation between body and soul, the survival of natural gifts after the fall, and God's infusion of general grace in all and special grace in some, forms the theological framework for Calvin's societal doctrine. When we take this into account, we find that Calvin did not entertain a societal doctrine that completely separated the heavenly and earthly realms, nor did he expound an integrationist societal doctrine that fused the two realms. Instead, his societal doctrine displayed a general consistency in

---

144. *CO* 51.222.
145. See *CO* 2.510 for Calvin's grounding of universal love in our God-createdness.
146. Kelsey, *Eccentric Existence*, 877.
147. See Butler, *Milton Friedman*, 191.

uniting, but not mingling, the two realms. Christians are at once citizens of both kingdoms. They cannot escape nor transcend the material realm to find refuge in a spiritual realm. In fact, they must realize that–as images of God–they are part of the family of humanity that lives as a neighbourhood in mutual obligation to each other. In this neighbourhood, believers should fulfill their vocation by renewing and transforming society according to the principles of God's moral law. Though the two kingdoms should be differentiated, they do not stand in adversity, but complement, aid and assist each other in the same way that the two compounds of the soul and body form one person. The moral law of the written word, for instance, promotes and enhances civil society, while the coercive powers of the civil realm provides a safe environment for the proclamation of the Gospel. Yet, the nature of the two kingdoms should not be mingled. The heavenly kingdom is spiritual, eternal and eschatological, while the civil kingdom is temporal and anticipatory in nature. The two kingdoms, therefore, cannot be equated with each other, nor should they be assimilated into one another.

This chapter has indicated that some of Calvin's social insights are implausible in a modern context, yet his theological-anthropological-infused social approach also contains rich perspectives that modern theologians can explore with great effect in a rapidly pluralizing and globalising social environment.

6

Women in Church and Society[1]

Introduction

THE ISSUE OF THE ordination of women in church offices has divided churches in the Calvinist Reformed tradition for a considerable period of time and has played either an aggravating or direct and decisive role in the many schisms that have taken place in this tradition. While some churches within the Calvinist tradition have been ordaining women from as early as 1917, other churches still do not allow women in the office or only ordain women in the office of deacon.[2] In some cases doctrinal differences on the issue have either directly resulted in schisms or are threatening to cause future schisms.[3]

1. This chapter is a shortened and slightly modified version of an earlier published article by Nico Vorster entitled "John Calvin on the Status and Role of Women in Church and Society" in *The Journal of Theological Studies* 68.1 (2017) 178–211. Reproduced by permission of Oxford University Press.

2. Examples of Calvinist Churches that ordained women in offices from an early period are the Congregation Church in England (1917); the Reformed Church of Zürich (1917); United Free Church of Scotland: deacons (1918), ministers, and elders (1929); the Reformed Church of Alsace-Lorraine (1930); and the Reformed Church in France (1949). The Reformed Churches in the Netherlands (Liberated) ordained women in offices in 2017. Examples of Calvinist Churches that still do not ordain women in offices are the Orthodox Presbyterian Church; the Free Reformed Churches of North America; the Reformed Churches in South Africa (only deacons are ordained); the Free Church of Scotland; the Free Church of Scotland (Continuing); the Christian Reformed Churches in the Netherlands; the Evangelical Presbyterian Church of Ireland; the Reformed Presbyterian Church of Ireland; and the Reformed Church in Japan. See Christensen, "Women Clergy and Ecclesiastical Territories."

3. In 1973, a group of conservative congregations within the Presbyterian Church of the United States broke away to form the Presbyterian Church of America (PCA). The main divisive issue was women in the office. The Christian Reformed Church experienced a schism after its 1995 decision to allow women in the offices. At present, the issue of women ordination is causing intense division in the Reformed Churches in South Africa (RCSA). The General Synod of the RCSA decided in January 2015 to convene a Special Synod to address the issue of women in the office in order to restore

The major question that churches in the Calvinist tradition face is whether the recognition of full gender equality in the church, will subvert the basic tenets of Calvinist theology. This issue surfaced repeatedly in the many official studies that churches in the Calvinist tradition have undertaken on the matter.

The abovementioned state of affairs necessitates a re-examination of Calvin's views on gender and its relation to other aspects of his theological corpus. This chapter attempts to provide an accurate historical interpretation of Calvin's doctrine on gender. Thereafter it evaluates the compatibility of Calvin's doctrine on gender with his broader theological corpus.

The structure of the chapter unfolds as follows. The first section discusses the current state of scholarly discourse on the matter. The second segment focuses on Calvin's understanding of the natural order and the createdness of women in the image of God; the third part analyzes Calvin's view of marriage and sexual relationships; while the fourth section examines Calvin's understanding of the role of women in the church and public sphere. The last section proceeds to enquire whether Calvin's understanding of gender relations is consistent with some of the basic tenets of his theological corpus, and whether the recognition of gender equality will require from the Calvinist tradition to subvert their theological heritage.

Scholarly Discourse on Calvin's View of Gender

Up to the 1980's most scholars agreed that Calvin's stance on women is consistently patriarchal and hierarchical in nature, and that his opinions do not deviate much from the views of his contemporaries. The relative consensus on the matter is probably the main reason why so little has been written on the topic until then. The situation changed when female scholars such as Jane Dempsey Douglass, Mary Potter, Suzannah Lipscomb and Mary McFulkerson entered the scene. They questioned the traditional interpretation by calling attention to egalitarian elements in Calvin's theology and his doctrine on gender.

Four lines of interpretation can be discerned on Calvin's understanding of the status and role of women, namely the hierarchical, the protofeminist, the perspectival and womanist interpretations. The hierarchical line of interpretation is followed by authors such as Ronald Wallace (1959), Andrè Bièler (1963), John H. Bratt (1976), Willis P. DeBoer (1976), Rita

---

unity in the church. This unheralded decision reflects the crisis that the church currently experiences on the question. The Special Synod eventually decided not to allow women in the offices of minister or elder.

Mancha (1976), John Lee Thompson (1988, 1989, 1994), and Jason Van Vliet (2009).[4] These authors agree that though Calvin granted women equality in the spiritual realm, he subordinated women in the earthly realm to the authority of men. Women may neither teach nor rule over men, because the order of nature demands it and is according to Calvin inviolable. God's grace does not suspend the created order. Women are therefore men's equals as far as matters of salvation are concerned, but in the familial, ecclesiastical and social spheres women occupy a subordinate status and therefore ought to submit themselves, not only to the authority of their husbands, but to all men. The abovementioned authors agree that Calvin did not challenge the social order of the time, but maintained the status quo.[5]

Though the hierarchical interpretation of Calvin's stance still represents the dominant line of thought in Calvin scholarship, the debate took a surprising turn with the 1985 publication of Jane Dempsey Douglass's book *Women, Freedom and Calvin*.[6] Douglass identified some proto-feminist elements in Calvin's thinking that presumably provide us with evidence that Calvin exhibited a theoretical openness to greater freedom for women in the church as new social contexts arise. Douglass argues that Calvin was open to greater freedom for women on theological grounds, but not willing to implement such changes in the patriarchal society of his time.[7] In contrast to the hierarchical line of interpretation, Douglass contends that Calvin did not believe that the issue of women's subordination belongs to God's eternal inviolable order, but to the realm of human law that is dynamic and open to change.[8] This allows Douglass to interpret Calvin's comment in Book 4 of the *Institutes*[9] that women's silence belongs to matters of *adiaphora* as a sign that he exhibited an openness to a new civil order where women can enjoy greater freedom. She states her argument as follows:

> Calvin sees strong biblical guidance for women's subordinate role in the public life of church and society, and though he finds it appropriate for his own society that women should

---

4. Wallace, *Calvin's Doctrine of the Christian Life*; Bièler, *L'Homme et la Femme*; Bratt, "Role and Status of Women," 1–17; DeBoer, "Calvin on the Role of Women." Also see Mancha, "Woman's Authority," 92; Thompson, "*Creatia ad Imaginem Dei*," 125–43; Thompson, *John Calvin and the Daughters*; Thompson, "Patriarchs, Poligamy and Private Resistance," 3–27; Van Vliet, *Children of God*.

5. See DeBoer, "Calvin on the Role of Women," 238.

6. Douglass, *Women, Freedom and Calvin*.

7. Douglass, *Women, Freedom and Calvin*, 80.

8. Douglass, *Women, Freedom and Calvin*, 24; Douglass, "Christian Freedom," 156.

9. CO 2.889–90.

be subordinate, he holds on principle that the order in which women are subordinate is one determined by human law, ecclesiastical and political. Such order can legitimately be adapted to changing circumstances.[10]

In an essay published in 1991,[11] Claude-Marie Baldwin also identifies progressive elements in Calvin's theology on gender. She calls attention to Calvin's affirmation of the fundamental equality of male and female in sexual matters,[12] accentuates that Calvin regarded a man who despises his wife as actually despising himself because he owes his origin to a woman,[13] and she highlights the fact that Calvin regarded male and female as equals in God's kingdom.[14] Baldwin concludes that there is room in Calvin's thought for the transformation of gender relations. He regarded male and female as spiritually and sexually equal, leading to the Genevan Consistory treating men and women "alike in matters of adultery and divorce."[15] Because of his commitment to order and the "immense task of reforming Geneva," Calvin held to the status quo and did not translate into practise his view of women's silence as *adiaphora*.[16]

Suzannah Lipscomb in a similar vein argues that Calvin's discourse on marriage departed significantly from "pre-Reformation concepts of sexuality."[17] Though Lipscomb acknowledges that Calvin did not escape the doctrine of female subjection; she posits that Calvin's emphasis on companionship and mutuality in marriage, his denial that marriage is purely a means for procreation, and his description of unmarried men as only half men, represents a major shift in the Christian understanding of marriage.[18]

Mary Potter Engel[19] follows a different and quite unique approach by calling attention to the perspectival nature of Calvin's theology. Calvin's seeming inconsistent view on gender relations are, according to Potter, in fact quite consistent. From the absolute perspective of the *cognitio Dei*, that is the eternal perspective of God, men and women are equal, and egalitarianism is the result. From the temporal perspective of the *cognitio hominis*,

---

10. Douglass, "Christian Freedom," 81.
11. Baldwin, "Ethics of Gender Relations," 133–43.
12. Baldwin, "Ethics of Gender Relations," 137.
13. Baldwin, "Ethics of Gender Relations," 138.
14. Baldwin, "Ethics of Gender Relations," 138.
15. Baldwin, "Ethics of Gender Relations," 142.
16. Baldwin, "Ethics of Gender Relations," 142–43.
17. Lipscomb, "Subjection and Companionship," 349.
18. Lipscomb, "Subjection and Companionship," 351.
19. Potter, "Gender Equality and Gender Hierarchy," 725–39.

that is the temporal perspective of human beings, all persons appear as part of an inviolable graded hierarchy, and hierarchism is the result. Potter concludes that Calvin's perspectival approach led him to an affirmation of gender equality, but simultaneously also to the endorsement of stringent hierarchical relationships in the social order.[20] Potter's interpretation differs from the hierarchical line of interpretation in that she posits that there is a bi-focal superstructure in Calvin's theology that combines his seeming inconsistent lines of thought.

Mary McClintock Fulkerson[21] presents a womanist line of interpretation. She is not so much concerned with a correct historical interpretation of Calvin's stance, but asks: What underlies Calvin's reformed logic? Her conclusion is that *semper Reformanda* is the guiding principle in Calvin's theology and must be utilised to liberate women from all kinds of oppression.[22] Fulkerson argues that Calvin's own reformed logic should be applied to new contexts, instead of seeking direct answers from his texts written in a totally different epoch. An affirmation of Calvin's spirit of *semper Reformanda* will unshackle other themes in Calvin's theology that have the potential to make Calvinist theology a true power of liberation.[23]

The abovementioned lines of interpretation clearly indicate that both gender egalitarians and gender complementarians will be able to find evidence in the works of Calvin to substantiate their claims. In an effort to assess the consistency of Calvin's doctrine on gender, the next three sections examine applicable passages in Calvin's letters, commentaries, sermons and the *Institutes*.

The Natural Order and the Image of Women

Earlier we have indicated that Calvin consistently depicted God's original creation as a mirror of God's glory that manifests his good works and eternal power.[24] The human being was placed in this theatre to behold the wonderful works of God.[25] Not only did Calvin regard creation as a theatre of

20. Potter, "Gender Equality and Gender Hierarchy," 136.
21. Fulkerson, "Imago Dei and the Reformed Logic," 95–106.
22. Fulkerson, "Imago Dei and the Reformed Logic," 100.
23. Fulkerson, "Imago Dei and the Reformed Logic," 100.
24. CO 23.10. *Luther's Werke* is referenced in this chapter as *LW*, the Weimar edition of Luther as *WA*, *Melanchton's Werke* as *MW*, and Zwingli's *Sämtliche Werke* as *ZSW*. All the references denote the volume number and page.
25. CO 23.7: "Et illud David est verissimum coelos, utcunque lingua careant, disertos tamen esse gloriae Dei preacones (Ps 19, 1): pulcherrimum hunc naturae ordinem silendo clamare quam admirabilis sit eius sapientia."

God's glory, but it was originally created "perfectly good" (*perfected bonum*); it is an artefact of "the highest perfection" (*summam perfectionem*).[26] This premise naturally implies that Calvin regarded the created natural order as an expression of God's divine will. Humankind may enjoy God's gifts and utilise its fruits, but they may not subvert the natural order of things.[27] This would be an insult to the Creator of all things.

What then is the natural order as far as gender relations are concerned? Calvin's *Commentaries on Genesis* (1554) originated later than his *Commentary on 1 Corinthians* (1546). In his exposition of Genesis 1:26 he clearly struggled with the fact that 1 Corinthians 11:7 seems to ascribe the *imago Dei* only to the male, while Genesis 1:26 awards the image to both male and female.

Calvin's predecessors and contemporaries grappled with the same problem and provided various solutions. Ambrose, John Chrysostom and Gratian's *Decretum* understood 1 Corinthians 11:7 as positing that women don't bear the image of God. Augustine and Aquinas, in contrast, described the image of the woman as secondary in nature. Augustine harmonised Genesis 1:26 and 1 Corinthians 11:7 by stating that the women is the image of God as far as the soul is concerned, while the man is image of God with regard to both soul and body. Adam, after all, was created first as *vir*, while Eve was created as *femina*, that is, as derived from the male. Since the female body is inferior, and the passive receiver in the act of procreation, her body cannot be regarded as the image of God. Augustine also distinguished between the higher masculine part of the soul, that contemplates eternal things, and the lower feminine part of the soul, that reflects on earthly things.[28] Aquinas, in turn, applied the secondary status of the woman's image to her subordinate status to the man in the family.[29]

Calvin's contemporaries generally attempted to find ways to grant women the image of God despite 1 Corinthians 11:7.[30] The result was theories that contained a mixture of equation and subordination. Musculus held that the woman shares God's image through her participation in the man after marriage, while Capito posited that the woman reflects the glory of the man, while the man reflects God's glory.[31] Melanchton argued that though the woman originally possessed the image in terms of reason, righteousness

---

26. CO 23.30.
27. CO 23.10.
28. See Paul, "Patriarchal Anthropology," 115.
29. Horowitz, "Image of God in Man," 179.
30. Thompson, *Daughters of Sarah*, 86; Horowitz, "Image of God in Man," 177.
31. See Thompson, *Daughters of Sarah*, 104.

and her knowledge of God, she holds it to a lesser degree than the man because she does not own the same kind of dominion as the man.[32] Thus, Melanchton thought in terms of dominion and degrees of honour. Luther attempted to harmonise the two texts by distinguishing between the image of the woman as far as spiritual affairs are concerned, and the image as far as external issues are concerned. With regard to spiritual affairs, she possesses the image in equal measure, but in external affairs she displays the image to a lesser degree.[33]

Calvin's exegesis on the matter resembles Luther and Melanchton's line of thought. He provided two proposals to solve the conundrum. His first solution was to harmonize Genesis 1:26 and 1 Corinthians 11:7 by using his often used distinction between the civil realm and the spiritual realm. According to Calvin, the man has superiority over his wife in the civil realm, which means that the man is superior in terms of honour (*gradu honoris*); while in the spiritual realm man and woman are equal before God as far as common humanity, sin and grace are concerned.[34] The question that immediately comes to mind is whether the spiritual realm, which presents the ideal state of things, has any bearing on the civil realm? Ought the ideal spiritual state not to find some way or another into the church and the civil realm?

As noted in the previous chapter, Calvin modeled the distinction between the civil and spiritual kingdoms on the human being's possession of a soul and body.[35] The spiritual realm corresponds to the soul and has bearing on spiritual things, while the civil realm corresponds to the body and pertain to present life.[36] Though these two realms do overlap in the sense that they assist each other, they each possess an integrity of their own and should therefore not be mingled.

When it comes to the relation between man and woman, Calvin was of the opinion that the spiritual equality between the different sexes belongs to the spiritual realm, but cannot be transferred to the civil realm because it would contradict the natural order of things that belong to the penultimate age. Calvin located man's earthly superiority over the woman not in

---

32. *MW* 4.56.
33. See *WA* 42.15; *LW* 27.281.
34. *CO* 23.27. See Thompson, *Daughters of Sarah*, 22.
35. *CO* 2.616; *CO* 2.1092.
36. *CO* 2.616.

the curse after the fall, but in the natural order of things.[37] The curse[38] is not the origin of the woman's subordination to her husband, but it aggravates the coercive nature of the created subordinate relationship so that it becomes a yoke. Whereas the subjection of the woman was previously "a liberal and gentle subjection" (*liberalis et minime*), now, she is cast into "servitude" (*in servitutem*).[39] Hence, Calvin is able to state that the divinely appointed order (*ordem divinitus*) demands that women should act as helpers of their husbands and should accept their husbands as their heads (*caput*) and leaders (*ducem*).[40] With regard to the conjugal and political order, man and woman are not equal.

Thompson sums up Calvin's position well when he states that Calvin teaches a doctrine of women's subordination which is rooted in creation, but which is made more severe by the fall.[41] Calvin, of course, was not alone in grounding women subordination in the original order of creation, he simply followed the same line of thought as Aquinas, Luther and Zwingli.[42] These theologians all regarded hierarchy as an integral part of creation, because without it there can be no order.

Calvin's second solution to solve the seeming contradiction between Genesis 1:26 and 1 Corinthians 11:7 was to redefine the meaning of the *imago Dei* when applied to the woman. As discussed in the first chapter, Calvin defines the *imago Dei* in three ways. First the *imago* indicates the original righteousness and uprightness that Adam initially possessed.[43] God created the human as good and therefore human beings cannot blame their Maker for their natural corruption. Sin is wholly attributable to the

---

37. CO 23.51: "Aliud praeterea notandum est, quum vocatur hoc loco mulier adiutorum viri, non attingi neccessitatem cui post Adae lapsum obnoxii sumus."

38. In contrast to some of his contemporaries, Calvin did not hold the view that Eve was more culpable for the fall than Adam. According to Calvin, when Paul refers in 1 Timothy 2:4 to the women as first deceived, not the man, he speaks only comparatively. Adam is as culpable as Eve because he was drawn by a fatal kind of ambition into her invitation. Moreover, says Calvin, Paul states in Romans 5:12 that sin came not by the woman, but by Adam himself. See CO 23.60.

39. CO 23.72

40. CO 23.47. Also see his sermon on 1 Timothy 2; CO 53.209.

41. Thompson, *Daughters of Sarah*, 21–22.

42. See Aquinas, *Summa Theologiae*, I.92.1.2; Luther, *WA* 42.46; Zwingli, *ZSW* 13.27; Calvin CO 51.735; CO 51.222. It needs to be noted that Luther often contradicted himself on this matter, yet the majority of his pronouncements on the issue point to the stance that the woman was created subordinate.

43. For a more extensive discussion on Calvin's understanding of the *imago Dei*, see Gerrish, "Mirror of God's Goodness," 14.

human being's own volition.⁴⁴ Second, the *imago Dei* is a relational concept that lifts human beings above the animal plane. Human beings are created as rational beings and are, in contrast to animals, able to stand in a filial relationship with God.⁴⁵ As noted in earlier chapters, Calvin emphasized the relational nature of the *imago* in reaction to the realist inclinations of Roman Catholic theology that posited that God creates human beings with natural properties such as habits that actualise their relationship with God. Human communion with God, for Calvin, does not depend on human nature being ontologically continuous with divine nature, but it rests solely on God, who enters through his grace into a relationship with humanity. Lastly, the image denoted for Calvin the original ability of the human being to be a living object and mirror in which the glory of God can be reflected.⁴⁶ For the purpose of this chapter it is important to note that Calvin initially did not regard *dominion* as part of the image. In his early work, *Psychopannychia*, Calvin described human dominion as excluded from the image, but in his Genesis commentary he included dominion as a "very small" (*exigua*) part of the image. He, however, still rejected Chrysostom's view that dominion defines the image.⁴⁷

With regard to the image of women, Calvin was not willing to extend the full implications of the image unconditionally to them. In fact, Calvin described in his comments on Genesis 1:26 the woman as image of God to a secondary degree (*licet secundo gradu, ad imaginem Dei creata*).⁴⁸ This telling statement in Calvin's exposition of Genesis 1:26 ought to be read in conjunction with his comments on 1 Corinthians 11:7. In his Commentary on 1 Corinthians 11:7 Calvin stated that as far as internal spiritual affairs are concerned, women are fully created in the image of God and they are required to reflect holiness and innocence in the same manner as men, but when it comes to external affairs, women do not reflect the glory of God to the same degree, since she is appointed as the helper of her husband and is subjected to him. That is why Paul only refers in 1 Corinthians 11:7 to men as created in the image of God.⁴⁹ Clearly, for Calvin the man reflects God's image to a larger degree than the woman, because control (*dominium*) is in his hands as father of the family and head of his wife.

---

44. Calvin, *Sermons on Genesis 1–11*, 12; SC 11/1.8; CO 23.67.
45. CO 2.138. Also see CO 23.35.
46. SC 11/1.57.
47. See CO 23.25–26.
48. CO 23.46.
49. CO 49.476.

John Lee Thompson correctly states that we find in Calvin's reflections on gender a twofold distinction between an outer and inner image that corresponds with his distinctions between a spiritual and civil realm:

> Calvin, in fact, has two distinct definitions of *imago Dei*. The first pertains equally to men and women and has to do with the invisible "inner good of the soul." That is to say, it primarily concerns salvation and sanctification insofar as these constitute the restoration of God's image in the elect who glorify God spiritually. Calvin's second definition has to do with the way the "headship" of man who is head of a family or the head of a state visibly reflects or "images" the glory of God.[50]

The question is whether Calvin is consistent in his definition of the *imago Dei*, because when he reflects on gender *dominium* suddenly becomes a leading principle in his description of the image, whereas he describes *dominium* in his *Commentaries on Genesis* as only a very small part of the image.[51] We will return to this question in the last section.

Marriage and Sexual Relationships

Witte[52] rightly describes Calvin's view of marriage as "a heterosexual monogamous union presumptively for life—a permanent joining of two opposites "male and female" who have the physical capacity and natural inclination to be united in love." Since God is its Author, Calvin perceived marriage as the most sacred of all human associations.[53] It constitutes a sacred and inviolable covenant that forms one of the roots of society and serves as a prototype for relations in society. The themes that dominated Calvin's reflections on marriage were the headship of the husband over his wife; the importance of mutual respect between husband and wife; their equality when it comes to their sexual relationship and the general unacceptability of divorce, celibacy and polygamy.

The biblical notion of headship featured strongly in Calvin's understanding of the marital relationship. He regarded society as consisting of various orders of authority that impose "yokes" (*subiectionis vinculum*) on the subjects. In his sermon on Ephesians 5:22–26 and his commentary on Ephesians 5:22, Calvin specifically identified the father-son, the

---

50. Thompson, "Women as the Image of God," 132.
51. *CO* 23.25.
52. Witte, "Marriage and Family Life," 459.
53. *CO* 23.49–50.

husband-wife and master-servant relationships as the yokes that God enacts on society to preserve order.[54] Thompson asserts that Calvin distinguished between a hierarchy of headship, that is, God over Christ, Christ over the husband and the husband over his wife.[55] Christ is equally the head of both man and woman in the spiritual realm, but in the civil realm Christ exercises his headship over the woman through the man.[56] The question is: What does the notion of headship entail?

Firstly, Calvin agreed with the vast majority of exegetes of his time that headship entails an element of superiority and authority (*honneur de superiorite*). The husband is the leader (*ducem*) who makes decisions, while the wife should submit. The wife, according to Calvin, has no authority over the man in marriage.[57] DeBoer remarks that "Calvin never relents on asserting the man's right and duty to take the first place and control of the household and its affairs."[58] In practice, Calvin associated the superiority of the husband with him providing for the welfare of his wife and helping her to maintain herself.[59] He regarded the superiority of the husband as *ex officio* embedded in the divinely ordained order of things, not in inherent superior qualities that the husband may possess. Calvin thus stated that the wife should honour her husband even if he displays severe shortcomings in his character.[60]

Calvin was clearly much more nuanced than other classic theologians when it came to the topic of the natural capabilities of women. Aquinas and Luther regarded the female as inferior because she does not possess the same natural capabilities as the male. In his exegesis of Genesis 1:27 Luther asserted that the woman has a weaker disposition (*ingenium*).[61] Satan specifically chose to tempt the woman, because she is the weak part of nature.[62] Aquinas argued on the basis of 1 Corinthians 11:3 and Ephesians 5:22 that God could only have appointed the male as head of the female, because the male is intellectually superior to the female.[63] Aquinas derived this idea from a long line of patristic theologians who viewed Adam and Eve as anthropo-

---

54. *CO* 51.735; *CO* 51.222.
55. Thompson, *Daughters of Sarah*, 375.
56. *CO* 49.474, 476.
57. *CO* 51.740. Also see Thompson, *Daughters of Sarah*, 120.
58. DeBoer, "Calvin on the Role of Women," 251.
59. *CO* 51.741–42.
60. *CO* 51.743–44.
61. *LW* 1.69: "et membra habet dissimilia et ingenium longe infirmius."
62. *LW* 1.151.
63. See George, "What Aquinas Really Said," 11.

logical symbols. Adam represents the superior intellectual component of humanity and Eve the lower affective element.[64] Calvin, however, stayed clear from this line of argumentation. Instead he based the subordination of the female simply on God's command. The man is superior in his degree of honour because he possesses a higher authority. The woman, however, was created equally competent, otherwise God would not have held her equally accountable for the fall.[65]

Secondly, Calvin held that the man's headship resembles Christ's headship over the church. This has implications for both husband and wife. The husband should rule over his wife with the same attitude that Christ reigns over the church. Though the husband is superior in authority, he should remember that his wife is part of his body. When a husband despises his wife or treats her cruelly and tyrannically, he despises God and openly defies God, since the superiority that God awards to the husband is intended to lead to good order, not to diabolical acts.[66] Instead, the husband ought to follow the example of Christ by exercising his authority in such a way that it reflects "companionship" rather than "kingship."[67] Conversely, as Christ rules over the church for her salvation, the wife ought to find safety and security in the headship of her husband:

> The women must understand that since marriage is like a lively image of the spiritual union between us and the Son of God, it is also for their benefit to be under their husbands and to yield them obedience. This will be much more for their profit than if they were at liberty to govern themselves and to do what they please, and to be without constraint.[68]

Despite his hierarchical understanding of the marital relationship, Calvin was adamant that showing mutual respect is a fundamental principle for the Christian marriage. God, after all, instituted marriage to foster "mutual love and support of husband and wife."[69] Calvin understood the reference in

---

64. See Zamfir, "Quest for the Eternal Feminine," 513.

65. *SC* 11/2.675.

66. *CO* 51.735–36.

67. English translation from Calvin, *Sermons on Ephesians*, 570; *CO* 51.740: "mais qu'ils ayent authorité plutost de compagnie que de royaume."

68. Calvin, *Sermons on Ephesians*, 572; *CO* 51.741: "et que les femmes cognoissent, d'autant que le mariage est comme une image vive de l'union spirituelle que nous avons avec le Fils de Dieu, que c'est aussileur bien d'estre sous leurs maris pour leur rendre obeissance et que cela leur sera beaucoup plus profitable que si elles avoyent toute licence pour se gouverner et faire tout à lear appetit et qu'il n'y eust point de bride pour elles."

69. Witte, "Marriage and Family Life," 461.

Genesis 1:27 to man as being created as male and female to signify that the male, and indeed the human race, was incomplete without the female. In fact, he described Adam's initial status as only that of a half man (*dimidium hominem*).[70] The woman thus was added to the male as a companion so that they may be one.[71] In his exposition of Genesis 2:18 Calvin balanced his earlier remarks regarding the woman as helper by making it clear that the husband has mutual obligations to his wife and that he should accept her as his associate. In contrast to Augustine, Aquinas and Luther, who held that women are primarily created for the purpose of procreation,[72] Calvin maintained that the woman was not made for the sake of mere propagation, but to serve as a personal companion.[73] Blanchard notes that Calvin used the biblical theme of the covenant to stress that marriage is not merely intended to order sexual relations, but it is instituted for the purpose of mutual love and companionship.[74]

Calvin further substantiated the need for mutual respect between husband and wife based on their common origin. Since God created male and female from the same source (*principiis*), man ought to be encouraged to recognise himself in his wife, while his wife should "submit herself willingly to her husband, as being taken out of him."[75] If they proceeded from different sources they would have had reason for contempt and envy, but God created Eve from Adam's own flesh so that Adam may embrace his wife as a part of himself.[76] In his expositions of Ephesians 5:22-30, Calvin also based the mutual subjection that ought to exist between husband and wife on their relationship with Christ. The husband ought to show his wife the same kind of strong affection that Christ bestowed on the church, while the wife should act as a helper of her husband, be obedient, avoid resisting the authority of the husband and bear her subjection "patiently" and with "voluntary affection" (*patiement et d'une affection volontaire*) in the same manner that the church obeys Christ.[77]

---

70. *CO* 23.49.

71. *CO* 23.28.

72. Cf. Aquinas, *Summa Theologiae*, I.92.1, and Luther, *LW* 1.116. Also see Reinis, "Catechism and *Querelle des femmes*," 192.

73. *CO* 23.48.

74. Blanchard, "Gift of Contraception," 227.

75. For English translation see Calvin, *Commentaries on Genesis*, 1:132; *CO* 23.48: "Heva quoque vicissim, ut se libenter viro subiiceret, tanquam ex eo sumpta." Also see Calvin, Sermons on Job, 47–52; *CO* 33.146–47.

76. *CO* 23.49.

77. *CO* 51.735–37; *CO* 51.225; *CO* 49.478.

Since husband and wife become one in marriage, Calvin regarded marriage as inviolable and therefore allowed for divorce only in extreme circumstances. In a sermon on Deuteronomy 23:24–24:4, Calvin stated that God allows for divorce in these verses only to preserve the civil order that cannot display perfection. Yet, this does not mean that God's original intention that marriage is inviolable does not stay in full force.[78] In general, he maintained that husbands and wives ought to stay together even if their marriage partners exhibit extreme character faults. Husbands ought to bear patiently the wife's faults, while the wife should obey her husband even if his a drunkard or gambler, because it is the yoke that God has placed on her.[79] Calvin's concern was clearly that married couples would be tempted to divorce for the slightest reasons. Instead he insisted that husband and wife should rather work on their relationship by bridling their wicked affections and keeping their eyes on their spiritual union with Jesus Christ.[80] However, when a husband displays violent behaviour towards his wife, Calvin thought it best that the married couple divorce so that the wife can live in peace.[81] In cases of adultery, Calvin regarded the ties of marriage as automatically severed.[82] He specifically sought to incorporate the right of women to divorce adulterous husbands in the *Marriage Ordinance* of 1547. Though scholars disagree on the extent of Calvin's openness to divorce, I agree with DeBoer that Calvin took a more egalitarian stance towards divorce "as was customary in his day."[83] Bièler also finds Calvin's efforts to have the city council promote fairer divorce legislation significant and as indicative of the manner in which Calvin's theology influenced his social philosophy.[84]

In contrast to the anti-sexual inclinations of some church fathers, specifically Jerome and Augustine, Calvin maintained the fundamental equality between husband and wife with regard to sexual relations. There is mutual accountability in marriage in sexual matters and adultery is equally sinful for both. The husband who despises his wife effectively despises himself.[85] In his comments on Matthew 19:9, Calvin stated that husband and wife have an equal and mutual obligation to fidelity. Even though the husband

---

78. *CO* 28.138.
79. *CO* 51.743.
80. *CO* 51.745.
81. *CO* 28.139.
82. *CO* 28.150.
83. DeBoer, "Calvin on the Role of Women," 255.
84. Bièler, *L'Homme et la Femme*, 73.
85. Baldwin, "Ethics of Gender Relations," 138.

has the upper hand in other matters, in his sexual relationship with his wife, she has the same rights as he because he is not master of his own body.[86]

Calvin viewed celibacy as an unnatural state since he regarded the male without a wife as incomplete. In his comments on Genesis 2:18 he stated that marriage is a common law of man's vocation (*humanae vocationis regulam*), since solitude is not good, except when a person receives a special calling.[87] Together with other Reformers, Calvin viewed the celibacy ideal as unsustainable and as driven by the unbiblical intention to attain salvation through good works.[88] The impact of the Reformation on the re-evaluation of celibacy was immense. Hans Küng notes that the Reformation established a new paradigm that replaced the "mediaeval priority of celibacy" with a heightened sense of the value of marriage.[89] Thompson remarks that marriage "became not only respectable but also religiously significant for Protestants as a vocation, a calling, a divine office in its own right."[90]

Calvin also dismissed polygamy as contrary to God's intended purpose and based his argument on the divine command in Genesis 2:24 that husband and wife will be one flesh:

> It remains, therefore, that the conjugal bond subsists between two persons only, whence it easily appears, that nothing is less accordant with the divine institution than polygamy.[91]

Though Calvin granted that polygamy was a custom in ancient eastern societies, he, in contrast to Luther and Bucer, maintained that the patriarchs erred by adopting these bad customs.[92] Thompson[93] rightly notes that Calvin was of the opinion that Christ did not "restore" monogamy, but that he "re-affirmed" it because the matrimonial law of monogamy was never "suspended."

---

86. *CO* 44.531.
87. *CO* 23.464.
88. Karant-Nunn, "Reformation, Society, Women and the Family," 436.
89. Küng, *Women in Christianity*, 63.
90. Thompson, *Daughters of Sarah*, 9.
91. English translation is from Calvin, *Commentaries on Genesis*, 1:136; *CO* 23.51: "unde facile apparet, nihil minus constaneum esse divinae institutioni quam polygamiam."
92. See Thompson, *Daughters of Sarah*, 228, 232.
93. Thompson, "Patriarchs, Polygamy and Private Resistance," 14.

Women in the Church and in Public

With regard to the role of women in the church and in the public sphere, Calvin was confronted by three seeming contradictions in Scripture. First, Galatians 3:28 appears to assert the fundamental equality between male and female, while 1 Corinthians 11, 14 and 1 Timothy 2 seem to posit the subordination of women. Second, 1 Corinthians 11:5 apparently allows women to pray and prophesy in Christian services as long as they wear scarves, while 1 Corinthians 14:34 and 1 Timothy 2:11 command that women be silent during services. The third problem Calvin faced was to explain the public leadership role that women such as Deborah, Huldah and Sarah play in the Bible, and how to harmonize this phenomenon with passages such as 1 Corinthians 11, 14 and I Timothy 2 which, according to most exegetes of the time, do not allow women to play a leading role in public affairs.

Calvin harmonized the apparent incompatibility of Galatians 3:28 and passages in 1 Corinthians 11, 14 and 1 Timothy 2, by again applying his Two Kingdoms doctrine. When Paul says in Galatians 3:28 that man and woman are equal, he is speaking of Christ's spiritual kingdom in which individual distinctions are not at stake. This pronouncement, according to Calvin, had nothing to do with the outward relationships of humankind or the mind, and therefore Paul can state that there is no difference between male and female.[94] Yet, when it comes to external arrangements and political decorum, Christ is the head of the man and the man is the head of the woman so that they are not on the same footing, but in fact are unequal (*sed locum habeat inaequilitas ista*).[95] Paul commands men not to wear head scarfs in the church because this will detract from the pre-eminence that God assigned them and will obscure their authority over the family through the exercise of which they ought to reflect the glory of Christ.[96] Women, conversely, ought to wear scarves as a sign of subjection in order to honour their head. Not wearing the scarf would be a sign of contempt for their husbands.[97] Calvin understood Paul to base the woman's inferiority in rank

---

94. CO 49.474: "Quum mulierem a viro differre negat, tractat de spirituali Christi regno ubi personae non aestimantur, nec in rationem veniunt: nihil enim ad corpus, nihil ad externam hominum societatem, sed totum in spiritu situm est."
  In his sermon on Galatians 3:28, Calvin, in a similar vein, stated that the distinctions mentioned in this verse pertains to God's grace not the relations of this world; that Paul did not intend to do away with the hierarchies whereby this world is ordered; and that the hierarchies of this world are of a penultimate nature. See CO 50.567–69.

95. CO 47.474.
96. CO 49.475.
97. CO 49.475.

on the woman deriving her origin from the man, and being created for the sake of the man.[98]

Concerning the problem that 1 Corinthians 11:5 seems to allow women to speak in the church, whereas 1 Corinthians 14:34 and 1 Timothy 2:12 command women to be silent during services, Calvin stated that 1 Corinthians 11:5 does not address the issue of prophecy. In fact, it is superfluous for Paul to state that women may not prophesy with her head uncovered, because in 1 Timothy 2:12 he totally prohibits women from speaking.[99] The intent of Paul in 1 Corinthians 11:5 is not to permit women to speak in the church, but he delays his condemnation of this vice (*vitii reprehensionem*) to chapter 14.[100] Another interpretation that Calvin provided in his commentary on Acts 21:9 is that the command in 1 Corinthians 11:5 applies to private gatherings in homes outside church services. In such instances, as was the case with the daughters of Phillip, it was admissible for women to prophesy provided that they wear scarves, because by prophesying in private they do not bring the public ecclesiastic office in disrepute.[101] In his comments on 1 Corinthians 14:34 Calvin maintained that teaching is inconsistent with subjection, because teaching entails presiding over men. Thus, women do not have the authority to teach in public. They also do not have the right to partake in public management, because female government is indecorous and inappropriate.[102] The question arises whether Calvin understood the Pauline commands that women ought to subject themselves to the authority of their husbands as eternal and perpetual laws, or was Calvin open to a future change in gender relations? What inspires this question is Calvin's remarks in his commentary on 1 Corinthians 11:2, 1 Corinthians 14:35 and Book 4 of his *Institutes* where he describes Paul's instructions on women wearing headscarves and them being silent during worship services as regulations framed for the sake of *decorum*, that is, for the sake of order and government (*decenter et ordine*). These issues are not decisive for salvation.[103] In his comments on 1 Corinthians 14:35 Calvin stated that churches do not necessarily have to follow the institutions and traditions of churches from an earlier era. Paul makes external arrangements in 1 Corinthians 14

---

98. *CO* 49.476.

99. *CO* 49.475.

100. *CO* 49.475.

101. *CO* 48.478.

102. *CO* 49.533: "Et saneubicunque valuit ipsa naturae honestas, mulieres omnibus saeculis a publica administratione exclusae fuerunt. Et sensus communis dictat, vitiosam turpemque esse gynaecocratian."

103. *CO* 49.474.

that should not be regarded as inviolable laws.[104] In his *Institutes*, Calvin included the silence of women during services and the wearing of scarves among issues that are not fixed. They are perpetual obligations, but can be suspended under certain circumstances.[105]

As noted earlier, Jane Dempsey Douglass deduces from the above-mentioned texts a proto-feminism in Calvin. She argues that Calvin derived his interpretation from the *querelle des femmes* debate in the humanistic circles of Europe on the superiority or inferiority of women.[106]

In response to Douglass it ought to be noted that though Calvin probably had knowledge about the *querelle des femmes* debate, his works do not provide any evidence that he either participated in or was influenced by the debate. Moreover, even though issues of polity are for Calvin not essential for salvation, and though they may be violated in cases of emergency, it does not mean that they are indifferent or unimportant for the decorum of the church.[107] Calvin's allowance for women to teach in emergencies, as was the case with Deborah, does not mean that he believed that the external order can be suspended altogether.[108]

Thompson rightly notes that despite Calvin's vague references to the silence of women in the church as an issue of *adiaphora*, he generally treated the matter as important. Calvin regarded women's silence "as a precept which is explicitly taught in Scripture and thus is not open to revision or amendment."[109] In addition, Calvin did not base the woman's subordination purely on human and ecclesiastical law, as Douglass suggests, but on the created order itself. Since the woman's subordination emanates from God's created order, not the curse, the nature of the male-female relationship is for Calvin not open to change.[110] In his comments on 1 Corinthians 11:12, Calvin stated explicitly that the divinely appointed order between the sexes is not open to change, but that the woman ought to be satisfied with her state of subjection.[111] He repeated these comments in his sermon on 1 Timothy 2 when he stated that once God has established an order in his sovereign rule, humankind must keep to that order. Women must accept their submission without complaint because human beings have no right to resist God's

---

104. *CO* 49.532–36.
105. *CO* 2.889–90.
106. Douglass, "Christian Freedom," 167.
107. See, Thompson, *Daughters of Sarah*, 392.
108. Thompson, *Daughters of Sarah*, 382.
109. Thompson, *Daughters of Sarah*, 361.
110. See *CO* 53.210.
111. *CO* 49.478.

order.¹¹² Shortly before identifying the silence of women as *adiaphora* in 1 Corinthians 14:35, Calvin stated the following in his comments on verse 34:

> The office of teaching in the church is a superiority in the Church, and is, consequently, inconsistent with subjection. For how unseemly (indecorum) a thing it were, that one who is under subjection to one of the members, should preside over the entire body.¹¹³

Calvin's stance can also be seen in his response to the question on how the church ought to deal with the biblical examples of women who occupied public positions. Calvin stated that these exceptions do not establish a new norm, but they represent an extraordinary state of affairs where God in his providence calls women to shame men and chastise their disobedience to God.¹¹⁴ God can and sometimes does suspend the natural order in his providence, but this does not mean that Christians have the right to dispense with God's natural order altogether. This would amount to a "mingling of heaven and earth" (*coelam quodammodo terrae*).¹¹⁵

Calvin wrote a revealing letter on this issue in May 1559 to William Cecil, Secretary of Elizabeth 1, to regain Elizabeth's support after John Knox distributed a strongly worded pamphlet against governance by women. In this letter Calvin diplomatically affirmed that there are extraordinary occasions that allow for government by women. In his providence God may sometimes raise women such as Deborah and Huldah to condemn the "supineness" of men. When God sets up such governments, men are not permitted to unsettle them. Yet, Calvin still maintained that a gynaecocracy is a deviation from the "established order of nature."¹¹⁶ In fact, in his Commentary on 1 Timothy 2 he called it *portenti*, that is, a monstrous thing or something that causes terrible things to happen.¹¹⁷ Thompson aptly states

---

112. *CO* 53.211: "Ainsi apprenons de suyvre la doctrine que sainct Paul nous monstre en ce passage c'est asçavoir de tenir l'ordre de Dieu: et quand une chose aura esté instituée de celuy qui a toute puissance, que ne repliiquions point là dessus, mais que ce nous soitla vraye regle et souveraine."

113. Translation from Calvin, *Corinthians*, 1:468; *CO* 49.533: "munus docendi praefecturam esse in ecclesia, ideoque pugnare cum subiectione. Quam enim indecorum fuerit, quae subiecta est uni membro, praeesse universo corpori?"

114. Cf. Thompson, "Women as the Image of God," 136.

115. *CO* 52.276.

116. Calvin, "To William Cecil," 211–15.

117. *CO* 52.275.

that Calvin's letter to Elizabeth 1 is a "prime example of Calvin's refusal to shift his stance even when it would have been pragmatic to do so."[118]

In conclusion, it seems that even though Calvin was under certain conditions open to future changes in the rites that arrange the external decorum of the church, he certainly was not prepared to compromise on the principle of decorum itself, nor the requirement of the natural order that women ought to subject themselves to men.[119] This entails that women cannot occupy any leading positions in either the church or in the public sphere. The practice of women occupying teaching offices in the church would not endanger the believer's salvation, and in cases of necessity woman teachers could indeed be used to prevent the church from falling in disarray. Yet, under normal circumstances it would certainly be indecorous and contrary to God's will for women to teach.[120]

Evaluation and Reflection

From the discussion so far it is clear that Calvin was neither a misogynist nor a proto-feminist regarding gender relations. His thoughts on the social status of women were indeed imbedded in the patriarchal and hierarchical thoughts of his time, yet he also deviated on some key points from his predecessors and contemporaries. The important question that follows is: How do Calvin's views on gender fit within his general theological corpus? How consistent was Calvin's doctrine on women? Are Calvin's thoughts on gender reconcilable with the basic tenets of his theology?

The Validity and Consistency of Calvin's Exegesis

Calvin professed the infallibility, consistency and unity of Scripture. When he detected possible contradictions in Scripture he often attempted to harmonize the applicable passages. His voluminous effort to harmonise the Gospels is a clear example of this approach. As noted already, Calvin had to make various exegetical choices to harmonise seemingly contradicting passages on the status of women. The question is whether the harmonizations are exegetically valid, or do they display an artificial effort to provide coherence to a theological system?

The first important exegetical choice that Calvin had to make pertains to the meaning of "helper" in Genesis 1:26. The term does not necessarily

---

118. Thompson, *Daughters of Sarah*, 76.
119. See Miles, "Theology, Anthropology," 305.
120. See Thompson, *Daughters of Sarah*, 381–82.

have a hierarchical meaning. Even if it denotes subordination, there is no evidence that it asserts inferiority. In fact, in the Psalms God is regularly called the human being's helper.[121] Calvin interpreted "helper" as denoting a divinely appointed order where the women is assigned as a help of the male who acts as her head and leader.[122] Without having any textual support, Calvin continued to describe the female as the lesser companion (*adiumentum inferius*).[123] Calvin thus understood "helper" as a state of subordination and of inferiority. Yet, for the discernible reader it should be clear that "helper" is used in the Genesis account within the context of companionship. God assigns the male a help to alleviate his loneliness. Calvin clearly imported here ideas from elsewhere, not the Genesis material. DeBoer[124] rightly notes that Calvin's reading of Paul made him confident that female subordination is in accordance with the order of creation, but Calvin never realised that the creation account itself provides little support for his view.

A second important exegetical choice relates to the question whether the Genesis account and Pauline texts pertain to all gender relations or only to husband-wife relations. Calvin asserted the latter. The male's headship does not only pertain to the household but is part of the whole order that God has created. Males are therefore heads of all women.[125]

Calvin grounded his decision in the notion that man was created first, while the woman came from the flesh of the man. In his sermon on 1 Corinthians 11:4-10, Calvin posited that the origination of the woman from the man establishes her in a position of subjection.[126] The Genesis account, in fact, does not make the claim that the male is superior because he was created first, but Calvin read the Genesis account through Pauline glasses without asking whether it is indeed rational to argue that something that originates from something else is necessarily subordinate to its origin. Moreover, Calvin never asked whether the passages he was explicating pertain to marriage or universal gender relations. He merely asserted that the hierarchical nature of the created order demands the universal superiority of men and the subordination of women. Thus, when commenting on 1 Corinthians 14:34 Calvin simply extended Paul's prohibition of women

---

121. See Zamfir, "Quest for the Eternal Feminine," 503; DeBoer, "Calvin on the Role of Women," 241. See Ps 30:11; 54:6; 115:9-11; 118:7.

122. CO 23.47.

123. CO 23.47.

124. DeBoer, "Calvin on the Role of Women," 244.

125. CO 49.724: "qu'il est chef. Et de qui? Des femmes: car il ne nous faut point regarder en une maison seulement, mais en l'ordre que Dieu a établi en ce monde."

126. CO 49.728-29.

speaking in the church to the sphere of public governance without having any textual support to do so.[127]

A third important exegetical choice pertains to the relation between Galatians 3:28 and 1 Corinthians 11, 14 and 1 Timothy 2. If Calvin was interested in making a case for gender equality he could have subordinated Paul's pronouncements in the latter texts to Galatians 3:28. This passage, after all, is Christological in nature and gives expression to the freedom that Christians across all classes and distinctions receive in Christ. However, Calvin's remarks in his commentary on Galatians 3:28 were very brief and simply stated that our hope for salvation does not depend on the law.[128] In his sermon on Galatians 3:28 he asserted that this new oneness only applies to the spiritual realm, not the established created order.[129] But why would Calvin not allow oneness of male and female in Christ to filter through to social relations? DeBoer[130] is probably correct when he states that Calvin removed gender equality from the "earthly realm and its relationships" to "do justice to Paul." In other words, he attempted to harmonize Pauline passages with the creation account, and Galatians 3:28 with 1 Timothy 2 and 1 Corinthians 11 and 14. In doing so, he chose for the patriarchal explanation rather than the egalitarian one. However, neither the Genesis accounts nor Paul himself ever applied this distinction between the earthly and spiritual realms. This, instead, is Calvin's own theological construction. DeBoer[131] rightly notes that there is a "discrepancy here not easy to solve."

The fourth choice Calvin had to make was how to harmonize the seeming inconsistency of 1 Corinthians 11:5 with 1 Corinthians 14:34. As noted earlier, 1 Corinthians 11:5 apparently allows women to pray and prophesy in the church on the precondition that they wear scarfs as a sign of subjection to their husbands, while 1 Corinthians 14:34 commands that women should stay silent during services. Calvin could have subordinated 1 Corinthians 14:34 to 1 Corinthians 11:5 as some exegetes do. Yet, Calvin chose to subordinate 1 Corinthians 11:5 to 1 Corinthians 14:34 by stating in his comments on Acts 21:9 that 1 Corinthians 11:5 alludes to gatherings at homes.[132] He, however, had no textual support to make such a claim. Contrary to his general approach to exegesis, he engaged here in pure speculation.

---

127. *CO* 49.533.
128. *CO* 50.223.
129. *CO* 50.567–568.
130. DeBoer, "Calvin on the Role of Women," 254.
131. DeBoer, "Calvin on the Role of Women," 254.
132. *CO* 48.478.

A further exegetical choice that confronted Calvin pertains to the meaning of "prophesy." Both Acts 2:17 and Joel 2:28 speak of women receiving the spiritual gift of prophesying. In his explications Calvin were at pains to explain that prophecy should be distinguished from teaching in public. In his Commentary on Joel 2:28 Calvin stated that prophecy relates to the gifts of understanding and wisdom, while in his comments on Acts 21:9 he commented that the gift of women to prophesy was restricted to private gatherings. Both explications, however, clearly did not do justice to the respective texts.[133] Calvin's final solution was to simply state that the gifts of prophecy ceased to exist. He provided various speculative reasons for the ceasing of the gift of prophecy, but these were also not based on any scriptural evidence.[134]

Lastly, Calvin had to deal with texts that seem to imply that there were women deacons in the early church. In 1 Timothy 5:9, for instance, Paul recommends Phoebe to the church in Rome and calls her *diakonos*. Since Calvin could not accept the notion of a female deacon in the church, he interpreted the passage as referring to the feminine order of widows that did charitable work in the early churches. This, of course, conveniently brought the passage back into harmony with Calvin's doctrine on gender.[135]

In conclusion, Calvin's exegesis on the status of women was remarkably consistent, but this consistency was artificial in nature. In fact, he alternated the meaning of some passages to provide a coherent doctrine that establishes the universal subordination of women to men. In doing so, his patriarchal mindset came to the fore. The basic pattern in Calvin's exegesis was to read biblical material on gender relations through the glasses of what he perceived to be the created natural order as explicated by Paul.[136]

Woman as imago Dei to a Secondary Degree

As indicated earlier, Calvin's doctrine on the *imago Dei* experiences difficulties as far as the application of the image to women are concerned. Calvin resisted Chrysostom's notion that *dominium* is part of the image, though he stated later on that *dominium* is only a very small part of the image.[137] However, when it comes to the image of the woman, *dominium* suddenly

---

133. CO 42.567; CO 48.477.

134. CO 48.477.

135. CO 52.310. See DeBoer, "Calvin on the Role of Women," 268.

136. In this regard, see DeBoer, "Calvin on the Role of Women," 269.

137. CO 23.25. For a more extensive discussion on the issue, see Van Vliet, *Children of God*, 23.

seems to be not only a small part of the image, but the leading interpretative principle in his definition of the *imago*. The woman is an image of God to a secondary degree, because she does not possess *dominium* in the human realm, and therefore does not reflect the glory of God to the same degree as the man. In his comments on 1 Corinthians 11:4, Calvin quite explicitly related the image of the male to *dominium*:

> For in his own home the father of the family is like a king. Therefore he reflects the glory of God, because of the control that is in his hands.[138]

The inconsistency is probably due to Calvin being forced to invoke *dominium* to harmonize Genesis 1:26 with 1 Corinthians 11:7. Thompson makes the following telling comment on this issue:

> It is no surprise to find Calvin equally forced to invoke "dominion" by the sheer intractability of 1 Cor. 11:7. It is not surprising; it is merely ironic, not only because Calvin seems unaware of the shift in his definition, but also having left Chrysostom so boldly by the front door, he must return to him now by way of the back.[139]

Calvin's view on the *imago Dei* displayed a tension between a spiritual equality that is exhibited by the inner image and hierarchicalism that is brought about by *dominium* as a reflection of the outer image.[140] What makes Calvin's distinction between an inner and outer image of the woman perplexing is that he initially resisted in *Psychopannychia* Osiander's outward notion of the image as something reflected by the body. Instead, Calvin held that the image be sought in the inner good of the soul, that is, in the spiritual qualities that the human possess.[141] Yet, when Calvin referred to the image of the woman he suddenly linked the image, not to the spiritual qualities of the human being, but to external relations of authority.

Conclusion

The question posed at the onset was whether the recognition of gender equality and the ordination of women in Calvinist churches will amount to

---

138. Calvin, *Corinthians*, 1:354; CO 49.475: "Est enim paterfamilias instar regis domi suae. Gloria enim Dei in eo relucet propter dominium quo pollet."

139. Thompson, *Daughters of Sarah*, 114.

140. See Potter, "Gender Equality and Gender Hierarchy," 731.

141. On the debate between Calvin and Osiander, see Gerrish, "Mirror of God's Goodness," 214.

a serious subversion of the essence of Calvinist theology. In order to answer this question this chapter attempted to provide an accurate historical interpretation of Calvin stance on the role and status of women. It also probed the consistency of Calvin's doctrine on gender and its compatibility with Calvin's theological corpus.

The finding of this chapter is that Calvin's view of the status of women in church and society was largely located within the patriarchal and hierarchical line of thought that was so dominant in his times. Calvin held to the generally accepted views of his time and made no fundamental attempt to reorder the status of women in society. Compared to his contemporaries, Calvin did display greater openness to gender equality on issues such as companionship in marriage, the right of women to divorce adulterous husbands, equality in sexual relationships and the equal rational competence of women. Calvin also did not indulge himself in the anti-women rhetoric so prevalent in the works of his contemporaries. These features set him apart from other classic theologians such as Augustine, Thomas Aquinas, Luther and Knox, yet they do not represent a major reformation of gender relations and can hardly be regarded as a form of proto-feminism.

On the question whether the recognition of gender equality will subvert Calvin's theology, this chapter argues that Calvin's exegesis on the matter was artificial and that he interpreted some texts, specifically the creation account, to fit his theological position. His patriarchal understanding of gender relations also stands in a tension with other aspects of his theology, such as the *imago Dei* and the original goodness of creation. His position on women therefore provided a mixed and often inconsistent picture rather than an authentic example of his theological project. Since Calvin was not able to provide a doctrine on gender that is fully compatible with some of the most important tenets of his theological corpus, the issue on whether Calvinist churches stay true to their tradition when granting women more rights in the church will not depend on whether they follow Calvin's explicit views on the issue of gender. The true challenge is rather to resolve issues such as women ordination while being true to the basic tenets of a Calvinist understandings of creation, scripture, the *imago Dei*, justification and regeneration, vocation, the universal priesthood of all believers, Christian freedom and the indwelling of the Spirit in the human being. In fact, the challenge for Calvinist churches is to reconcile the Calvinist doctrine on gender with the whole Calvinist theological corpus—something which Calvin himself was not quite able to do.

7

Summary[1]

CALVIN'S ANTHROPOLOGY CAN BE typified as theocentric, since he grounds all being in God who is the Origin of life and breaths energy into all things. Calvin depicts the human person as a microcosmic image of God that reflects God's glory the brightest within the hierarchy of created mirrors in God's creation. The brightness of the human mirror consists in her being created in order to relate to God through the Mediator Christ. By contemplating God's works, the human person ought to develop a sense of God's magnificent power and infinite grace and should be inspired to glorify God. Chapter 1 analyzed Calvin's understanding of the created structure of the human being by exploring his views on the human's position in creation; the original goodness of the human being; the human beings' created relatedness to Christ; the relation between body and soul; the faculties of the soul and the meaning of the *imago Dei*. Reflections on these topics show that Calvin's anthropology is decisively influenced by the ontological premise that the divine and human realms are united but not mingled (*unitis non confusis, distinctio sed non seperatio, coniunctus non confundis*). The human being radiates God's glory by resembling the attributes of God, but does not share the essence of God. Calvin opposes all kinds of monism that might fuse divine and human essence or compromise the integrity of the spiritual and material realms.

---

1. The summary contains material of the following published articles by Nico Vorster: "Calvin on the Created Structure of Human Nature: The Influence of His Anthropology on His Theology" in the *Journal of Theology for Southern Africa* 151 (2015) 162–82; "Assessing the Consistency of John Calvin's Doctrine on Human Sinfulness" in *HTS Teologiese Studies* 71.33 (2015) 1–8; "And Behold a Ladder'. Descent and Ascent in Calvin's Soteriology" in *In Luce Verbi* 49.1 (2015) 1–8; "John Calvin on the Christian's Social Responsibility. Cultural Activist or Modest Social Reformer?" in *Dialog: A Journal of Theology* 56.4 (2018) 441–48; "Calvin on Human Reason" in *In Luce Verbi* 48.1 (2014) 1–9; "'United but Not Confused': Calvin's Anthropology as Hermeneutical Key to Understanding His Societal Doctrine" in the *Journal of Church and State* 58.1 (2016) 117–42; and "John Calvin on the Status and Role of Women in Church and Society" in the *Journal of Church and State* 68.1 (2017) 178–211. These articles are used by permission.

SUMMARY

The historical section in chapter 1 was followed by a critical evaluation of Calvin's understanding of the created structure of the human being. Critical questions were asked about the biblical basis of Calvin's understanding of the human faculties and his hierarchical understanding of creaturely reality. The chapter identified Calvin's theocentric premise as the most promising and theologically important feature of his anthropology. Calvin decentered the human being by locating the center of human existence outside "human self-determination and human self-consciousness in a life of communion with God and fellow human beings."[2] Calvin relates the I, We and It to a Thou, thereby assisting us in avoiding reductionist anthropologies that treat proximate contexts as ultimate contexts.[3] Calvin's grounding of human dignity in the human's divinely created status stands in stark contrast to the Kantian tradition that approached human dignity, rights and ethical conduct from the perspective of the innate rational capacities of the human being.[4] For Calvin humans ought to treat each other with dignity, not out of a respect for innate human properties, but as a result of their respect for the Creator. This theocentric premise of Calvin's anthropology allows for a Christian ethics that can be applied universally to all human beings and created things. Secondly, Calvin avoided the theological abstraction of realist ontological speculation, by presenting Christ as the "paradigmatic example" of the *imago Dei* who shows us what imaging God is all about.[5] This feature of Calvin's theology enables him to articulate a theology that is practical and pastoral in nature. Lastly, Calvin's theocentric anthropology provides a bridge to promising eco-ethical perspectives, since he relates creation in the first place to God not the human person. Creation is a theatre of God's glory and a macrocosmic mirror of God's goodness that humans need to treat as a blessing of God.[6]

The accusation is often leveled at Calvin that his doctrine on sin is inconsistent, contradictory, deterministic and culpable of making God the Author of sin. Chapter 2 probed the validity of these accusations by analysing the consistency of John Calvin's doctrine on human sinfulness and by asking whether Calvin's understanding of sinful human nature is theologically valid. In doing so, the investigation kept in mind the structural makeup of his theology, the rhetorical intent of his utterances, and the devices he employed to harmonize possible inconsistencies in his theology.

2. Vorster, "Theocentric Premises," 107.
3. Vorster, "Theocentric Premises," 110.
4. See Kelsey, *Eccentric Existence*, 278.
5. See Vorster, "Theocentric Premises," 111.
6. Vorster, "Theocentric Premises," 113.

The first section discussed the rhetorical and theological intent of Calvin's doctrine on sin. It argued that Calvin used the sinful nature of the human being as a foil to emphasize the glory of God's grace. His denigrating depictions of fallen human nature should not blind us to the fact that he regarded God's restorative grace as enjoying precedence over the destructive power of sin. This fundamental position of Calvin can be easily obscured if the dialectical nature of Calvin's construction is not taken into account.

The following section discussed the relation between divine sovereignty and human accountability in Calvin's theology. Calvin employed the notion of relative necessity, in contrast to necessity as coercion, to claim that though humans sin necessarily, they are not coerced into sinning by external compulsion. Humans are therefore liable and accountable for their own actions. Calvin furthermore utilized the two causes doctrine of Aristotle and Thomas Aquinas to argue that though God is not the Author of sin, sin does not fall outside of God's will. The sovereign God is the first cause of all things, and in this sense wills everything. Yet, the secondary causes that emanate from first causes are instrumental and contingent in nature. Since humans operate within the field of secondary causes, they are culpable for their own actions. Nonetheless, due to God's grace, secondary causes don't have the final say because God directs all things to serve his ultimate aim, which is good and pure.

The third section examined Calvin's view on the effects of sin on the *imago Dei*. Calvin's initial position was that the fall destroyed the *imago Dei*. However, as Jason Van Vliet rightly indicates, Calvin modified his position after his debate with Pighius to hold that sin corrupts all parts of human existence without totally destroying the image in us.[7] What remains after the fall are remnants of our original excellence. Calvin explained this dialectic by distinguishing between our natural and supernatural gifts. The fall has destroyed our supernatural gifts and our ability to turn to God by ourselves and to conquer sin through our own efforts. Yet, sin does not destroy or dehumanize us. God's common grace prevents humanity from descending into chaos by preserving their natural gifts, such as an innate sense of right and wrong and the ability to practice arts and sciences.

The chapter concluded by evaluating Calvin's doctrine on sin and exploring its constructive potential for modern reformed anthropology. It argued that characterizations of Calvin's doctrine on sin as deterministic, logically inconsistent and culpable of making God the Author of sin are not well founded. Factors often overlooked are the dialectical nature of his theological reflection on sin, the chronological evolution of his thought on

---

7. Van Vliet, *Children of God*, 256.

sin and the fact that he does not regard God and human beings as operating on the same ontological level. When these factors are taken into account, Calvin's doctrine on sin proves to be fairly consistent and reconcilable with the rest of his theology.

Calvin's doctrine on sin contains rich impulses that can be fruitfully contextualized. In contrast to modern secular culture's inclination to resist notions of guilt, Calvin's articulation of the systemic nature of sin puts the issue of collective and historical guilt on the table. How should societies deal with the systemic aftereffects of colonialism, genocides, political oppression and economic exploitation? Liberal democratic systems are, seemingly, not well equipped to address these issues because of their difference-blind approach to individual rights and human autonomy that often show little regard for historic patterns of social discrimination. Another significant feature of Calvin's doctrine on sin is his depiction of idolatry, materialism and self-deception as the ultimate effects of sin. Idols and materialistic attitudes naturally arise when humans become carnally minded. The question is whether excessive consumerism and materialism are not the by-products of secular culture's rejection of transcendent beliefs and its adoption of an imminent frame of mind? Lastly, Calvin's distinction between God and the world of secondary causes, might help us to find an alternative to forms of monism that compromises human integrity by deifying all things, and ontological dualism that deride God's sovereignty by recognizing certain aspects and spheres of reality as able to function independent and outside of God's reign.

Union with Christ is a fundamental theme in Calvin's theology, and in a sense, expresses his understanding of the essence of the Gospel. The third chapter started by discussing Calvin's doctrine on the two natures of Christ. His criticisms of Nestorianism, ubiquitism, Stancarism and Eutychianism was discussed, as well as the ontological presuppositions that underlie his understanding of Christ's two natures. The next section discussed Calvin's soteriology within his scheme of descent and ascent. This scheme denotes a cycle of exchange between the infinite God and finite beings: because of Christ's descent to earth, we can ascend to heaven, through Christ's appropriation of mortality, we acquire immortality, and because of Christ's submission to weakness, we receive heavenly strength.[8] Our depravity prevents us from ascending to God through our own efforts; instead, Christ descends to us through the incarnation. He is the perfect mirror of God's image and reflects God's glory to us in an unparalleled bright and direct sense. Christ's descent to earth culminates in his substitutionary work whereby he makes

8. *CO* 2.1003.

the great exchange possible. With Christ's glorification, a second cycle of ascent and descent follows. When Christ's human nature ascends to heaven, he sends the Spirit as his substitute who is the bond between us and Christ, bestows Christ's benefits on us, and unites us with Christ. The Holy Spirit engrafts believers in the body of Christ and makes it possible for believers to have communion with God without being assimilated into divine nature.

Calvin regarded justification and sanctification as the twofold benefit of our union with Christ. He employed the dictum of *distinctio sed non seperatio* to explain the relation between justification and regeneration. This terminology resembles the formulas that he utilized to describe the relation between the two natures of Christ and the relation of the human body and soul (*unitis non confusis and coniunctus non confundis*). Justification denotes our forensic acquittal, whereas regeneration (sanctification) signifies the gradual communication and transfusion of Christ's righteousness to the believer. The restoration of God's image in the believer occurs through a mortification of our sinful desires and a simultaneous vivification (ascent) of our spirit to God. Self-denial, cross-bearing and meditation on the future life are the three key characteristics of our life in union with Christ. The administration of the sacraments serves as vivid reminder of God's descent to us in order to raise us up to him through the Spirit of Christ.

The last section of the chapter commented on recent debates about theosis in Calvin's theology and probes the constructive potential of Calvin's doctrine on the believer's union with Christ. The argument offered was that Calvin understood the Spirit as imparting his energy to human beings without fusing divine and human essences. Calvin, moreover, utilized the notion of descent-ascent as a tool to weave together juridical and mystical categories in his soteriology. By using the dynamic notion of a Spirit enabled descent-ascent cycle in our union with Christ, Calvin was able to integrate juridical and participationist soteriological motifs without absorbing them into another. The descent-ascent scheme also qualifies Calvin's soteriology as profoundly theocentric, since we cannot ascent to God if God does not descend to us and enables us through his Spirit to ascent to him. True to Calvin's ontological premise of united but not mingled, the ascent-descent scheme allows Calvin to differentiate between the transcendent and immanent realms, yet also correlate them. Finally, the scheme endows his soteriology with a strong pneumatological and eschatological orientation since the believer is "bound up;" in the glorified Christ and is continually involved in a process of "being raised up."

Chapter 4 analyzed Calvin's profound scepticism in human reason. The chapter commenced by discussing the intellectual environment of Calvin's day; something that inevitably influenced his thinking on reason.

SUMMARY

Calvin rejected the Aristotelian and Scholastic notion that human beings possess innate properties or habits that, when cultivated, enable them to reach their telos. Instead, he related the problem of knowledge to the predicament of the self. Calvin regarded reason as an endowment of God that is unique to the human and that enables her to surpass all other creatures. In its original state, reason was a noble faculty that acted as the guide and ruler of the soul enabling human souls to raise up to God and experience eternal happiness. Sin, however, corrupted human reason to such a degree that human beings are no longer able to ascend to God. They are plunged into darkness and epistemological blindness, incapable of penetrating the mysteries of God's kingdom. Not only does sin "blind" the human mind, but it also causes him to create and venerate earthly idols in the place of God. Without God's grace, humans would be totally helpless. However, God preserves through his common grace some remnants of the *imago Dei*, most importantly, the faculties of reason and will. With regard to reason, Calvin distinguished between heavenly and natural knowledge. As far as heavenly things are concerned, the human person is totally blind and unable to secure his salvation. When it comes to natural knowledge human persons still possess a sense of right and wrong, an awareness of God's existence, the ability to practise arts, and a desire to preserve the social order. The survival of these remnants are not due to indestructible properties in the human person, but the Spirit's presence in human lives, including, the unregenerate. Though Calvin's was indeed sceptic about the ability of reason when it comes to knowing God; his position did allow for a universally shared social ethics and the cultivation of virtues. He, afterall, posited that the *imago Dei* was not totally destroyed by sin and that even non-believers are able to acquire virtue through the common grace of God.

The next section discussed Calvin's perspective on the relation between grace and reason. According to Calvin, the Spirit opens our eyes through the eyeglasses of God's Word that dissipates the darkness in our lives and shows us God's grace. Our knowledge of God, however, is inherently analogical in nature and consists in a knowledge of God's works, rather that the essence of his being. The Holy Spirit regenerates us by working faith in us and renewing our faculties of reason and will. His work is not instantaneous nor coercive in nature, but gradually transforms our faculties by directing it towards God's will. Whereas depraved reason posits its own autonomy, faithful reason submits the human person to God's Word. The chapter concluded with perspectives on the constructive potential of Calvin's epistemology. It argued that Calvin's scepticism of the powers of reason is highly relevant in a postmodern age. Calvin demythologized reason by relating it to the predicament of the self and the self's inclination to create idols in the place of God. Detached from God, human reason tends to seek replacements for God by attaching an ultimate significance to things that belong to the penultimate realm. This reality necessitates a continuous deconstructive critique of human thinking in the spirit of *semper Reformanda*. Calvin, moreover, indicated that reason can not function properly without faith. Faith binds us to the true source of Wisdom. Detachment from this source inevitable leads to "carnal mindedness."

There is confusion among scholars on the exact nature and structure of Calvin's societal doctrine. Various scholars hold that Calvin made a sharp distinction between the spiritual and civil realms; others argue that Calvin had a theocratic outlook on society; while some describe Calvin's societal doctrine as ambiguous. Chapter 5 maintained that Calvin's doctrine of society is mainly informed by his theological anthropology, which regards the human being as a microcosm of reality, which is the macrocosm. Calvin grounded the roots of society in the created characteristics of the human person and in God's grace. The *imago Dei* indicates that all people have a common origin and shared dignity, while our createdness as male and female signifies that we are social beings with an innate desire for communion. Community is made possible by the diversity of gifts that God bestow on humans and the divine calling that every person receives to exercise a distinct duty within a particular mode of life.

Calvin, furthermore, modeled the relation between the heavenly and civil kingdoms on the "united but not mingled" relation between the human's body and soul, which, in turn, exemplifies the two natures of Christ. As the human body and soul are two distinctive compounds that contain their own peculiar properties, the two kingdoms have distinct characteristics and ought not to be fused. Yet, as the soul and body predicate their properties to one human person, the two kingdoms jointly serve the one reign of God. These hermeneutical keys help us to understand that Calvin entertained a societal doctrine of differentiation and relation that is neither "otherworldly" nor "socially utopian." Calvin does not separate the heavenly and earthly realms in an absolute sense, nor does he expound an integrationist societal doctrine that fuses the two realms. Instead, his societal doctrine displayed a relative consistency in uniting, but not confounding the two realms.

Despite his emphasize on Christian vocation, Calvin was adamant that the coming ultimate order does not suspend the penultimate natural order. Christ's reign is present in that it restores the original natural and moral order of God, but the present order will only be replaced with an eschatological order at the Consummation. Christians therefore have no right to subvert or undermine social structures that are part of God's original intended order.

The chapter concluded by discussing the constructive potential of Calvin's societal doctrine. It argued that Calvin's notions of common grace and the survival of natural gifts, despite sin, provides reformed theologians with resources to develop a global ethics based on natural law principles that can generate the minimum ethical consensus needed to safeguard social stability in plural societies. Calvin's position that only God can consummate history serves as an important caveat against eschatological oriented social metanarratives that seek to create optimum societies. Utopian metanarratives inevitably end up in anarchy and excessive social control. Calvin also provides us with a symbiotic approach to social ethics that correlate duties and rights closely to each other. For Calvin, the art of associating exists in human persons recognizing their mutual relatedness and reciprocal dependency, as well as, their common obligation to serve each other through their gifts. Lastly, Calvin's doctrines on vocation and the three offices of the Christian (*munex triplex*), provide important impulses for Christians to be responsible citizens and for churches to become communities of truth (prophets), justice (kings) and mercy (priests).

Churches that find their theological origin in the Calvinist Reformation seem to experience difficulty establishing theological clarity on the role that modern women ought to play within the church. The question that the modern Calvinist tradition faces and chapter 6 addressed is whether greater openness to gender equality in the church will amount to a serious subversion of the essence of Calvinist theology. The chapter commenced with an overview of the state of current scholarly discourse on Calvin's understanding of gender. Four lines of interpretation were discerned namely, the hierarchical, proto-feminist, perspectival and womanist interpretations.

The following sections in chapter 6 analyzed Calvin's view on the created status of women, husband-wife relations and the role he ascribed to women in the church and in the public sphere. Calvin's stance on the image of women was that male and female are created as equals as far as common humanity, sin and grace are concerned. However, when it comes to external relations women do not reflect God's glory in the same manner as men, because God ascribes rule to the male as the father of the family and the head of his wife. Women are image of God only "to a secondary degree."

Calvin's reflections on marriage were characterized by an emphasis on the headship of the husband; the importance of mutual respect between husband and wife; the equality of the sexual relationship and the general unacceptability of divorce, celibacy and polygamy. Though Calvin deviated on some key points from his predecessors and contemporaries, his thought on marriage was embedded in a hierarchical line of thought. This is also true with regard to his position on women in public positions. Calvin did not endorse the idea of women occupying church offices or any public office, because this would be contrary to God's intended natural order. The natural order demands that women act as helpers of their husbands and that they accept the divinely appointed authority of men.

The chapter concluded by evaluating the consistency of Calvin's exegesis and the compatibility of his doctrine on gender with the basic tenets of his theology. The finding is that Calvin's exegesis on the status of women is forced and that he alters the meaning of texts, specifically the creation account, to provide a coherent doctrine that establishes the universal subordination of women. His patriarchal understanding of gender relations also created tension with other aspects of his theology. For example, when Calvin discussed the image of women he treated dominion as a definitive feature of the *imago Dei*, whereas his general doctrine of the *imago Dei* depicted dominion only as a very small part of the image. Secondly, whilst recognizing that male and female are "spiritually" equal before God and affirming that the church belongs to the spiritual realm; Calvin did not allow the order of the church to be framed by the notion of spiritual equality of the sexes. Calvin's position on women therefore provided a mixed and often inconsistent picture, rather than an authentic example of his theological project. As a result, Calvinist churches might be forced to move beyond Calvin himself to develop a doctrine on gender that fits within the Calvinist theological corpus.

Bibliography

Althusius, Johannes. *Politica: An Abridged Translation of Politics Methodically Set Forth and Illustrated with Sacred and Profane Examples*. Translated and edited with an introduction by Frederich S. Carney. Indianapolis: Liberty, 1964.

Aquinas, Thomas. *Disputed Questions on the Virtues*. Translated and edited by E. M Atkins and Thomas Williams. Cambridge: Cambridge University Press, 2005.

———. *Divi Thomae Aquinatis Summa Theologica: Editio altera Romana ad emendatiores editiones impressa, et noviter accuratissime recognita*. Rome: Forzani, 1920.

———. *Summa Theologiae*. Translated and edited by Timothy McDermott. Maryland: Westminster Christian Classics, 1989.

Baker, J. Wayne. "Church, State and Dissent: The Crisis of the Swiss Reformation, 1531–1536." *Church History: Studies in Christianity and Culture* 57 2 (1988) 135–52.

Bakker, Peter, et al. "Report of Deputies Male/Female in the Church." http://godgeneratedlife.com/downloads/2014male_female_report.pdf.

Baldwin, Claude-Marie. "John Calvin and the Ethics of Gender Relations." *The Calvin Theological Journal* 26 (1991) 133–43.

Balserak, Jon. "The Accomodating Act Par Excellence? An Inquiry into the Incarnation and Calvin's Understanding of Accommodation." *Scottish Journal of Theology* 55 (2002) 408–23.

Bandstra, Andrew J. "Law and Gospel in Calvin and in Paul." In *Exploring the Heritage of John Calvin*, edited by David E. Holwerda, 11–40. Grand Rapids: Baker, 1976.

Bavinck, Herman. *Gereformeerde Dogmatiek*. Vol. 4. Kampen: Kok, 1930.

Beeke, Joel R. "Calvin's Piety." *Mid-America Journal of Theology* 15 (2004) 33–65.

———. "Twelve Reasons Calvin is Important Today." In *Calvin for Today*, edited by Joel R. Beeke, 241–76. Grand Rapids: Reformation Heritage, 2009.

Berkhof, Louis. *Christian Faith*. Grand Rapids: Eerdmans, 1986.

Berkouwer, Gerhardus C. *Dogmatische Studien: De Mens het Beelds God*. Kampen: Kok, 1957.

Bièler, Andrè. *L'Homme et la Femme dans la Morale Calviniste: La doctrine Rèformèe sur l'mour, Le mariage, Le cèlibat, Le divorce, L'adultère et la Prostitution, Considereè dans son Cadre Historique*. Geneva: Labor et Fides, 1963.

Billings, J. Todd. "John Calvin's Soteriology: On the Multifaceted 'Sum' of the Gospel.'" *International Journal of Systematic Theology* 11.4 (2009) 428–47.

———. "Milbank's Theology of the 'Gift' and Calvin's Theology of Grace: A Critical Comparison." *Modern Theology* 21.1 (2005) 87–105.

———. "United to God Through Christ: Assessing Calvin on the Question of Deification." *Harvard Theological Review* 98.3 (2005) 315–34.

Blanchard, Kathryn D. "The Gift of Contraception: Calvin, Barth, and a Lost Protestant Conversation." *Journal of the Society of Christian Ethics* 27.1 (2007) 225–49.

Blochner, Henri. "The Atonement in John Calvin's Theology." In *The Glory of Atonement*, edited by Charles E. Hill and Frank. A James III, 279-303. Downers Grove: Intervarsity, 2004.

Bolt, John. "Eschatological Hermeneutics and Women's Ordination." *Calvin Theological Journal* 26.2 (1991) 370-88.

———. "Spiritus Creator: The Use and Abuse of Calvin's Cosmic Pneumatology." In *Calvin and the Holy Spirit*, edited by Peter de Klerk, 17-34. Grand Rapids: Calvin Studies Society, 1989

Bouwsma, William J. *John Calvin: A Sixteenth Century Portrait*. Oxford: Oxford University Press, 1988.

Bratt, John H. "The Role and Status of Women in the Writings of John Calvin." In *Renaissance, Reformation, Resurgence: Colloquiem on Calvin and Calvin Studies*, edited by Peter de Klerk, 1-17. Grand Rapids: Calvin Theological Seminary, 1976.

Butin, Philip Walker. *Revelation, Redemption and Response: Calvin's Trinitarian Understanding of the Divine-Human Relationship*. New York: Oxford University Press, 1995.

Butler, Eamonn. *Milton Friedman—A Guide to His Economic Thought*. New York: Universe, 1985.

Calvin, John. *The Bondage and Liberation of the Will*. Edited by A. N. S. Lane and translated by G. I. Davies. Grand Rapids: Baker, 1996.

———. *Catechism or Institution of the Christian Religion*. Translated by Ford Lewis Battles. Pittsburgh: Pittsburgh Theological Seminary, 1972.

———. *Commentaries on the Catholic Epistles*. Translated by William Pringle. Edinburgh: Calvin Translation Society, 1855.

———. *Commentaries on the Epistles of Paul to the Galatians and Ephesians*. Translated by John Pringle. Edinburgh: Calvin Translation Society, 1854.

———. *Commentaries on the Epistles of Paul to the Hebrews*. Translated by John Owen. Edinburgh: Calvin Translation Society, 1853.

———. *Commentaries on the First Book of Moses Called Genesis*. Vol 1. Translated by John King. Edinburgh: Calvin Translation Society, 1847.

———. *Commentaries on the First Book of Moses Called Genesis*. Vol 2. Translated by John King. Edinburgh: Calvin Translation Society, 1850.

———. *Commentaries on the Last Four Books of Moses Arranged in the Form of a Harmony*. Vol. 4. Translated by C. W Bingham. Edinburgh: Calvin Translation Society, 1855.

———. *Commentaries on the Prophet Jeremiah and the Lamentations*. Vol. 1. Translated by John Owen. Grand Rapids: Eerdmans, 1850.

———. *Commentary on a Harmony of the Evangelists, Mathew, Mark and Luke*. Vol. 2. Translated by William Pringle. Edinburgh: Calvin Translation Society, 1845.

———. *Commentary on the Book of Psalms*. Vol. 1. Translated by James Anderson. Edinburgh: Calvin Translation Society, 1845.

———. *Commentary on the Book of Psalms*. Vol. 3. Translated by James Anderson. Edinburgh: Calvin Translation Society, 1847.

———. *Commentary on the Book of Psalms*. Vol 5. Translated by James Anderson. Grand Rapids: Eerdmans, 1949.

———. *Commentary on the Book of the Prophet Isaiah*. Vol 1. Translated by William Pringle. Grand Rapids: Eerdmans, 1958.

———. *Commentary on the Epistles of Paul the Apostle to the Corinthians.* Vol. 1. Translated by John Pringle. Edinburgh: Calvin Translation Society, 1848.

———. *Commentary on the Epistles of Paul the Apostle to the Corinthians.* Vol. 2. Translated by John Pringle. Edinburgh: Calvin Translation Society, 1849.

———. *Commentary on the Epistles of Paul the Apostle to the Philippians, Colossians and Thessalonians.* Translated by John Pringle. Edinburgh: Calvin Translation Society, 1851.

———. *Commentary on the Epistle of Paul the Apostle to the Romans.* Vol 1. Translated by John Owen. Edinburgh: Calvin Translation Society, 1859.

———. *Commentary on the Gospel according to John.* Vol. 1. Translated by William Pringle. Edinburgh: Calvin Translation Society, 1847.

———. *Commentary Upon the Acts of the Apostles.* Vol. 1. Translated by Henry Beveridge. Edinburgh: Calvin Translation Society, 1844.

———. *Concerning the Eternal Predestination of God.* Translated by J. K. S. Reid. London: Clarke, 1961.

———. "Confession on the Trinity." Translated by Casey Carmichael. *Kerux* 29.3 (2014) 4–9.

———. "Election: the Ground and Source of the Christian Life: A Sermon on Ephesians 1:3–4." In *The Christian Life*, edited by John H. Leith, 83–101. San Francisco: Harper & Row, 1973.

———. *Institutes of the Christian Religion.* Translated by Henry Beveridge. Peabody: Hendrickson, 2008.

———. *Institutes of the Christian Religion 1536.* Translated by F. L. Battles. Grand Rapids: Eerdmans, 1975.

———. *Ioannis Calvini Opera quae supersunt omnia: Ad fidem editionum principium et authenticarum ex parte.* Edited by Gulielmus Baum et al. Brunswick: Scwetschke, 1864–1900.

———. *Psychopannychia: Tracts and Treatises in Defense of the Reformed Faith.* Vol. 3. Translated by Henry Beveridge. Grand Rapids: Eerdmans, 1958.

———. *Sermons on Genesis 1–11.* Translated by Rob R. McGregor. Edinburgh: Banner of Truth, 2009.

———. *Sermons on Job.* Translated by A. Golding. Londini: Bishop, 1574.

———. *Sermons on the Epistle to the Ephesians.* Translated by Arthur Golding. Edinburgh: Banner of Truth Trust, 1975.

———. *Supplementia Calvinia: Sermons Inédit.* Moderated by James I. McCord. Neukirchen-Vluyn: Neukirchner, 1961.

———. "To William Cecil." In *Letters of Calvin*, edited by Jules Bonnet, 206–8. Bonnet ed. Edinburgh: Banner of Truth Trust, 1980.

Canlis, Julie. "Beyond Tearing One Another to Pieces: Union with Christ in Reformed Fellowship." *Journal of Reformed Theology* 8.1 (2014) 79–88.

———. *Calvin's Ladder: A Spiritual Theology of Ascent and Ascension.* Grand Rapids: Eerdmans, 2010.

Christensen, Martin Iversen. "Women Clergy and Ecclesiastical Territories." https://guide2womenleaders.com/women_clergy.htm.

The Christian Reformed Church. *Acts of Synod 1995.* Grand Rapids: Christian Reformed Church, 1995.

———. *Report Committee to Review the Decision Regarding Women in Office for Synod 2000.* Grand Rapids: Christian Reformed Church, 2000.

Combrinck, Bernard. "Die Krisis van die Skrifgesag in die Gereformeerde Eksegese as 'n Geleentheid." *NGTT* 31.3 (1990) 325–35.

Couenhoven, Jesse. "Grace as Pardon and Power: Pictures of the Christian Life in Luther, Calvin and Barth." *Journal of Religious Ethics* 28.1 (2000) 63–88.

DeBoer, Willis P. "Calvin on the Role of Women." In *Essays in Honor of John H Bratt: Exploring the Heritage of John Calvin*, edited by David E. Holwerda, 236–72. Grand Rapids: Baker, 1976.

De Jong, Peter Y. "Calvin's Contributions to Christian Education." *Calvin Theological Journal* 2.2 (1967) 162–207.

Denlinger, Aaron. "Calvin's Understanding of Adam's Relationship to His Posterity: Recent Assertions of the Reformers 'Federalism' Evaluated." *Calvin Theological Journal* 44 (2009) 226–50.

Die Nederduitse Gereformeerde Kerk in Suider Afrika. *Acta*. Kaapstad: Nederduitse Gereformeerde Kerk in Suider Afrika, 1990.

———. *Acta*. Kaapstad: Nederduitse Gereformeerde Kerk in Suider Afrika, 1982.

———. *Skema van Werksaamhede*. Elsiesrivier: Nederduitse Gereformeerde Kerk in Suid-Afrika, 1953.

———. *Skema van Werksaamhede*. Kaapstad: Nederduitse Gereformeerde Kerk in Suid-Afrika, 1970.

Douglass, Jane Dempsey. "Christian Freedom: What Calvin Learned at the School of Women." *Church History* 53.2 (June 1984) 155–73.

———. *Women, Freedom and Calvin*. Philadelphia: Westminster, 1985.

Edgar, Brian. "Calvin and the Natural Order: Positives and Problems for Science-Faith Dialogue." *Christian Perspectives on Science and Technology* (2010) 1–15.

Edmondson, Stephen. *Calvin's Christology*. Cambridge: Cambridge University Press, 2004.

Engel, Mary P. *John Calvin's Perspectival Anthropology*. Atlanta: Scholars, 1988.

Esser, Hans-Helmut. "The Contemporary Relevance of Calvin's Social Ethics." In *Toward the Future of Reformed Theology*, edited by David Willis and Michael Welker, 366–86. Grand Rapids: Eerdmans, 1999.

Evans, William B. "Déjà Vu All Over Again? The Contemporary Reformed Soteriological Controversy in Historical Perspective." *Westminster Theological Journal* 72 (2010) 135–51.

Fisk, Philip. "Calvin's Metaphysics of Our Union with Christ." *International Journal of Systematic Theology* 2 (June 2007) 309–31.

Fulkerson, Mary McClintock. "The Imago Dei and the Reformed Logic for Feminist/Womanist Critique." In *Feminist and Womanist Essays in Reformed Dogmatics*, edited by Amy Plantinga Pauw and Serene Jones, 95–106. Columbia Series in Reformed Theology. Louisville: Westminster John Knox, 2006.

Gamble, Richard. "Calvin's Bibliography." In *Tributes to John Calvin: A Celebration of His Quincentary*, edited by David W. Hall, 419–35. Phillipsburg: P. & R., 2010.

Ganoczy, Alexandrè. "Calvin's Life." In *The Cambridge Companion to John Calvin*, edited by Donald K. McKim, 25–41. Cambridge: Cambridge University Press, 2004.

Garcia, Mark A. "Imputation as Attribution: Union with Christ, Reification and Justification as Declarative Word." *International Journal of Systematic Theology* 11.4 (2009) 415–27.

———. *Life in Christ: Union with Christ and Twofold Grace in Calvin's Theology*. Eugene, OR: Wipf & Stock, 2008.

Gatis, Joseph. "The Political Theory of John Calvin." *Biblioteca Sacra* 153.612 (1996) 449–67.
George, Marie I. "What Aquinas Really Said About Women." *First Things* (1999) 11–13.
Gerrish, Brian A. "The Mirror of God's Goodness: Man in the Theology of Calvin." *Concordia Theological Quarterly* 45.3 (1981) 211–22.
Godfrey, W. Robert. "Kingdom and Kingdoms." *Evangelium* 7.2 (2009) 6–9.
Graham, W. Fred. *The Constructive Revolutionary: John Calvin and His Socio-Economic Impact*. Atlanta: John Knox, 1978.
Gregory, Brad. *The Unintended Reformation. How a Religious Revolution Secularized Society*. Cambridge: Harvard University Press, 2012.
Hauerwas, Stanley. *A Community of Character: Toward a Constructive Social Ethic*. Notre Dame: University of Notre Dame Press, 1981.
Helm, Paul. *John Calvin's Ideas*. Oxford: Oxford University Press, 2006.
Holwerda, David. "Eschatology and History: A Look at Calvin's Eschatological Vision." In *Exploring the Heritage of John Calvin*, edited by David E. Holwerda, 110–40. Grand Rapids: Baker, 1976.
Horowitz, Maryanne Cline. "The Image of God in Man: Is Woman Included?" *Harvard Theological Review* 72.3/4 (1979) 175–206.
Horton, Michael S. "Union and Communion: Calvin's Theology of Word and Sacrament." *International Journal of Systematic Theology* 11.4 (2009) 398–414.
Jeon, Jeong Koo. "Calvin and the Two Kingdoms: Calvin's Political Philosophy in Light of Contemporary Discussion." *Westminster Theological Journal* 72.2 (2010) 299–320.
Johnson, Marcus. "Luther and Calvin on Union With Christ." *Fides et Historia* 39.2 (2007) 59–77.
———. "New or Nuanced Perspective on Calvin? A Reply to Thomas Wenger." *Journal of the Evangelical Theological Society* 51 3 (2008) 543–58.
Jones, David Clyde, "The Curious History of Calvin's *Golden Booklet*." *Presbyterion* 35 2 (2009), 82–86.
Jooste, Simon. *Recovering the Calvin of the Two Kingdoms? A Historical-Theological Enquiry in the Light of Church-State Relations in South Africa*. Stellenbosch: Sun, 2013.
Karant-Nunn, Susan C. "Reformation, Society, Women and the Family." In *The Reformation World*, edited by Andrew Pettegree, 433–61. London: Routledge, 2000.
Keesecker, William J. "The Law in John Calvin's Ethics." In *Calvin and Christian Ethics*, edited by Peter de Klerk, 1–21. Calvin Studies Society Papers. Grand Rapids: Calvin Studies Society, 1987.
Kehm, George. "Christ and Man in Calvin's Theology." *Perspective* 12.3 (1971) 197–216.
Kelsay, John. "Prayer and Ethics: Reflections on Calvin and Barth." *Harvard Theological Review* 82.2 (1989) 169–84.
Kelsey, David. *Eccentric Existence: A Theological Anthropology*. 2 vols. Louisville: Westminster John Knox, 2009.
Kőnig, Adrio. *God waarom lyk die Wêreld so? Kan ons sê God is in Beheer*. Wellington: Lux Verbi, 2007.
Küng, Hans. *Women in Christianity*. Translated by John Bowden. London: Continuum, 2005.
Kuyper, Abraham. *Souvereiniteit in Eigen Kring*. Kampen: Kok, 1930.

Lane, A. N. S. "Did Calvin Believe in Free-Will?" *Vox Evangelica* 12 (1981) 72–90.

Leith, John H. *John Calvin's Doctrine of the Christian Life*. Louisville: Westminster John Knox, 1989.

Leithart, Peter J. "Stoic Elements in Calvin's Doctrine of the Christian Life: Part III: Christian Moderation." *Westminster Theological Journal* 56.1 (1994) 59–85.

Lief, Jason. "Is Neo-Calvinism Calvinist? A Neo-Calvinist Engagement of Calvin's 'Two Kingdoms' Doctrine." *Pro Rege* 37.3 (2009) 1–12.

———. "Two Kingdoms Perspective and Theological Method: Why I Still Disagree With David Van Drunen." *Pro Rege* 41.1 (2012) 1–5.

Lipscomb, Suzannah. "Subjection and Companionship: The French Reformed Marriage." *Reformation & Renaissance Review* 6.3 (2004) 349–60.

Little, David. "Calvin and Natural Rights." *Political Theology* 10.3 (2009) 411–30.

Malan, F. S. "Hoe verstaan 1 Timoteus die Posisie van die Vrou in die Diens van die Gemeente." *Nederduitse Gereformeerde Teologiese Tydskrif* 29.4 (1988) 305–16.

Mancha, Rita. "The Woman's Authority: Calvin to Edwards." *Journal of Christian Reconstruction* 6 (Winter 1979–80) 86–98.

Marko, Jonathan S. "'Free Choice' in Calvin's Concepts of Regeneration and Moral Agency: How Free Are We?" *Ashland Theological Journal* 42 (2010) 41–60.

McCormack, Bruce L. "Union with Christ in Calvin's Theology: Grounds for a Divinization Theory?" In *Tributes to John Calvin: A Celebration of His Quincentary*, edited by D. W. Hall, 512–16. Phillipsburg: P. & R., 2010.

McGrath, Alister E. A. *Iustitia Dei*. 2nd ed. Cambridge: Cambridge University Press, 1998.

———. *Life of John Calvin: A Study in the Shaping of Western Culture*. Oxford: Basil Blackwell, 1990.

Miles, Margaret R. "Theology, Anthropology and the Human Body in Calvin's 'Institutes of the Christian Religion.'" *Harvard Theological Review* 74.3 (1981) 303–23.

Mosser, Carl. "The Greatest Possible Blessing: Calvin and Deification." *Scottish Journal of Theology* 55.1 (2002) 36–57.

Muller, Richard. *Calvin and the Reformed Tradition: On the Work of Christ and the Order of Salvation*. Ada, MI: Baker, 2012.

———. "Christ in the Eschaton: Calvin and Moltmann on the Duration of the *Munus Regium*." *Harvard Theological Review* 74.1 (1981) 31–59.

———. *Divine Will and Human Choice: Freedom, Contingency and Necessity in Early Modern Reformed Thought*. Grand Rapids: Baker Academic, 2017.

———. "Grace, Election and Contingent Choice: Arminius's Gambit and the Reformed Response." In *Grace of God, the Bondage of the Will: Historical and Theological Perspectives on Calvinism*, edited by Thomas R. Schreiner and Bruce A. Ware, 2:251–78. Grand Rapids: Baker, 1995.

———. "The Starting Point of Calvin's Theology: An Essay Review." *Calvin Theological Review* 36 (2001) 314–41.

———. *The Unaccommodated Calvin: Studies in the Foundation of a Theological Tradition*. Oxford Studies in Historical Theology. Oxford: Oxford University Press, 2000.

Murphy, Gannon. "Reformed Theosis?" *Theology Today* 65.2 (2008) 191–212.

Nürnberger, Klaus. *Informed by Science—Involved by Christ: How Science Can Update, Enrich and Empower the Christian Faith*. Pietermaritzburg: Cluster, 2013.

Oberman, Heiko A. *The Dawn of the Reformation*. Grand Rapids: Eerdmans, 1992.

———. *The Two Reformations*. Edited by Donald Weinstein. Yale University Press: New Haven, 2003.
Ollerton, Andrew J. "'*Quasi Deificari*': Deification in the Theology of John Calvin." *Westminster Theological Journal* 73.2 (2011) 237–54.
Osiander, Andreas. *Gesamtausgabe*, edited by Gottfried Seebass & Gerhard Müller, 3:176–79. Gutersloh: Gutersloher Verlagshaus, 1975–97.
Palmer, Timothy P. "Calvin the Transformationist and the Kingship of Christ." *Pro Rege* 35.3 (2007) 32–39.
Paul, Shelly L. "Patriarchal Anthropology: Spiritual Equality/Natural Subordination." *Ex Auditu* 13 (1997) 114–25.
Pitkin, Barbara. "Nothing but Concupiscence: Calvin's Understanding of Sin and the *Via Augustini*." *Calvin Theological Journal* 34 (1999) 347–69.
———. "The Protestant Zeno: Calvin and the Development of Melanchthon's Anthropology." *Journal of Religion* 84.3 (2004) 345–78.
Potter, Mary. "Gender Equality and Gender Hierarchy in Calvin's Theology." *Signs* 11 (1986) 725–39.
Plaatjies, Mary-Anne. *Vroue in die Teologiese Antropologie van die Afrikaanse Gereformeerde Tradisie*. Pretoria: Unisa, 2003.
Pruyser, Paul W. "Calvin's View of Man: A Psychological Commentary." *Theology Today* 26.1 (1969) 51–68,
Quistorp, Heinrich. *Calvin's Doctrine of the Last Things*. Translated by Harold Knight. London: Lutterworth, 1955.
Raitt, Jill. "The Saving Work of the Holy Spirit in Calvin." In *Calvin and the Holy Spirit*, edited by Peter de Klerk, 13–16. Grand Rapids: Calvin Studies Society, 1989.
Reinis, Austra. "Catechism and *Querelle des femmes* (1556–4689): Lutheran *Haustafel* Sermons as Contributions to the Debate About Women." *Lutherjahrbuch* 79 (2012) 183–209.
Schwöbel, Christoph. "Human Being as Relational Being: Twelve Theses for a Christian Anthropology." In *Persons, Divine and Human*, edited by Christoph Scwöbel and Colin E. Gunton, 141–65. Edinburgh: T. & T. Clark, 1991.
Senior, John. "Cruciform Pilgrims: Politics Between the Penultimate and Ultimate." *Journal of the Society of Christian Ethics* 32.1 (2012) 115–32.
Sewell, Leni A. *Calvin, the Body and Sexuality: An Inquiry into His Anthropology*. Amsterdam: VU University Press, 2012.
Shih, Shu-Ying. *The Development of Calvin's Understanding of the Imago Dei in the Institutes of the Christian Religion from 1536–1559*. Heidelberg: Ruprechts Karl University, 2004.
Slater, Jonathan. "Salvation as Participation in the Humanity of the Mediator in Calvin's Institutes of the Christian Religion: A Reply to Carl Mosser." *Scottish Journal of Theology* 58.1 (2005) 39–58.
South Africa. *The Constitution of the Republic of South Africa, 1996; As Adopted on 8 May 1996 and Amended on 11 October 1996 by the Constitutional Assembly*. https://www.wipo.int/edocs/lexdocs/laws/en/za/za107en.pdf.
Southgate, Christopher. "Re-reading Genesis, John, and Job: A Christian Response to Darwinism." *Zygon* 46.2 (2011) 370–95.
———. "Responses to Darwin in the Religious Traditions." *Zygon* 48.2 (2011) 439–53.

Spykman, Gordon J. "Sphere Sovereignty in Calvin and the Calvinist Tradition." In *Exploring the Heritage of John Calvin*, edited by David E Holwerda, 163–209. Grand Rapids: Baker, 1976.

Steinmetz, David. "The Theology of John Calvin." In *The Cambridge Companion to Reformation Theology*, edited by D. Bagchi and D. C Steinmetz, 113–29. Cambridge: Cambridge University Press, 2004.

Sytsma, David S. "The Exegetical Context of Calvin's Loci on the Christian Life." *Calvin Theological Journal* 45 (2010) 256–79.

Tamburello, Dennis E. *Union with Christ: John Calvin and the Mysticism of St. Bernard*. Columbia Series in Reformed Theology. Louisville: Westminster John Knox, 1994.

Taylor, Charles. *A Secular Age*. Cambridge: Belknap, 2007.

Thompson, John Lee. "*Creata ad Imaginem Dei, Licet Secundo Gradu*: Women as the Image of God according to John Calvin." *Harvard Theological Review* 81.2 (1988) 125–43.

———. *John Calvin and the Daughters of Sarah: Women in Regular and Exceptional Roles in the Exegesis of Calvin, His Predecessors, and His Contemporaries*. PhD diss., Duke University, 1989.

———. "Patriarchs, Polygamy and Private Resistance: John Calvin and Others on Breaking God's Rules." *The Sixteenth Century Journal* 25.1 (1994) 3–27.

Tipton, Lane G. "Union with Christ and Justification." In *Justified in Christ: God's Plan for Us in Justification*, edited by K. Scott Oliphint, 23–51. Tain: Christian Focus, 2007.

Torrance, Thomas F. *Calvin's Doctrine of Man*. Grand Rapids: Eerdmans, 1957.

Tylenda, Joseph. "Christ the Mediator: Calvin Versus Stancaro." *Calvin Theological Journal* 8.1 (1973) 1–16.

Beek, Abraham van de. *Een Lichtkring om het Kruis: Scheppingsleer in Christologisch Perspectief*. Zoetermeer: Meinema, 2014.

———. *Lichaam en Geest van Christus: De Theologie van de Kerk en de Heilige Geest*. Zoetermeer: Meinema, 2012.

van den Brink, Gijsbert, and Cornelius van der Kooi. *Christelijke Dogmatiek: Een Inleiding*. Zoetermeer: Uitgevery Boekencentrum, 2012.

VanDrunen, David. "The Context of Natural Law: John Calvin's Doctrine of the Two Kingdoms." *Journal of Church and State* 46.3 (2004) 503–25.

———. "The Importance of the Penultimate: Reformed Social Thought and the Contemporary Critiques of the Liberal Society." *Journal of Markets and Morality* 9.2 (2006) 219–49.

———. *Natural Law and the Two Kingdoms: A Study in the Development of Reformed Social Thought*. Grand Rapids: Eerdmans, 2010.

———. "The Two Kingdoms: A Reassessment of the Transformationist Calvin." *Calvin Theological Journal* 40 (2005) 248–66.

———. "Two Kingdoms and Reformed Christianity: Why Recovering an Old Paradigm is Historically Sound, Biblically Grounded, and Practically Useful." *Pro Rege* 40.3 (2012) 31–38.

Van Eck, John. *God, Mens, Medemens: Humanitas in De Theologie Van Calvijn*. Franeker: Van Wijnen, 1992.

Van Til, Henry R. *The Calvinistic Concept of Culture*. Reprint, Grand Rapids: Baker, 2001.

Vliet, Jason Van. *Children of God: The Imago Dei in John Calvin and His Context*. Reformed Historical Theology 11. Göttingen: Vandenhoeck & Ruprecht, 2009.
van Wyk, Jan Harm. *Homo Dei: 'n Prinsipiële Besinning oor Enkele Mensbeskouings: Waaronder die van Calvyn*. Pretoria: In die Skriflig, 1993.
Van't Spijker, Wim. "'Extra Nos' and 'In Nobis' by Calvin in a Pneumatological Light." In *Calvin and the Holy Spirit*, edited by Peter de Klerk, 39-62. Grand Rapids: Calvin Studies Society, 1989.
Venema, Cornelis P. "Calvin's Understanding of the 'Twofold Grace of God' and Contemporary Ecumenical Discussion of the Gospel." *Mid-America Journal of Theology* 18 (2007) 67-105.
Vorster, Jakobus M. "Calvin and Human Rights." *The Ecumenical Review* 51.2 (1999) 209-20.
Vorster, Nico. "'And Behold a Ladder': Descent and Ascent in Calvin's Soteriology." In *Luce Verbi* 49.1 (2015) 1-8.
―――. "Assessing the Consistency of John Calvin's Doctrine on Human Sinfulness." *HTS Teologiese Studies* 71.33 (2015) 1-8.
―――. "Calvin on the Created Structure of Human Nature." *Journal of Theology for Southern Africa* 151 (2015) 162-82.
―――. "Calvin on Human Reason." In *In Luce Verbi* 48.1 (2014) 1-9.
―――. "Calvin's Modification of Augustine's Doctrine of Original Sin." In *Restoration Through Redemption: John Calvin Revisited*, edited by Henk van der Belt, 45-63. Leiden: Brill, 2013.
―――. "Die Westerse Mens en Betekenisverlies." *Tydskrif vir Geesteswetenskappe* 53.1 (2013) 30-44.
―――. "John Calvin on the Christian's Social Responsibility. Cultural Activist or Modest Social Reformer?" *Dialog: A Journal of Theology* 56.4 (2018) 441-48.
―――. "John Calvin on the Status and Role of Women in Church and Society." *Journal of Church and State* 68.1 (2017) 178-211.
―――. "The Nature of Christ's Atonement: A Defence of Penal Substitution Theory." In *Strangers and Pilgrims on Earth: Essays in Honour of Abraham van de Beek*, edited by Eddy Van der Borght and Paul van Geest, 129-47. Leiden: Brill, 2012.
―――. "The Theocentric Premises of Calvin's Antropology: Its Significance for Modern Theological Anthropologies." In *Reformed Theology Today: Biblical and Systematic Theological Perspectives*, edited by Nico Vorster and Sarel Van der Walt, 103-14. Durbanville: AOSIS, 2017.
―――. "'United but Not Confused': Calvin's Anthropology as a Hermeneutical Key to Understanding his Societal Doctrine." *Journal of Church and State* 58.1 (2016) 117-41.
Wallace, Ronald S. *Calvin's Doctrine on the Christian Life*. Edinburgh: Oliver & Boyd, 1959.
Waugh, Barry G. "Reason Within the Limits of Revelation Alone: John Calvin's Understanding of Human Reason." *Westminster Theological Journal* 72.1 (2010) 1-21.
Welker, Michael. *God the Revealed: Christology*. Grand Rapids: Eerdmans, 2013.
Wendel, François. *Calvin: The Origins and Development of His Thought*. Translated by Philip Mairet. London: Collins, 1963.
Wenger, Thomas L. "The New Perspective on Calvin: Responding to Recent Calvin Interpretations." *Journal of the Evangelical Theological Society* 50.2 (2007) 311-28.

Willis, Edward David. *Calvin's Catholic Christology: The Function of So-called Extra Calvanisticum in Calvin's Theology*. Leiden: Brill, 1966.
Winecoff, David K. "Calvin's Doctrine of Mortification." *Covenant Seminary Review* 13 (1987) 85–101.
Witte, John. "Law, Religion and Human Rights: A Historical Perspective." *Journal of Religious Ethics* 26.2 (1998) 257–62.
———. "Marriage and Family Life." In *The Calvin Handbook*, edited by Herman J. Selderhuis, 455–64. Grand Rapids: Eerdmans, 2009.
———. "Moderate Religious Liberty in the Theology of John Calvin." *Calvin Theological Journal* 31 (1996) 359–403.
———. *The Reformation of Rights: Law, Religion and Rights in Early Modern Calvinism*. Cambridge: Cambridge University Press, 2007.
Wolterstorff, Nicholas. *Until Justice and Peace Embrace*. Grand Rapids: Eerdmans, 1983.
Zachmann, Randall C. "'Deny Yourself and Take Up Your Cross': John Calvin on the Christian Life." *International Journal of Systematic Theology* 11.4 (2009) 466–82.
Zamfir, Korinna. "'The Quest for the Eternal Feminine': An Essay on the Effective History of Gen 1–3 with Respect to the Women." *Annali di Storia deli'Esegesi* 24.2 (2007) 501–22.
Zimmerman, Jacquelyn A. K. "The Christian Life in Luther and Calvin." *Lutheran Quarterly* (1964) 222–30.
Zylstra, Carl E. "Serious Education for Serious Christians." *Pro Rege* 39.4 (2011) 39–42.

www.ingramcontent.com/pod-product-compliance
Lightning Source LLC
Chambersburg PA
CBHW051742230426
43670CB00012B/2132